RELATIVE *Intimacy*

RELATIVE *Intimacy*

FATHERS, ADOLESCENT DAUGHTERS,

AND POSTWAR AMERICAN CULTURE

Rachel Devlin

The University of North Carolina Press

Chapel Hill and London

© 2005
The University of North Carolina Press
All rights reserved
Manufactured in the United States of America
Set in Arnhem and Bickham types
by Tseng Information Systems, Inc.

The paper in this book meets the guidelines for
permanence and durability of the Committee on
Production Guidelines for Book Longevity of the
Council on Library Resources.

Library of Congress Cataloging-in-Publication Data
Devlin, Rachel.
Relative intimacy : fathers, adolescent daughters, and
postwar American culture / Rachel Devlin.
    p. cm. — (Gender and American culture)
Includes bibliographical references and index.
ISBN 0-8078-2946-3 (cloth : alk. paper) —
ISBN 0-8078-5605-3 (pbk. : alk. paper)
1. Teenage girls—Family relationships. 2. Fathers and
daughters. 3. Fathers and daughters in literature.
I. Title. II. Series.
HQ798.D3995   2005
305.235′2—dc22   2004025409

cloth   09 08 07 06 05   5 4 3 2 1
paper   09 08 07 06 05   5 4 3 2 1

CONTENTS

Acknowledgments vii

Introduction 1

CHAPTER 1 The Oedipal Age:
Postwar Psychoanalysis Reinterprets the
Adolescent Girl 17

CHAPTER 2 Delinquent Girls and the Crisis of
Paternal Authority in the Postwar United States 48

CHAPTER 3 Adolescent Authorities:
Teenage Girls, Consumerism, and the Cultural
Transformation of Fatherhood 78

CHAPTER 4 Coming-of-Age:
A Paternal Rite of Passage, 1948–1965 109

CHAPTER 5 Affection, Identification, Skepticism:
Situating Men in Relation to Adolescent Daughters 141

Epilogue 171

Notes 175

Bibliography 221

Index 245

ILLUSTRATIONS

A 1959 *Life* magazine photograph 79

A 1937 *Parents' Magazine* photograph 80

Publicity still from *Junior Miss* (play), 1941 89

Illustration from *Life with Teena*, 1944 99

Illustration from *Father of the Bride*, 1948 115

Illustration from "Mr. Banks' Other Daughter,"
  Good Housekeeping, 1950 123

Cover of the book *Junior Miss*, 1959 125

A 1950 advertisement for Chanel perfume from
  Seventeen magazine 126

Cover of a 1957 issue of *Ebony* magazine 132

Cover of a 1962 issue of *Jet* magazine 133

Publicity still from *Kiss and Tell* (play), 1943 142

Advertisement for *Kiss and Tell* (film), 1945 143

Photographs of F. Hugh Herbert from the *New York Post*, 1951 144

ACKNOWLEDGMENTS

We all write with an audience in mind, and this project bene-
fited enormously in its early stages from the fact that Nancy F. Cott and
Jean-Christophe Agnew were mine. Nancy F. Cott advised the dissertation on which this book is based at Yale University. Her quick eye and
succinct questions galvanized both research and argument, while her
own scholarship has been a constant source of inspiration. The idea
for the project grew out of a paper for Jean-Christophe Agnew's memo-
rable seminar titled "The American Century." His approach to cultural
history animates my thinking throughout the book; his intellectual
generosity and enthusiasm helped me see it through to completion.

Support from the Mrs. Giles Whiting Foundation and a Mellon Fel-
lowship for Research allowed me to complete research on the dissertation on which this book is based. Grants from the Sexuality Research
Program of the Social Science Research Council, the Larry Hackman
Research Program of the New York State Archives, and the Tulane University Committee on Research, allowed me to do additional research
and to take time off to finish the writing.

Much of the research for this book was conducted at various arms
of the New York Public Library, including the Schomburg Center for
Research on Black Culture; the Science, Industry, and Business Library; and the Library for the Performing Arts. Archivists at the Billy
Rose Theatre Collection helped me wend my way through midcentury
drama—a field that, without this collection, might not have made it
into my historical imagination. Jim Holts at the New York State Archives in Albany did a great deal to help, even when searches proved
frustrating.

Two Medievalists, Bonnie Wheeler and Caroline Walker Bynum,
were early models of intellectual reach and precision; both gave me
much-needed encouragement early on. Robert Griswold answered
questions at the beginning of this project and generously shared
sources. Regina Kunzel helped me situate some of my thinking as I
set out to turn the dissertation into a book. Jeannie Rhee helped me

think through legal history and Sherrie Inness prompted me to make it more readable.

Catherine Stimpson read the entire manuscript and posed important questions at a critical juncture. At a time when I needed an audience, Martha Hodes arranged for me to give a presentation at the Program in the History of Women and Gender at New York University. James Boyden and Linda Pollock generously read chapters when I asked them to and offered useful suggestions.

This book rests on the shoulders of those who transformed the history of youth and their doings into the recognized and richly researched topic that it is today. I very much appreciate that Paula S. Fass and Beth L. Bailey, two such pioneers, read and commented extensively on a late draft of the manuscript.

In New Orleans, the friendship of Larry Powell, Laura Watts, Richard Watts, Alisa Plant, Kate Haulman, Natalie Ring, Daniel Hurewitz, Peggy Simon, Randy Sparks, and Justin Wolfe has helped see me through the day-to-day work of teaching and writing. Sylvia Frey has been a steadfast intellectual ally, and the simple knowledge of her presence was often reassuring. Beth Willinger, at the Center for Research on Women, and Cynthia Lowenthal, dean of Newcomb College, have helped make this city a hospitable home for thinking about women and gender. I have counted on Pamela Smith and Donna Deneen for their help with the office-based work of writing and travel.

In New York, Kio Stark read various chapters and offered helpful advice. Sabrina Banes and Tenea Johnson assisted with the often dreary business of tracking down sources on microfilm. Joshua Beckman helped with the arcana of photo editing.

Genuine thanks to my editor at the University of North Carolina Press, Sian Hunter, for giving me the "rigorous review process" she promised and for her thoughtful advice. Thanks also to Mary Caviness, David Hines, and all at the University of North Carolina Press who have helped with the production of this book.

I thank Debby Applegate, Elizabeth Barnes, Virginia Blaisedale, Pamela Haag, Amy Kesselman, Trip McCrossin, and Susie Steinbach for their friendship and provocative conversation during the years spent on the dissertation and after. I am grateful to Cynthia Gooen Lesser and Deborah Rieders more than they know for making me laugh so much for so many years and for their patience with this book.

Bernard Devlin looked up citations for me at the public library when I could not be in New York, and James E. Devlin helped on the financial end. I am indebted to Tony Lacavaro for various literary tips.

The friendship of Rosanne Marion Adderley has been a most unexpected gift, and it has sustained me during the time it has taken to finish this project. Athena Devlin has read every page of the book several times over; her insight has been invaluable. I do not know how to thank her enough. A room of one's own is one thing, but in the age of Dr. Sears it is quite another to give oneself permission to go there. I am deeply grateful to Stephen Sollins for his endless conversations on all sides of this question, his generous help, and his unwavering faith in this project. Thanks to Jonah Sollins Devlin for making life outside of that room so rich, interesting, musical.

RELATIVE *Intimacy*

Introduction

> *His daughter's room was full of life. His own old microscope stood on*
> *Margaret's desk and around it was a litter of slides. . . . The books were*
> *beginning to be too many for the small bookshelf, starting with* The
> Little Family *and going on to his own soiled copy of* The Light That
> Failed*. . . . The dolls were no longer so much to the fore as they once*
> *were, but they were still about. . . . And he stood contemplating the*
> *room with a kind of desolation of love for it.*
> —Lionel Trilling, "The Other Margaret," 1945

The week that Pearl Harbor was bombed, *Life* was the only major magazine that did not have time to change its cover. Rather than an image of battleship guns ablaze or military commanders, *Life*'s cover on December 15, 1941, featured a picture of a sixteen-year-old girl: pretty, smiling coyly, and utterly oblivious to the national tragedy that had occurred a few days earlier.[1] The girl was Patricia Peardon, and she played a thirteen-year-old daughter in *Junior Miss*, a coming-of-age story that was Broadway's biggest hit of the 1941 season. Based on a series of encounters—alternately difficult, confused, and fawning—between Peardon and her father, *Junior Miss* depicted growing up as a process that was defined by moments of sexual recognition and appreciation that took place between an adolescent girl and her father. In chronicling these moments, *Junior Miss* was a harbinger of what would become a national preoccupation with the meaning—particularly the erotic meaning—of the father-daughter relationship in the aftermath of America's entrance into World War II. Indeed, in retrospect, what was probably a publishing mishap for *Life* looks like a prescient emblem of the cultural concerns of the war and postwar period.

At least since the mid-1920s, child psychologists had discussed the "happy girl who . . . has a father whom she can make the embodiment of her ideals."[2] Some of the more daring child experts incorporated Freudian notions of Oedipal attachment into their vision of female adolescence. But even in the best father-daughter relationships, the famed child psychologist G. Stanley Hall warned in 1925, "there are dangers. For if her fondness for her father is too intense . . . this may make it impossible for her ever to be happy if mated to a man not in the father image."[3] After America's entrance into World War II, warnings about overly intense Oedipal father-daughter relationships disappeared; they were discarded by a society suddenly—and universally—convinced of the special value of a father's contribution to his adolescent daughter as she began to sexually mature.

In the early 1940s, the father began to be portrayed as the most important witness to his daughter's transformations at adolescence: he was amused when she tried on her first pair of high heels, astounded when she appeared in her first cocktail dress, and weak-kneed when she emerged for her first junior prom. It became the common sense of an era—through the repetition of such scenes in parenting manuals, magazine fiction, advertising, Broadway plays, literature, journalism, and psychoanalytic studies of childhood—that this kind of paternal response to a daughter's transformation from child to young adult was how affection was—or should be—manifested. The moment at which, as one father put it, "he discovered that his baby had grown into quite a girl" was imbued with fresh meaning in the 1940s and 1950s, celebrated with unambiguous pleasure and eventually institutionalized as a highly ritualized event.[4] Such moments became definitive—socially, psychologically, and sexually—for daughter and father alike.

This book examines the unprecedented scale of interest in the father-adolescent daughter relationship during the war and postwar era, the sexual themes that informed its representation, and the decline of any detectable caution, particularly on the part of psychoanalysts, in espousing the benefits of the female adolescent's Oedipal attachment to her father. It argues that because of these developments, the relationship between father and adolescent daughter came to be understood, in ways both subtle and overt, as primarily—if not exclusively—erotic in nature. Taken separately, transformations either in scholarly thinking about female adolescent development or in popular representations of fathers and daughters would comprise noteworthy historical developments. Together, they reflect a fundamental shift in the social meaning of the father-daughter relationship and challenge us to consider its significance to postwar sexual culture.

I begin with the most authoritative—and striking—changes in

thinking about adolescent girls' relationship with their fathers produced by psychoanalysts practicing in the United States during and just after World War II. I then consider some of the events that prompted psychoanalysts to reformulate their assumptions about adolescent girls, particularly a steep rise in female juvenile delinquency cases in the 1940s and the growth of institutions created to monitor and control girls' behavior. I argue that the diagnosis collectively embraced by psychoanalysts working with "wayward girls" —that antisocial behavior originated in Oedipal disturbance during adolescence—played a major role in establishing the father as the sexual focal point of female adolescent psychology. I then examine the idiom of eroticism that informed virtually every representation of adolescent girls and their fathers in popular culture. I begin with the earliest, often subtle, erotic links that appeared between 1941 and 1948 in plays, marketing campaigns, advice books, and works of fiction. The next period, 1948–60, saw the triumph of the eroticized view of the father-daughter relationship in popular culture, a period when the celebration of paternal economic indulgence, frank sexual interest, and rituals of paternal sexual recognition held sway. A final chapter is devoted to exploring literature and plays that took a more skeptical view of men's motivations in dealings with their adolescent daughters. Father–adolescent daughter eroticism leads, in these works, to empty sexual banter, abject paternal sexual desire, or father-daughter incest. While some writers explored the moral dimensions of incestuous relationships, others simply exploited, caricatured, or satirized the eroticism of the modern father-daughter relationship—a fact that provides some clues to weakness inherent in its conceptualization.

Most of the material on girls and their fathers was considered "fluff" when it appeared and has since been forgotten. Much of the psychoanalytic literature has been rejected by current practitioners. As with so much of women's history, ideas and images have been thrown out, superseded, and, most important, condemned as silly. Meanwhile, texts both popular and academic about boys (and very often their fathers) have been canonized and reprinted. Arthur Miller's *Death of a Salesman* (1949), Paul Goodman's *Growing Up Absurd: The Problems of Youth in an Organized Society* (1960), J. D. Salinger's *Catcher in the Rye* (1945), and Erik Erikson's *Childhood and Society* (1950)—our impressions of the midcentury relationship between parents and children, youth and authority, have been molded by these texts. In many instances, the material on girls and their fathers simply does not measure up to these works; in others, texts have been unjustly forgotten. Yet we must keep in mind that at the time of their creation, works involving ideas about fathers and daughters were just as influential and very often more popular. To name just a few: Helene Deutsch's towering work of psychoanalysis, *The Psychology of Women* (1944); the hit plays (and films) *Kiss and Tell* (1943; film, 1945) and *Janie* (1942; film, 1944); Carson McCullers's *Member of the Wedding* (book, 1946; play, 1950; film, 1952); Grace Metalious's record-breaking blockbuster, *Peyton Place* (1956; film, 1957); Edward Streeter's best-selling book of humor, *The Father of the Bride* (1948; film, 1950); Douglas Sirk's melodrama *Imitation of Life* (1959); and William Styron's acclaimed first novel, *Lie Down in Darkness* (1951).

The proposition that there was a pervasive cultural interest in fathers' relationships to their teenage daughters during the postwar years is at odds with several received ideas about the period. First, the 1940s and 1950s have widely been envisioned as the historical moment when teenagers dramatically and self-consciously separated themselves from adults, including their parents, and America became an "age stratified society." [5] The achievement of near-universal high school attendance, the segregation of high schools from lower schools, and the rapid growth of teen incomes—a $10 billion market by 1958—have supposedly been the key factors behind a rupture between adolescents and the rest of society. [6] In the face of large and increasingly bureaucratic public high schools, teenagers created— through fads, fashions, magazines, and private rituals—a world of their own. The gradual but definitive acceptance of sexual liberalism on the part of parents was particularly important for girls. [7] Girls reported a sharp decline in conflict with their parents about "how often to date and appropriate places to go." [8] At the same time, however, the system of "going steady," according to historian John Modell, remained threatening to adult observers, who thought it offered "premature liberties, dominated by a code of alien design." [9] Apparent sexual precocity was accompanied by a steady decline in the ages at which girls married, from 20.5 in 1947 to 20.1 in 1956. By the late 1950s, the most common age at which girls married was 18. Histories of postwar youth have thus emphasized the increasing independence of adolescents, beginning with what Joseph Kett has called an "insulated value system" during the high school years, followed by early marriage and the creation of their own families.[10]

Assumptions about adolescent separateness during the postwar period began with contemporary observers' perceptions of teenage alienation. Erik Erikson famously recommended that children be given a "social moratorium" during adolescence; Holden Caulfield railed against "phony" adults in *Catcher in the Rye*; and popular books regularly bemoaned the distance between parents and children with titles such as *"But You Just Don't Understand"* (1950), *"Where Did You Go?" "Out," "What Did You Do?" "Nothing"* (1957), *The Adolescent Society* (1961), and *Teen-Age Tyranny* (1963).[11] The advent of *Seventeen* magazine in 1944, the screaming idolatry of Elvis in the mid-1950s, the insularity of "hep" language and fashions—all seem to have reduced parents to marginal figures in girls' lives. With their daughters' bedroom doors closed, the music blaring, and the soda shop beckoning, parents became irrelevant. Parents were to provide the funding, the schooling, and the opportunities, and then, in the name of sexual liberalism and American freedom, kindly step aside. Not only did social commentators envision American childhood in this manner at mid-century, it is a form of coming-of-age that many believe to be one of our most important social inheritances from the postwar period. As the historian Christopher Lasch wrote in his influential book on the modern family, *Haven in a Heartless World: The Family Besieged*, "parents accept their obsolescence with the best grace they can muster, voluntarily relegating themselves to the background of their children's lives."[12]

The other dominant perception of the 1950s that is challenged by the fascination with eroticism between fathers and adolescent daughters is the image of social and sexual conservatism that is so central to our understanding of the period, despite thoroughgoing revisions by such prominent historians as Elaine Tyler May, Beth L. Bailey, and Joanne Meyerowitz. According to this still-prevalent view, postwar Americans effectively exchanged the sophisticated, worldly, politicized values of the New Deal era for what appeared to be a safer path: isolationism, political disengagement, and a bland, anesthetized culture. Some rebelled, but most capitulated to what one journalist recently called "the country's platonic image of itself at mid-century"

—an image of America as wholesome, cheerful, and churchgoing.[13] There was, as Stephen J. Whitfield has described it, a "proclivity to hang a giant Do Not Disturb sign over the nation."[14]

Because of this powerful image of the decade, the historiographical debate has centered on the extent of the impact of the family ideal, rather than the nature of its expression. How did women and men absorb the ideal of "family togetherness"? Did older, progressive movements for social change "survive" or did they disappear?[15] Were women "happy" in their new homes or "miserable"?[16] Did the 1950s represent a throwback to more "traditional" family life, or was it a "bridge" or "link" to the social movements of the 1960s?[17] One problem with these inquiries is that, for many historians, the real interest is not with the 1950s but with how we got to the 1960s. For others, in contrast, it has been impossible to get out from under the sentimental yearnings attached to the 1950s. It is a decade, to many, of exemplary moral strength and singular cultural innocence, one that has become, in Frederic Jameson's words, a "privileged lost object of desire."[18] The seductive appeal of this notion of the 1950s has often made it difficult to make the postwar period feel in any sense real, even when those who have written its history actually lived through it.

The seismic shifts in ideas about family life that occurred in the postwar period, however, suggest a form of interaction between fathers and adolescent daughters that required anything but "naive innocence" on the part of the American public.[19] What we see in the father-daughter relationship is something very different: a culture that provided fresh opportunities for eroticism and ever more sophisticated modes of sexual self-understanding. Though adolescent girls might have been more "on their own" in certain ways, in others, their relationship with their fathers was imbued with unprecedented intimacy, sexual power, and cultural prominence (significantly, at the expense of their relationships with their mothers). While girls might have been segregated from parents on a day-to-day basis, they were newly depicted as fundamentally motivated by their Oedipal needs, dependent upon paternal sexual approval, and interested in their fathers' romantic lives. The locus of the father's role might have shifted —from protector and occasional "companion" to Oedipal object— but in the process the paternal role was actually enhanced rather than diminished.

Why did American culture become so consumed with the question of the sexual significance of the relationship between adolescent daughters and their fathers at midcentury? Why did psychoanalysts, the popular media, and the American public become fascinated with the dynamics of the father-daughter relationship and the increasingly seductive exchanges that became its chief characteristic? What did the eroticization of "normal" father-daughter relationships have to do with the enormous popularity of literary and dramatic representations of father-daughter incest? Or with larger historical developments, including the end of the war and the rise of youth culture, the growing influence of psychoanalysis and economic prosperity?

In some measure, scholarly interest in fatherhood was inspired by demographic shifts caused by the war. The return of soldiers after World War II prompted widespread discussion about the place of men in the American family. Wartime absence—of fathers, husbands, and sons—affected almost one-fifth of the nation's families.[20] As William M. Tuttle has shown, the reintegration of a father into the family could prove difficult: children grew used to life without him and were sometimes afraid or resentful upon his return.[21] Social scientists "discovered" that boys had trouble establishing male identity in a culture in which they were brought up primarily (or during the war exclusively) by their mothers.[22] In the face of such social anxieties, sociologists and psychologists redoubled their efforts to explain the particular nature of the paternal contribution to the rearing of children. Combining "sex-role sociology" with Freudian ideas about Oedipal attraction, sociologists and psychologists argued that although girls identified directly with their mothers, their fathers served as an exemplar of the kind of man they would one day marry, and thus fathers should think of themselves as their "daughters' first boyfriend."[23]

More important, the rise of psychoanalysis in the United States after the Second World War had a profound impact on ideas about the father-daughter relationship.[24] The insights of psychoanalysis went virtually unquestioned among social scientists during this era, its methods were respected if not revered among much of the literary and artistic intelligentsia, and psychoanalytic concepts were popularized and made glamorous in the mainstream media by journalists' enamored portrayals of individual psychoanalysts.[25] So, in seeking to understand why the father-daughter relationship was eroticized in the 1950s, another obvious answer might be that the culture as a whole began to see parent-child relationships in Freudian terms. The psychoanalytic perspective, we might deduce, simply transformed the way in which human personality and family relationships were perceived, locating needs and conflicts in a dense web of projections, identifications, and subconscious fantasies, much of it stemming from the Oedipal drama. One might say that the father-daughter relationship was not so much eroticized during this period as perceived through the lens of the Oedipus complex.

To make such an interpretation, however, would be to mistake a complicated cultural shift in perceptions about the meaning of the father-adolescent daughter relationship in the 1940s and 1950s for the intellectual paradigm in which it took place. For postwar culture did not simply lift ideas about fathers and daughters wholesale from a bedrock of established psychoanalytic principles. Rather, social change, popular culture, and psychoanalytic theory influenced each other. Had psychoanalysts, playwrights, or screenwriters chosen to represent eroticism between mothers and sons in a manner that assumed its normalcy, they could have found the evidence they needed in early psychoanalytic literature. But they did not.

Indeed, postwar culture exhibited an *anxiety* about mother-son eroticism that, much like the new attitudes toward father-daughter eroticism, went beyond and ultimately transformed the prewar psychoanalytic perspective. Michael Rogin has argued that in the popular imagination maternal love for sons—often portrayed as entrapping and incestuous—was connected to primitive fears about boundary invasion and Communist infiltration. The movies *My Son John* (1952) and *The Manchurian Candidate* (1962), he writes, "located the threat to the free man less in the alien Communist state than in his loving mother."[26] As Rebecca Plant has also shown, sexual anxieties about the mother-son relationship were central to the peculiarly American problem of "momism"—as it was described within both the social sciences and popular culture—during the postwar period.[27] Unsurprisingly, in the psychoanalytic case histories of the postwar period, mother-son eroticism inevitably lead to neurosis on the part of the boy.[28] Fears about eroticism between mother and son may yet prove to be intimately bound up with the celebration of father-daughter eroticism during the 1940s and 1950s.

Though it was not often openly discussed, the question of paternal authority was necessarily a historical factor as well. In the 1940s and 1950s paternal authority was officially on the wane, if not extinct, in the United States. With anxieties about authoritarianism abroad and the rise of sexual liberalism at home, the postwar period has often been viewed as the end point in a process of the erosion of patriarchal power that began in the nineteenth century. The primacy of mothers, according to Mary Ryan, replaced that of fathers in the early nineteenth century when the corporate—and patriarchal—economy gradually gave way to market conditions that removed men from the home. "Mother love," she writes, "filled the vacuum left by paternal indifference as men became preoccupied with secular, economic concerns outside the household."[29] With the departure of men an emphasis on will-breaking and discipline was replaced with a commitment to tenderness and more gradual forms of socialization.[30] When at the turn of the century attempts were made to reinvigorate middle-class men's relationship to their children, efforts were geared toward shared leisure, particularly activities that would channel boys' energies into what Margaret Marsh has described as "manly" outlets such as sports and camping.[31]

Still, despite the growing ideal of "masculine domesticity," men's influence over their families, according to historians of fatherhood, continued to decline over the course of the twentieth century. The state expanded its power over children through the family court system, parent education movements aimed themselves almost exclusively at women, and consumer culture increasingly absorbed children's energies and attention.[32] Representations of "bumbling" fathers in comic strips and on television in the 1950s—if not the distraction of television itself—has been viewed as the final blow to paternal authority, the cultural genesis of the social reality of "poor old dad."[33] Overwhelmed by such a panoply of forces, men supposedly ceded power over their children, as well as a stake in maintaining it. By the 1950s, fathers, it seems, had been firmly relegated to an extracurricular role in American family life.[34] "In few societies," observed the anthropologist Geoffrey Gorer in 1948, "is the role of father more vestigial than in the United States."[35]

The kind of man who fostered romantic attraction in his daughter, whose attitude was one of fond indulgence or admiration of her physical charms, does indeed seem to cut a modest figure, to be the very opposite of the supposedly "heavy-handed, despotic male parent" of the past.[36] This image, however, does not mean that paternal power disappeared. Instead, what power men did hold over their daughters, I argue, was reconfigured—culturally—in terms of erotic bonds between father and daughter. The eroticization of the father–adolescent daughter relationship reformulated paternal power by several means: by establishing that girls' psychological health was *inescapably* dependent upon a good—and most certainly unrebellious—relationship with their fathers; by maintaining that girls' sexual acts were not autonomously undertaken but always reflected prior, Oedipal feelings for their fathers; and, finally, by establishing social conventions that instilled the idea that girls should (and inevitably would) look to their fathers, before anyone else, for sexual approval. This new kind of bond between father and adolescent daughter helped to preserve paternal authority without encroaching too implacably on the tenets of sexual liberalism or threatening the ideal of egalitarian family life so central to America's vision of itself in the aftermath of World War II.[37]

The eroticized father–adolescent daughter relationship also helped negotiate an important commodity in modern life: time. For the kind of father-daughter relationship we see portrayed during the postwar period was one that did not require any kind of sustained activity, prolonged engagement, or even much mutual interaction. Fathers offered instantaneous assessments of their daughters' looks. The banter and flirtatious encounters we see represented on stage, in film, and in literature represented brief episodes of exchange rather than shared activity. The big occasions—the walk down the aisle, the first dance at a coming-out party, the presentation of gifts—were singular events that nonetheless managed to convey a great deal of meaning. Which is not to say that such rituals were not important—quite the opposite—but simply that the father's role took little time to perform. In a recent study of middle-class families living in California in the 1950s, Jessica Weiss found that over 45 percent of fathers worked over fifty hours a week (a number that does not include the often long commutes to and from the suburbs). Robert Griswold has argued that the mounting pressure on men after World War II to provide for rising standards of living intruded upon their ability to spend time with their families.[38] Hence the elaboration of these middle-class rituals allowed fathers to maintain a distinct and even preeminent role in their daughters' lives despite the demands of professional life.

Perhaps the most compelling answer to the question of why the father-adolescent daughter relationship was eroticized during the postwar period can be found in the thematic links between psychoanalysis and popular culture. Case histories, Broadway plays, and popular literature all shared the assumption—often couched as diagnosis—that it was the father's role to recognize his daughter's need for sexual approval. A father should participate in—rather than guard against—the new forms of sexualized consumerism in which his teenage daughter was involved. He should not only condone but delight in the sexual transformations suggested in her new use of lipstick, her first pair of high heels, her strapless junior prom gown. It was this revised understanding of the father-daughter relationship that allowed for and helped facilitate the massive commercialization and sexualization of "girls' culture" at midcentury. What direct authority fathers may have given up was replaced with the subtle, psychological power of erotic attraction. Indeed, it is impossible to conceive of the emergence of the glamorous postwar teenage girl without her father, not simply because his permission was technically necessary for her to procure these new accoutrements, but because he was so consistently imagined as a central character within her sartorial and cosmetic coming-of-age.

Finally, by rendering the pleasures and privileges of the eroticized father-daughter relationship in ways that were expressly limited to the rituals of white middle-class life, this particular kind of paternal power—or lack of it—became an important marker of class and racial identity. For instance, there was, in black middle-class culture, a similar fascination with bobby-soxers in the 1950s. Depictions of the consumerism, achievements, and debutante balls of the black middle-class teenage girl were a staple of *Ebony* magazine, which began publication in 1945. However, such depictions, up until the early 1960s, included fathers and daughters pictured in ways that were much more restrained and physically distanced than they were in white culture. The formality characteristic of black middle-class representations of the father-daughter relationship stands in stark contrast to the casually erotic representations of the white father-daughter relationship—a reminder both of the latitude available to white culture in creating its own image and of the sexual imperatives inherent in the project of black aspirations for middle-class identity.[39]

Chapter 1 begins with an examination of the most famous and influential text on girlhood of the period, Helene Deutsch's groundbreaking book, *The Psychology of Women*. Peter Blos and Phyllis Greenacre—prominent scholars in the later postwar period but largely unfamiliar today—followed in Deutsch's footsteps, contributing to the general presumption that a girls' adult sexual identity depended upon her Oedipal experiences with her father at adolescence—an idea that became axiomatic in the field of psychoanalysis in the 1950s. Postwar therapists working in the United States did not invent the concept of a child's romantic and/or sexual desire for the parent of the opposite sex, or his/her competition with the parent of the same sex to secure those affections. What was new about the American postwar psychoanalytic perspective was the overriding concern with what Deutsch called the "second edition" of the Oedipus complex at puberty in *girls* (boys eradicated Oedipal desire with the onset of puberty) and lack of engagement with the question of how girls resolved—or grew out of—their Oedipal relationships with their fathers.[40] As a group, postwar psychoanalysts working in the United States were far more invested in the benefits of a healthy father-daughter Oedipal eroticism, and less concerned with its possible dangers, than those who came before or after them, in either the United States or Europe.

The social context within which psychoanalysts found themselves in the United States in the 1940s helps to explain their concerns. Psychoanalysts—in their private practices, at juvenile court clinics, and at government-sponsored youth centers—were confronted with behavior that seemed confrontational, disobedient, even hostile. One of the least understood aspects of the postwar interest in adolescent girls is that much of it was sparked by the rise in female juvenile delinquency, an increase that began in the mid-1940s and was characterized by behavior that was considered "anti-social"—truancy, running away, smoking, vandalizing property, forming gangs, and fighting with both parents and peers. In Chapter 2 I consider this steep rise in girls' crime, especially relative to boys', both on its own terms and in terms of the effect it had on psychoanalysts. Girls who defied authority often found themselves under the purview of a court clinic, and it was from experiences with these girls that many psychoanalysts formulated their theories of female adolescent Oedipal longing, frustration, and dysfunction.

The psychoanalytic response to female juvenile delinquency, however, comprises only one element of the rise of what was a multifaceted interest in the erotic nature of the father–adolescent daughter relationship in the United States in the 1940s and 1950s. Depictions of the father-daughter relationship emerged as a forum in which to discuss public curiosity about changes in the dress and demeanor of girls during the war. Much of the transformation in girls had to do with rising levels of income (both their own and their parents'), the growth of the youth market, and girls' individual creativity. However, no matter her delinquencies and sartorial daring, the perception of the adolescent girl that became dominant in the 1950s was the one invented by journalists, advertisers, and screenwriters: indulged and adored, the "teenage girl" became the symbol of an economic recovery that, confounding all expectations, continued after demobilization. As *Newsweek* explained in 1954, "when our editors decided to do a cover story on Atlanta's remarkable industrial progress, they all agreed that the cover picture should be of a typical Atlanta schoolgirl . . . a fresh, bright teen-ager would best symbolize the growth and vitality of the New South."[41]

Celebration of the economic good fortune of adolescent girls was usually couched in terms of the positive effects of ego-building and success with peers. Popularity in high school and personal attractiveness were attributed to a father's capacity to give his daughter all of the emotional and financial equipment necessary to achieve the look of "natural confidence" that new magazines for teenage girls like *Seventeen* endorsed.[42] This social/economic exchange between father and daughter gave positive sanction to the booming economy: social commentators and magazine editors might complain about wives spending their husband's paychecks during the 1950s, but the social approbation for a daughter's consumerism, when conducted within the bounds of paternal approval, knew no bounds.[43] Chapters 3 and 4 examine the father-daughter erotic/economic exchange that was constantly imagined as existing at the center of postwar economic growth and social change.

The potential for paternal lasciviousness in the performance of modern forms of paternal duty was noted, in different contexts, with humor, with dismay, and, perhaps surprisingly, with pleasure. Chapter 5 examines the ways in which playwrights and fiction writers interpreted, agonized over, and exploited the eroticism of new forms of paternal involvement—usually with great commercial success. The most successful was F. Hugh Herbert, creator of Corliss Archer, character of stage, screen, and radio. Though almost entirely forgotten today, Herbert was a self-consciously sophisticated, urbane, and fantastically prolific playwright and screenwriter. He deserves attention here in part because of the enormous and heretofore unexamined impact his portrayal of Corliss Archer had on more serious, culturally weighty depictions of American father-daughter dynamics in William Styron's *Lie Down in Darkness* and Vladimir Nabokov's *Lolita* (1955).

In this work, I have drawn more from imaginative literature, and less from sociological sources, than most studies of the immediate past. There are good reasons for historians to turn to longitudinal studies in particular. Orderly sets of questions issued to ordinary individuals offer a thorough, on-the-ground account of a period and often a democratic perspective. The sources for this project are the ones that, for the most part, the topic led me to.[44] It is perhaps telling that the more traditional sources on fatherhood and family life—the minutes of parenting classes, the *Senate Hearings on Drafting Fathers*, to name just a few—had less to say about fathers and daughters than did playwrights and novelists. Any study can only make partial claims about the dreams and desires that animate a society at a given moment in history; one among many ways to proceed is to locate and interpret what people found entertaining. If, as historians of women and sexuality have been pointing out since the 1970s, ideology and pleasure are inextricable, we must think about the off-the-record parts of people's lives, the places—whether real or imagined—where they found comfort, excitement, or amusement.[45] As Keith Thomas put it, "If we are to understand the minds of people in the past, to go on reading until we can hear them talking, it is partly to literature that we must turn."[46]

The point of examining *Lolita*, or for that matter other iconic cultural products of the postwar period, is not exegesis and re-interpretation (I leave this work to specialists in their respective fields) so much as it is an attempt to situate them in the day-to-day journalism, popular books, and lesser-known plays and public information in which they trafficked. Works on fathers and daughters relied on ideas produced elsewhere in the culture, if sometimes only in an indirect manner, sharing what the historian William H. Prescott has called "the informing spirit which gives life to the whole."[47] Of course, this approach assumes that an informing intellectual perspective can be reconstructed—a point upon which there is some debate. And yet, when disparate elements of midcentury culture are assembled side by side, a coherence emerges, comprised of moments between fathers and adolescent daughters that are magnified, resonant, and reiterated.

That the eroticized father-daughter relationship was consistently envisioned in so many places at once does not mean, however, that ideas about it were internally coherent.[48] For all the problems that the eroticized father-daughter relationship seemed to resolve—the need for a new, more psychologically "modern" conception of fatherhood, the lack of time available to breadwinners, and the assertion of class and racial status in a mobile society—this relationship is as remarkable for the questions that it raised as for the answers it provided. Eroticizing the father-daughter relationship was an inherently vexed proposition, one that privileged the father-daughter relationship in unprecedented ways while rendering its nature and actual practice more elusive, its fundamental laws potentially susceptible to the suggestion of incestuous transgression. Father-daughter eroticism was both titillating and anxiety producing, both an answer to the problem of representing a model of father-daughter intimacy and a cause of its demise. Ultimately, the contradictions at the heart of the discourse on fathers and daughters operated to sustain the relationship's status as a *dilemma* rather than to facilitate a set of everyday practices. The cultural force of the eroticized father-daughter relationship grew out of and manifested itself in the questions it raised and left unanswered, hinted at and then failed to address. The effect was to render masculine domesticity—at least insofar as it related to girls—a fragile and unresolved proposition.

Chapter 1

THE OEDIPAL AGE

> *Born ten years and yet an aeon*
> *Too early for the twenties,*
> *Mother, you smile*
> *As if you saw your Father*
> *Inches away yet hidden, as when he groused behind a screen*
> *Over a National Geographic Magazine,*
> *Whenever young men came to court you*
> *Back in those settled years of World War One.*
> *Terrible that old life of decency*
> *Without unseemly intimacy*
> *Or quarrels, when the unemancipated woman*
> *still had her Freudian papa and maids!*
> —Robert Lowell, "During Fever," Life Studies, 1956

In 1960, Kata Levy, a psychotherapist who worked with children and adolescents, published an article in the *Psychoanalytic Study of the Child* about "Debby G.," an adolescent girl who suffered from "school phobia." Afraid to interact with children her own age, or even leave the house in the morning, Debby eventually had to withdraw from high school. "Fear, clinging to her mother, aggressive outbreaks, and obsessional habits were the surface manifestations" of a child who could not bear to strike out on her own.[1] After making little headway with her patient, Levy recommended that Debby's mother, "Mrs. G.," undergo treatment as well. Levy found that Mrs. G. was an "overprotective" mother and that, though she "consciously wished to loosen the ties by which her daughter was attached to her," she could not bring herself to "relinquish her pathological hold on the child." However, Mrs. G.'s overprotection was not, according to Levy, unhealthy because it prevented Debby from achieving independence and personal autonomy. Rather, the attachment between mother and daughter interfered with a far more important goal for Debby: her Oedipal relationship with her father. Mrs. G., Levy discovered, had attempted to "isolate and separate father and daughter" because she wanted to "keep her husband for herself." Debby, for her part, complained that her mother "excluded her from their relationship." Levy's final diagnosis was that Debby's social phobias stemmed from the fact that her Oedipus complex "was belated and unsolved."[2] The cure was to allow Debby access to her father and for her adolescent Oedipal desire to be given an outlet for expression.

Though mother and daughter are the only actors in this case history, "Mr. G." is at the center of Levy's analysis. As long as Debby was a child, according to Levy, the exclusive and overinvolved relationship between mother and daughter, while unhealthy, did not keep Debby from maintaining a fairly normal routine. But with the onset of adolescence — a moment when sexual needs asserted themselves with renewed vigor — Debby's lack of contact with her father became a crisis. For Levy, the Oedipus complex was the most powerful and determinative experience of adolescence. The Oedipal relationship was the route through which Debby would grow into sexual maturity, explore the wider world, and find her way among her peers.

In this chapter I will explore how, during the 1940s and 1950s, American psychoanalysts came to view the adolescent girls' Oedipal relationship with her father as the preeminent and defining experience of her development. When Sigmund Freud first introduced the notion of the Oedipus complex in the nineteenth century, and when his followers elaborated upon and enlarged his ideas in the early years of the twentieth century, the conversation about the "Oedipal wish" had revolved around discussions of young children. It was not until World War II that psychoanalysts began to think extensively about how Oedipal desire might influence the process whereby girls matured into women.

The issue proved compelling: whereas with young children knowledge of relations between the sexes was limited, and most likely filled with misconceptions, in the case of adolescent girls, Oedipal desire took place within the psyche of a person who was on the cusp of adulthood, a person who had the capacity to realistically understand the nature of heterosexual desire. Psychoanalysts seized upon the depth and consequential nature of adolescent sexual drives and shaped a theory of female identity and sexuality that was entangled at all levels with Oedipal drives. A successful Oedipal father-daughter relationship began to be viewed as the key to psychological health, and a diagnosis of "Oedipal conflict" applied to a wide range of adolescent disturbances. Analysts endeavored to understand how girls mobilized Oedipal fantasies in the course of "normal" adolescent development and to assess the impact of frustrated Oedipal desire on female juvenile delinquency and antisocial behavior. Studies appeared on the role that female adolescent Oedipal desire played in sexual assault and father-daughter incest. In short, postwar interest in the female adolescent Oedipus complex exploded.

The Oedipus complex is, of course, the defining discovery of the science of psychoanalysis. What distinguishes war and postwar psychoanalysts, however, from their prewar counterparts is their belief in the relative psychological power of the adolescent Oedipus complex in girls and, somewhat contradictorily, their perception that American girls were failing to adequately enter into the adolescent Oedipal situation. The reasons for postwar interest in the female adolescent Oedipus complex cannot be entirely accounted for. However, the timing is tellingly commensurate with the rising anxiety within the profession about the overwhelming—even dangerous—influence of mothers on child development. By the late 1950s almost any and every kind of childhood disorder, like a fingerprint, had come to be seen as the stamp of a certain kind of mothering. There was the "seductive" mother, the mother who was "cold," and the "rejecting" mother.[3] Most famously, there was, as we saw in the case of "Mrs. G.," the "overprotective" mother, first delineated (in psychoanalytic terms) by David Levy in 1943. "Maternal overprotection," according to Levy, was synonymous with "excessive maternal care" and the prevention of independent behavior.[4] It was within this context that the emphasis on the necessity of paternal intervention into the mother-daughter relationship emerged. Indeed, one of the most striking aspects of the depiction of female adolescence during the postwar period is the extent to which a girl's engagement with her father was invariably represented as a form of psychological progress—simply because Oedipal feelings led away from the mother.

The changing behavior of adolescent girls themselves was also an important historical factor. Psychoanalysis, though rarified enough, did not exist in a vacuum. It was animated by the dominant preoccupations of the period—rising rates of juvenile delinquency among adolescent girls, sexual precocity, and the sense that paternal authority in particular was threatened by transformations in youth culture in the United States. When psychoanalysts recorded their case histories on adolescent girls, many—as we shall see in later chapters—had these larger social concerns in mind.

However, psychoanalytic theories, it is important to point out, both mirrored larger social desires and anxieties in America and drove them. Indeed, the father-daughter relationships depicted in a range of cultural forms over the course of the postwar period—from the sexual crisis induced by the absent father in Carson McCullers's novel (and play/movie) *The Member of the Wedding* (1946), to the description of the ideal father-daughter relationship in Dr. Spock's *Common Sense Book of Baby and Child Care* (1945), to the depiction of father-daughter incest in William Styron's *Lie Down in Darkness* (1952)—were all informed by the psychoanalytic perspective. Playwrights, screenwriters, authors of fiction, and social scientists viewed the father-daughter relationship, to greater and lesser degrees, through the lens of contemporary psychoanalytic theory. The conceptualization of the erotic content of the father–adolescent daughter relationship elsewhere in postwar culture is unimaginable without the emphasis on girls' Oedipal desire that occurred in psychoanalysis during this time.

The impact of the psychoanalytic perspective on female adolescence on American culture was due, in no small part, to the stature of psychoanalysis itself during and just after World War II. Embraced simultaneously by the psychiatric profession and by a postwar public eager for explanations of "war neuroses," psychoanalysis had a kind of authority during these years that was unparalleled, not just in the history of psychiatry, but in the history of social-scientific ideas. During the first wave of interest in psychoanalysis in the 1920s, Freudian concepts were glamorized by the urban upper classes and the bohemian avant-garde, who sought, in the adventurous spirit of sexual modernism, to challenge the taboos of Victorian culture, to revalue female sexuality, and to explore what Joel Pfister has called the "primitive within."[5] The second wave of interest in psychoanalysis, after World War II, was far more sober and wide-reaching. A large majority of

American physicians, according to Nathan Hale, simply came to feel that "psychoanalysis possessed a superior explanatory power."[6] The brand of psychoanalysis that was embraced with such enthusiasm during the 1950s was one that was easily reconcilable with the conservative social values of the day. Adopted less as a tool of individual liberation than as a way to understand family dynamics, it was used primarily as a technique for interpreting what has been called "intra-familial erotic life."[7]

It was also the golden age of popularization.[8] Journalistic accounts were more expert and favorable than they had once been, and detailed exegeses of psychoanalytic theories appeared in publications like *Scientific American*. The analyst, complete with couch and notepad, was so ubiquitous that he soon became a cartoon stereotype. Despite the ambivalence that these caricatures reflected, they also embodied, according to John Burnham, "an astonishing popular belief in [the analyst's] knowledge and power."[9] Indeed, by 1956, Freud had come to be seen as the equal of Copernicus or Galileo by the general public; and largely because of the popular interest and faith in psychoanalysis, the entire psychiatric profession took on a mantle of wisdom, even omnipotence.[10] "Vulgarizations" of Freudian ideas—very often ideas about fathers and daughters—appeared in publications ranging from *Time* to *Mademoiselle*, and small paperback publications explaining the theories of psychoanalysis, with titles like *The Story of My Psychoanalysis* (1950) and *The Fifty Minute Hour: A Collection of True Psychoanalytic Tales* (1956), proliferated.[11] But perhaps just as important to the process of popularization, the liberal intelligentsia embraced Freud's teachings. The number of Hollywood screenwriters and New York playwrights who were psychoanalyzed in the late 1940s and 1950s was legion, and they often dealt with questions of psychoanalysis directly in their writing.

Nonetheless, the psychoanalytic portrayal of the Oedipal father-adolescent daughter relationship—no matter the enormity of its social relevance and scientific authority—was of a delicate, and ultimately unstable, design. For the pervasive enthusiasm about the benefits of the Oedipal father-daughter relationship overwhelmed the question of how girls *grew out of or resolved the Oedipus complex*—an issue that had, in the period before World War II, been an integral part of the debate among psychoanalysts. The postwar perspective that viewed the onset of Oedipal desire solely as a positive achievement —rather than as a quandary that presented difficult psychological obstacles—ultimately threatened the very foundation of the father-daughter relationship itself: the incest taboo. In fact, some psycho-analysts became so convinced of the positive nature of the adolescent Oedipus complex that they came to view father–adolescent daugh-ter incest as a relatively benign event—one that was bound up with a healthy sexual attachment to the father on the part of the adolescent girl.

Psychoanalysts and Adolescence in the
United States: World War II and Beyond

Though psychoanalysts like to call Sigmund Freud's case his-tory of "Dora" (1905) the "first analysis of an adolescent girl," little was published on the subject up to the end of the Second World War.[12] In the years before World War II, questions about early childhood female development predominated; indeed, rancorous debate on the subject prevailed. Writing in Berlin, England, and Central Europe, the most important early figures of the psychoanalytic movement, such as Helene Deutsch, Jeanne Lampl–De Groot, Karen Horney, Ernst Jones, and Melanie Klein, did battle over the concepts of penis envy, the masculinity complex, genital transference, and the genesis of homo-sexuality. According to Mari Jo Buhle, the "disharmony in the ranks" over early childhood female sexuality lasted over a decade, from the mid-1920s through the late 1930s, and eventually forced Freud him-self to attempt to stem the controversy by clarifying his own views on the matter, which he did in his essay "Female Sexuality," published in 1932.[13]

By the time the psychoanalytic community became interested in the nature of female adolescence, much had changed. Over the course of World War II, many of the most prominent psychoanalysts had emigrated to the United States, finding positions in New York, Chi-cago, Boston, and Baltimore; many found work through contacts with American-born doctors and analysts who had once sought them out as teachers in Europe.[14] Following the political tenor of their adopted country, these analysts tended toward consensus rather than discord and were influenced by the development of psychiatric institutions as they had begun to emerge in the United States. The child guidance clinic, developed in the United States by Ethel Sturges and William Healy at the turn of the century, had become a well-established part of American urban life by the mid-1940s, employing large numbers of psychoanalysts.[15] With the exception of Anna Freud, who continued to live and work in London, the American refugee analysts and their native-born protégés worked on the question of adolescence with the most vigor.[16]

Many of the new children's agencies and clinics addressed problems of adolescent adjustment, juvenile delinquency, and sexual precocity. Psychoanalysts were not only confronted with a steep rise in juvenile crime during the war; they were also influenced by sensational reports of teenage girls flocking to soldiers' training camps, "determined to have one fling or better" while they could.[17] The behavior of the "amateur girls" during the war, the rapidly declining age at which girls married, and new dating practices such as "going steady" that emerged in the 1950s all contributed to concern about precocious female sexuality.[18] The émigrés were especially struck by the social anxiety and generational misunderstandings surrounding youth culture in the United States, and they applied their formidable analytical skills to addressing these problems.

Thus, when the most influential psychoanalysts moved from Europe to the United States, they began to ask new questions about female sexuality and the issues most hotly contested in the prewar era—penis envy, homosexuality, and the masculinity complex and/or castration complex—were superseded by a new research agenda. Psychoanalysts now asked how it was that girls managed to mature into heterosexual adults, how they succeeded in separating themselves from their mothers, and, finally, what role fathers played in both processes. Questions of maturity and adult heterosexuality were not limited to the study of girls, but as the interest in adolescence grew, articles about girls predominated in psychoanalytic journals.[19]

Adolescent girls, according to many psychoanalysts, made a more interesting study than boys because the goal of male adolescence—independence—was unequivocal. "The only difficulties he has to solve," wrote Helene Deutsch, "are the dissolution of the old object ties, the discovery of new ones, and the mastering of passive tendencies."[20] (In psychoanalytic terminology the person to whom a child is attracted, or to whom he attaches his needs, is called an "object," usually a parent.)[21]

Both boys and girls go through two phases of the "Oedipus complex," defined as attraction to the parent of the opposite sex and rivalrous hostility toward the parent of the same sex. The "first" Oedipus complex, which occurs in early childhood (approximately ages three to five) affects both male and female children with equal force. The "little man," Freud writes, "wants his mother all to himself, finds his father in the way . . . and shows his satisfaction when the father goes away or is absent." In little girls, "things proceed in just the same way, with the necessary reversal."[22] After experiencing the sexual or Oedipal intensity of the early years, children enter the latency period: from ages six to twelve sexual development comes to "a standstill or retrogression is observed."[23] However, during puberty or adolescence—at which time the sexual drives reassert themselves and Oedipal desire is revived—the experiences of boys and girls can take a radically different course. During World War II, psychoanalysts fully defined the differences between male and female sexuality at puberty. According to Helene Deutsch, girls experienced "the second edition of the Oedipus situation" with far more intensity than boys.[24] When Oedipal desire recurred among boys at adolescence, it was immediately repressed. Indeed, the prohibition against the drive was simultaneous with the onset of the drive itself. The adolescent boy, as one psychoanalyst put it, "denies the goal by rejecting his parents. He may evaluate his mother as physically unattractive, mentally stupid and emotionally silly."[25] Hence, as Anna Freud theorized in *The Ego and the Mechanisms of Defense* (1946), (male) adolescents became "touchy" and ascetic because they were actively involved in defending against the return to old objects. Self-imposed isolation, she says, is "prompted by the general antagonism to instinct" and directs itself "against the subject's fixation to all the love-objects of his childhood."[26]

In girls, the recrudescence of sexual drives after latency reactivated the Oedipus complex in its old form, and they found their way back into an Oedipal relationship with their father. Repression, renunciation, isolation, rejection, and withdrawal took place only in relationship to one object: her mother. However, accomplishing this attitude toward her mother, something that was characterized as very difficult for girls to do, was only her first "task of adolescing," as Erik Erikson put it.[27] Her second task was to reinterpret and remold her sexual identity as it related to an earlier object: her father. At the center of this design for female development was a single, basic contradiction: girls were to find their way out of early sexual ties through the re-experiencing of those ties at puberty. In other words, they were to mature out of the matrix of family sexuality through the sexual experience of the family itself.

This rather vexed aspect of postwar thinking about female adolescence is one that rested on highlighting and re-describing the female adolescent Oedipus complex as Freud had originally envisioned it, rather than changing its fundamental definition. When Helene Deutsch laid the foundation for the shift in thinking on the female adolescent Oedipus complex in *The Psychology of Women* (1944), she achieved much through the unique tone she employed to talk about fathers and daughters, and through her description of the extent to which what she called "female eroticism" rested on a girl's experience of her relationship with her father.

Helene Deutsch and The Psychology of Women

Helene Deutsch's two-volume work on female adolescent development and womanhood, *The Psychology of Women*, was, for a dense work on psychoanalysis, a phenomenal success. The most widely read work on adolescence during the postwar period after Erik Erikson's *Childhood and Society*, it underwent sixteen printings between 1944 and 1965. It was consulted more than almost any other psychoanalytic text in professional social-scientific journals, and, until the rise of feminism in the early 1960s, remained the unchallenged authority on all aspects of girls' psychological passage from girlhood to womanhood.[28] Yet Deutsch is a marginal figure in histories of psychology and psychoanalysis. She is often omitted in psychology reference books, and she has garnered nothing approaching the attention given to her contemporary and longtime adversary, Karen Horney.[29] The disinterest in her work today on the part of psychologists and psychoanalysts reflects a decades-long attempt by the profession to distance itself from Freud's most overtly sexist ideas. Once called "Freud's Darling," Deutsch, unlike Horney, remained faithful to Freud, both personally and in terms of her basic perspective on women, throughout her life.[30] Perhaps most devastating to her reputation, *The Psychology of Women* was used as the primary authority in support of the polemics of Marynia F. Farnham and Ferdinand Lundberg in their best-selling antifeminist treatise *Modern Woman: The Lost Sex* (1947). Farnham and Lundberg's theory that the "denial of the feminine in childhood" was responsible for the "loss of capacity for satisfaction in both tenderness and sexuality" in adult women was based entirely on Deutsch's conceptualization of girls' erotic nature and development.[31] Thus Deutsch's ideas were overtly deployed in an effort to return women to the home during the demobilization period after World War II, to disavow feminism, and to limit women's roles to those directly connected to sexuality and reproduction.

That Deutsch's ideas were put to such an antifeminist purpose is not without irony. Born in 1884 to a middle-class Jewish family in Austrian Poland, Deutsch was one of only three women to receive a medical degree from the University of Vienna in 1914. She was an ardent feminist and socialist during these years, lobbying cabinet ministers to let women study law, leading a strike of women textile workers in the Polish town of Przemysl, and working tirelessly for the Polish Social Democratic Party.[32] She was one of two women to join the Vienna Psychoanalytic Society in 1918, and she quickly established herself as one of Freud's most promising followers. From her earliest years as an analyst she dreamed of establishing an institution to treat neurotic and psychotic adolescent girls; in 1925 she became the first psychoanalyst to write a book on feminine psychology.[33] Renowned especially as a teacher, she was the director of the Vienna Psychoanalytic Society's Training Institute from 1924 to 1935.[34] August Aichorn, Edward Bibring, Ruth Mack Brunswick, Anna Freud, Heinz Hartmann, and Wilhelm Reich all taught under her. She would later call upon some of these powerful figures for assistance when she fled the Nazi occupation in 1935.

This history is evident in *The Psychology of Women* in her interest in the psychic processes whereby women become selflessly dedicated to higher political causes. Yet her attitude toward "careers" for women was contradictory at best. On the one hand, she claimed that too many women entered careers because it was the "fashionable" thing to do, and that professionalization could, in fact, threaten their basic "femininity." On the other, she stated that those women who were most "driven" deserved to be "creators and organizers in all the departments of peaceful life."[35] Women were capable of "brilliance" in artistic and, of course, psychoanalytic fields and "heroism" in political causes—particularly when they made use of the kind of intuition and ability for selflessness with which nature had so amply endowed them.[36] These women were the exception, however, and family life was described as "the exclusive source of women's well being."[37]

An overriding sense of foreboding about the current state of feminine adolescence gives the book a flavor of a later modernity, one that reflected a pervasive anxiety, even pessimism, that was characteristic of the World War II period.[38] Perils lay in store for the adolescent girl, both in the world at large and in the abundance of psychic obstacles inherent in adolescence itself. Gang activity, delinquency, and "promiscuity," all of which were exacerbated by what Deutsch called "the war problem," were described as dangerous pitfalls into which the adolescent girl could stumble in the event of psychic disturbance.[39]

Deutsch's perspective reflected a far darker outlook than the works on female adolescence produced in the United States before the war. In the prewar period, the most important psychoanalytic texts on adolescent girls in the United States were Phyllis Blanchard's *Adolescent Girl: A Study from the Psychoanalytic Viewpoint* (1930) and her less specialized book, *New Girls for Old* (1924). Much like Deutsch's work, these books dealt with the problem of defining new roles for girls in the context of rapidly changing mores, particularly sexual mores. But whereas Deutsch viewed the liberalization of attitudes toward sex as threatening to the feminine psychological makeup, Blanchard saw a new opportunity for girls to emancipate themselves from debilitating forms of repression. Blanchard labeled the emergent sexual liberalism of the 1920s the "new freedom" and likened what she called the "New Girl" to the celebrated idea of the "New Woman."[40] In the first volume of *The Psychology of Women*, in contrast, the future always feels uncertain and precarious, the psychic burden of modern choices overwhelming, and the path from girlhood to womanhood treacherous.

The "Feminine-Erotic Woman"

In addition to presenting a sweeping explanation for the "core" of the feminine personality, the book's nontechnical language and everyday descriptions of relationships between girls and their friends, teachers, and parents no doubt helped *The Psychology of Women* to appeal to a wide spectrum of social scientists, social workers, and practicing therapists. Like many who have written on adolescents, Deutsch herself was clearly captivated by her subject, and one could go so far as to say that the book is lovingly written. The complexity, subtlety, and life-altering importance attributed to the events of adolescence, in combination with the sense of high purpose with which Deutsch wrote, gives the book a passionate tone that is exceptional in the field.

The Psychology of Women is essentially a pyramid in form. Deutsch takes the reader through the various stages of female adolescence, beginning with "pre-puberty," then on through "early puberty," adolescence proper, and the impact of menstruation. She reaches her pinnacle at the center of the book, with a description of the ideal woman —the "feminine-erotic woman"—who shares a trinity of traits: "eroticism," "passivity," and "masochism." She then descends back through various possible psychic disturbances, many taken from case histories discussed in her earlier work: the masculinity complex, homosexuality, and various environmental traumas. Deutsch characterized the path into a "feminine-erotic" type as a veritable obstacle course of complex challenges. Most dangerous of all, to Deutsch, was the threat presented by a girl's relationship with her mother. It was the potentially destructive power of the mother-daughter relationship that accounted, in no small way, for the subsequent celebration of the adolescent girl's relationship with her father.[41]

Early on, Deutsch states flatly that "in pre-puberty attachment to the mother represents a greater danger than attachment to the father." Eventually, an "attempt at liberation from the mother that has failed or was too weak can . . . leave a definitely infantile imprint on the woman's entire personality."[42] If a girl failed utterly to disengage from her mother, avoiding the necessary hostility, conflict, and devaluation involved in separating herself, it resulted in "an emotionally crippled personality."[43] The element of totality (as well as alarming peril) here stands in contrast to other psychic challenges in a woman's sexual and emotional life; other kinds of developmental problems could impede or alter the course of a girl's emotional and sexual life, but continued emotional dependence upon her mother rendered her permanently emotionally disabled. Moreover, the adversarial nature of the mother-daughter relationship during adolescence was not a byproduct of the girl's change of object but inherent in the relationship itself. "The hate tendencies" that a girl displayed in relation to her mother, according to Deutsch, "originate not so much in the Oedipus situation as in her anger at the fact that her mother prevents her from being grown up." Hatred toward the mother, for Deutsch, was as much a sign of progress as was the rediscovery of the father as an object. "She wanted to be grown up," Deutsch concludes in one case history, "belong to a gang, and feel free — and to her, freedom meant everything that implied a protest against her mother."[44]

When a girl did not "act out," by joining a gang or becoming a juvenile delinquent, she found more socially acceptable ways to give up her attachment to her mother. In prepuberty she located objects of identification to substitute for her mother — usually characters found in books, films, or plays.[45] Then later in adolescence she formed new ego ideals that replaced her mother in her estimation — teachers, group leaders, and girlfriends.[46] At the same moment that a girl started to supplant her mother with new "ego ideals" and objects of identification, she also began to substitute other men for her father in her imagination — but, in the case of her father, the exchange served not as a way out of an attachment but instead as a way back into an Oedipal relationship that had been abandoned at the onset of latency. Substitutions took place on many levels, but for different purposes: with her mother, as a form of distancing herself from a former tie; with her father, as a way of re-experiencing Oedipal desire in a way that is psychologically acceptable.

There were several different "types" of feminine-erotic women, all of whom Deutsch celebrated in a strikingly warm and effusive manner. In so doing she went one step beyond the search for a "normal" psychology, an endeavor that had begun at the turn of the century, and ranged into the territory of the ideal.[47] "Feminine" women were described as harmonious and tolerant, quick to love and easy to satisfy, uncompetitive though capable of achievement, and, above all, intuitive. They all shared similar traits and had managed to move successfully through the various stages of adolescent development: disengagement from their mothers, sublimation of sexuality, a directing of "activity inward" (passivity), and a heightened engagement in fantasy. These women shared basic elements in their psychic makeup, including "a passive-masochistic character" and a "narcissistic ego." However, the feminine woman's "predominant trait," according to Deutsch, was "eroticism."[48] Eroticism, meanwhile, depended upon the capacity for fantasy. "Those who put no limit on their longings and their effervescent fantasies," she wrote, "have more opportunities for development of femininity."[49]

The first object available for fantasy, indeed the most appropriate object, as the adolescent girl experienced the regressive pull of adolescence, was her father. The emergence of Oedipal fantasy was viewed as the most important sign of sexual progress during puberty, despite the fact that the attraction to the father as an object represented a regressive impulse. "The regressive nature of adolescent fantasies is manifested in the fact that as a rule the real objects that are chosen strongly resemble earlier objects—that is to say, father."[50] Deutsch claimed that "in these fantasies we always find the old object formations[,] and in the platonic, ardently yearned-for lover we often recognize the features of the father."[51] Hence, an object that substitutes for the father, or reflected the desire for him in some way, was the first material to which the adolescent girl turned as she began to experience the sexual drives of puberty. In this way, her father became a kind of set point for the function of fantasy throughout her sexual life. Feminine sexuality, for Deutsch, depended upon idealization, longing, and fantasy—all of which were learned through the process of Oedipal yearning. Hence, the Oedipal became the bridge into sexuality itself for adolescent girls, a form of desire that included multiple forms of attraction all taking place at once: platonic, ideal, *and* sexual.

Deutsch saw the relationship with the father as existing at the center of the psychology of the "feminine-erotic woman." The positive experience of the adolescent Oedipus complex was, above all other experiences, predictive of the achievement of her ideal. She was explicit on this point: "The woman who is harmoniously erotic, who is most 'feminine' and represents the best achievement of her Creator, often declares in the evening of her rich and happy love life: 'I have not always been faithful, but actually I have been in love only once.' Some crumpled picture in her album or an image in her memory represents for her a figure to which in her early youth she attached her great yearning and readiness to love, and through which she unconsciously preserves her faith to her first love object, her father." [52] Describing the woman who was subconsciously "faithful" to her father as "the best achievement of her Creator" attached a beatific quality to the Oedipus complex; in this moment Deutsch has intertwined the metaphysical with the scientific—a rare if not singular move within the history of psychoanalysis. Moreover, in describing the Oedipus complex as not only a relationship upon which a woman's life happiness depends but also one that continues to inform her mature sexual relationships, Deutsch decidedly enlarged and intensified its impact.

Sigmund Freud was typically contradictory on the subject of the female Oedipus complex: in one treatise he claimed that women abolished their Oedipus complex late and even then incompletely; elsewhere he claimed that the female Oedipus complex inevitably dissolved "from its lack of success." [53] Early articles on female sexuality by psychoanalysts Ernst Jones (1927), Melanie Klein (1928), and Jeanne Lampl–De Groot (1927) all described the process whereby girls *overcame* their Oedipus complex as a (if not *the*) definitive event in their psychological development. [54] Oedipal resolution was a pivotal and central element in the prewar understanding of female childhood. Hence, to assert that the degree of happiness a woman experienced in her love life might in some way *depend* upon her ongoing attachment to her father was truly novel. In Deutsch's hands, the father-daughter bond became eroticism itself: a kind of kinetic energy that both initiated and animated the entirety of a girl's and eventually a woman's sexual life. And in the process of describing this phenomenon, Deutsch deployed a language—of faithfulness, nostalgic memories, lifelong loves—that effectively transformed what psychoanalysts had previously discussed as a problem of libidinal drives darkly and dangerously at odds with the taboo of incest into the paramount romance of a woman's life.

Passivity, the other major attribute of the feminine woman, was also achieved through the adolescent girl's relationship with the father. Here again, Deutsch magnified and celebrated the paternal role in a distinctive way. [55] Deutsch believed that although young girls' aggressive tendencies were weaker than boys', girls did not renounce their aggressive drives until late adolescence. Passivity was eventually achieved by the growth of the girl's natural inhibitions and the influence of the environment. "The social environment," she says, "offers the woman's ego a kind of prize or bribe" for renouncing her aggressions. The phrase "social environment" referred not to the world at large but to the father.[56] "The bribe offered to the little girl by the father, as a representative of the environment, is love and tenderness. For its sake she renounces any further intensification of her activity, most particularly her aggressions." Feminine passivity, then, was brought about through a social bargain with the father—aggression was exchanged for love. "In brief," Deutsch summarized, "the girl gives up her aggressions . . . chiefly because of the love prize given her as compensation."[57] Love as a bribe, or a "love prize" in return for renouncing aggression, made for a rather indeterminate set of gifts between father and daughter. (Emotional and erotic bribing also played a central role in popular depictions of the modern father-daughter relationship, as discussed in Chapters 4 and 5). Deutsch did not explain what she meant by a "love prize," nor did she distinguish it from the love a father might give a son. "Love," of course, has a variety of meanings: affection arising out of kinship, attraction based on sexual desire, or benevolent devotion. However, based on her description of a woman's "readiness to love" a husband, which she learns as an adolescent through her relationship to her father, Deutsch's definition was surely meant to be inclusive of sexuality. Like eroticism itself, the "love prize" contained a spectrum of attitudes—admiration, idealization, fondness, and sexuality—combined. What the father gave his daughter was, essentially, the gift of the eroticization of his attitude toward her.

At the moment when the father bartered his "love" for his daughter's aggression, Deutsch claimed, "the real personality of the father plays a particularly important part." However, Deutsch did not specify what aspects of his personality were important or what, ideally, this personality should be like. Neither fatherhood in the abstract nor fathers of specific patients in case histories, of which there were many, were explored in detail. The successful father, according to Deutsch, was loving but ultimately formless. He was really only knowable through the values and emotions that he signified, never as an actual person. A "representative of the environment" and "represented by" a crumpled picture in an album, he remained one step removed from reality; he was made invisible by an endless series of substitutions, a phantom of his daughter's Oedipal imagination.

Hence, *The Psychology of Women* managed to invest the adolescent girl's father with new meaning while rendering his actual role in her everyday life vague. The obfuscation of the paternal in *The Psychology of Women*, however, occurred not despite the fact of his enlarged significance but because of it. This was in part because the father's prescribed role was better evoked than elucidated: idealized and yearned for, the father was necessarily divorced from the everyday. The new role assigned to fathers in Deutsch's magnum opus was aggrandized, sexualized, and powerful. But this eroticized role also tended toward the contradictory, for it constantly threatened to transgress the sexual limits fundamental to the definition of fatherhood itself. Deutsch delicately worked around these limits by connecting a girl's ongoing "love" for her father to "platonic" forms of fantasy. Nonetheless, the point at which platonic love ends and erotic love begins was, within the terms of the schema that she herself laid out, impossible to pin down. It is this kind of inherent, nagging imprecision that accounts for the distancing effect that Deutsch's portrayal of the Oedipal father ultimately achieved.

The Specter of Oedipal Desire: Case Histories

When fathers failed their daughters, as they sometimes did in the case histories presented in *The Psychology of Women*, they were men whose downfall was passivity rather than abusiveness. However, because the behavior of fathers was not scrutinized like that of mothers, it is impossible to say how accurate (or real) this depiction was. Whatever the case, Deutsch perceived a fundamental difference in the types of father-daughter relationships brought to the attention of analysts over the course of the Second World War. Whereas from the turn of the century through the 1920s, she claims, girls' psychological problems were predominantly linked to an overinvestment in their fathers, girls' relationships with their fathers in the 1940s were most often too weak, particularly in comparison to the mother-daughter bond. She says:

It is a remarkable fact that the types of neurosis we encounter nowadays with increasing frequency reveal . . . a passive . . . infantile relation to the mother more clearly than did the older types, whose main content was found to be dependence on the father tie. . . . In the cases we have in mind the relation to the father often takes the form of a twofold accusation. There is first the reproach that he did not help the girl sufficiently in her *active effort* to liberate herself from her mother; second—and this reproach has a more erotic character—he is accused of having failed to prevent by his love the girl's return to her mother.[58]

Deutsch was certainly correct in noting a shift in psychoanalytic interpretations of female adolescent sexual development. "Father-fixation," an occasional diagnosis in the United States in the 1920s, was a form of neurosis in which a girl's attachment to her father prevented her from "falling in love outside the family circle."[59] It occurred when a father's overbearing nature, unconventional behavior, or personal charisma made it difficult for his adolescent daughter to move beyond his influence: she was transfixed by him. These girls, it was believed, developed an overinvestment in their fathers and the Oedipus complex.[60] One textbook on girls' psychology published in 1925 warned, "As we know from our studies of women nervously ill, a girl often becomes so much attached to her father that she cannot be happy except with a man who resembles him, or she may even be completely unable to transfer her affections . . . so that she does not marry at all."[61] After World War II, however, "father-fixation" ceased to be a diagnostic category. What psychotherapists witnessed instead was "Oedipal conflict."

Oedipal conflict was a broad concept meant to describe any situation in which a girl's attachment to her father was troubled in some way. However, it arose most often when adolescent Oedipal desire was frustrated or forestalled rather than too strong. Hence, the concern that informed virtually all postwar diagnoses of adolescent girls was not the overcoming of the Oedipus complex, or its successful resolution, but rather potential obstacles surrounding a girl's *entry into* the Oedipus complex as a starting point. This became the great anxiety, the consuming problem, of the postwar psychoanalysts. The achievement of a fully developed Oedipus complex was the *goal* of these diagnoses—the solution or cure for the girl's psychosexual disturbances. As a goal rather than a problem, the Oedipus complex was both exalted and ignored. The beneficial aspects of the entrance into the Oedipus situation were self-evident, hence its particular functioning required little if any interrogation.

There were two dominant paradigms for explaining why an adolescent girl might have trouble entering into the Oedipus complex at the outset of adolescence: either she herself hesitated to enter into it (or repressed it) out of a general fear of sexuality, or difficulties with her mother prevented her from forming an appropriate Oedipal attachment to her father.[62] The most important analysis of a repressed adolescent Oedipus complex was Phyllis Greenacre's "The Prepuberty Trauma in Girls," which first appeared in the *Psychoanalytic Quarterly* in 1950 and was republished in her highly acclaimed book *Trauma, Growth, and Personality* in 1952. Greenacre was one of the more illustrious of the American-born female psychoanalysts. She received her B.S. from the University of Chicago in 1913 and then took a degree in medicine from Rusch Medical College in 1916. After working at Johns Hopkins University Medical School and serving as a consultant for the Department of Child Welfare in New York, she taught clinical psychiatry at Cornell University. She was president of the New York Psychoanalytic Institute from 1948 to 1950, and of the New York Psychoanalytic Society in 1956–57.[63] Greenacre's book, especially the chapter "The Prepuberty Trauma in Girls," was second only to Deutsch's *Psychology of Women* in its influence on the postwar understanding of female adolescence. Indeed, the events Greenacre described in these case histories (and her analysis of them) were recounted in general textbooks, surveys of adolescence, and studies of female development throughout the 1950s and early 1960s.[64]

"The Prepuberty Trauma in Girls" examined one case of sexual abuse that, according to Greenacre, was representative of many cases involving adolescent girls she had treated. The case chronicled the history of a young woman who was sexually assaulted by an adult male stranger during prepuberty. Greenacre borrowed Deutsch's terminology to designate an early stage of adolescence, describing prepuberty as the time when "the unconscious begins to prepare for puberty."[65] Greenacre called this kind of sexual attack on girls "traumata of an Oedipal pattern": some girls reacted to the first glimmer of the reemergence of the Oedipus complex at the onset of puberty with profound fear. Fear of sexual feelings stemmed from memories of intense but frustrating Oedipal experiences that had taken place during early childhood. These girls responded to Oedipal anxiety by provoking a sexual attack by an adult man; the trauma inflicted by the assault then served as a defense against the revival of Oedipal desire during adolescence.

In this case, the sexual assault occurred when the patient was approximately ten years old. She "was roller-skating in the cellar of her own home," Greenacre writes, "when a man entered to read the gas meter." She asked the man to lift her so that she could see the movement of the little hands upon the dials of the meter. When the man lifted her, he put his hands underneath her dress and "stimulated her genitals." The patient managed to free herself, and the man quickly left. Subsequently, the girl suffered from pathological shyness, an inability to execute basic tasks, and, later in life, sexual dysfunction. The patient believed that this traumatic experience was the cause of her current problems. But Greenacre disagreed and diagnosed the incident instead as a "screen memory" for earlier, more profound experiences. The girl had, according to Greenacre, a "peculiarly difficult Oedipal period" in her early childhood. Because of the "vigorous romping and tickling by her father . . . she developed an unusual kinesthetic erotism [sic]. There were memories of having been swung and tossed in the air by her father until she got into states of almost frantic exhilaration; and from reconstructed memories it appeared that these reached climactic states of genital stimulation but no true orgasm." This "peculiar" father-daughter encounter, in addition to a few others, led her to develop a defense against her revived "Oedipal wishes" during the prepuberty period, which were then "acted out" in the provocation of the man who had come to read the gas meter.[66] "The child herself became victimized by the trauma which she had precipitated, and the unhappy event was then used as a dramatic defense against entering into the struggles of puberty."[67] The "provocation" reflected the simultaneous sexual desire for her father and her fear of it. In this case, "the child had initiated the experience," Greenacre claims, "by asking the man to lift her up and show her the meter which was hung high on the wall." Since she was ten years old and tall, "this was especially seductive and it contained the unconscious wish to be tossed in the air as she used to be by her father."[68]

One striking element of this study is Greenacre's narrow and relentless search for an Oedipal etiology. For Greenacre, the sexual attack was *only* understandable in Oedipal terms, a perspective that reflects the extent to which she viewed female sexuality as solely Oedipal in nature. The girl's reaction to the sexual abuse, as well as her other libidinal wishes, fears, and frustrations—all were reduced to the "Oedipal struggle," over and above other mediating factors or impulses. According to Greenacre's circular logic, all sexual experiences grew out of and then inevitably referred back to the Oedipus complex. Hence, it becomes difficult, if not impossible, to imagine a sexual event that has any independent meaning for this girl. An unhealthy Oedipal relationship was not one among many experiences that contributed to her emerging sexuality; it was equivalent to those experiences: "Oedipal traumata," for Greenacre, *was* sexual traumata.

Ironically, for all of Greenacre's insistence on the pathology created by the denial of Oedipal feelings, the ultimate effect of her analysis was to render the nature of the female Oedipus complex more mysterious. According to Greenacre, the patient attempted to repress her experience of Oedipal desire because "too vigorous romping and tickling" had led to sexual frustration of the most literal sort—"genital stimulation but no true orgasm."[69] The girl attempted to cope with her subsequent sexual anxieties first by provoking a sexual attack and then disengaging from her father during the adolescent Oedipal stage. "Throughout adolescence," Greenacre writes, "the girl was encased in a 'cast' of defensive irritability and silence directed against her father."[70] But Greenacre's diagnosis of frustrated and then repressed sexual/Oedipal desire as the cause of later sexual dysfunction ultimately raised more questions than it answered. The most important revolved around the question of the role of Oedipal frustration in adolescent development.

Before World War II, the terms "Oedipus frustration" and "Oedipus conflict" were used interchangeably with "Oedipus complex." For instance, in an article published in 1928 titled "Early Stages of the Oedipus Conflict," Melanie Klein claimed that over the course of a girl's lifetime, her admiration for her father was normally "shaken by the Oedipus frustration." Nonetheless, Klein concluded, this frustration constituted "one of the fundamental features of the woman's relation to the man [because] later, when full satisfaction of the love-impulses is obtained, there is joined with this admiration the great gratitude ensuing from the long-pent-up depravation."[71] In other words, frustration—which was the presumed destiny of Oedipal desire—played a constructive developmental role. It helped women transfer their affections from their fathers to other men. In "The Prepuberty Trauma in Girls," Greenacre takes the opposite view. Oedipal frustration leads to a fear of sexuality, which leads to "Oedipal traumata," which in turn results in the evasion of the Oedipus complex at puberty and sexual dysfunction. In short, the frustration of Oedipal desire was portrayed as pathogenic—a problem, moreover, with no obvious solution. For Greenacre leaves open the question of how a girl's intense Oedipal feelings might be relieved or resolved, how she might work through a successful Oedipal period that involved frustration as a matter of course. Greenacre's was an analysis informed by the same fundamental anxiety we saw in Deutsch's *Psychology of Women*: the sense that what was *most* dangerous to the adolescent girl was the possibility that she might fail to become sufficiently engaged in—or deny altogether —the adolescent Oedipal relationship, rather than that she might not overcome it.

Incest and the Adolescent Oedipus Complex

If the frustration of the Oedipus complex was pathogenic, and healthy psychological development depended upon a positive experience of the Oedipal relationship during adolescence, then a healthy adolescent Oedipal experience was necessarily the reference point for these analyses. What Greenacre (and those she later influenced) seemed to have been endorsing when asserting the need for a healthy adolescent Oedipal stage was a form of ongoing father-daughter eroticism like that experienced by the ideal "feminine-erotic woman" described by Deutsch in 1944. The conceptual difficulty of the position that Deutsch, Greenacre, and others put themselves in, as we have seen, is evinced by the fact that the nature of a healthy adolescent Oedipus complex eluded description. Further complicating these analyses is the fact that the Oedipus complex is constituted by a desire that is, by definition, both unconscious and taboo. How does one go about prescribing a healthy engagement with an inaccessible, inadmissible wish? One answer is to describe female adolescent Oedipal desire as both more conscious, and less taboo, than your predecessors. This is exactly what happened when psychoanalysts began to look at case histories of father-daughter incest in the 1940s and 1950s.

Of all the ways in which new ideas about the female adolescent Oedipus complex affected the interpretation of girls' behavior over the course of the 1940s and 1950s, the new interest in father-daughter incest that developed during World War II, while less broadly influential than theories about normal adolescent development, was perhaps the most dramatic. Within psychoanalysis, a sustained, singular attention to case histories of father-daughter incest represented a departure in the priorities and interests in psychoanalysis overall.[72] Though a few analysts considered cases of father-daughter incest before 1940, they did so only within the context of general inquires into the sexual experiences of children with adults. Prewar case histories, moreover, mostly involved girls under the age of ten. In contrast, all of the cases published between 1940 and 1965 concentrated on incestuous encounters that occurred during the prepuberty and adolescent stages, from the ages of ten through eighteen.

None of the postwar authors stated why they chose to investigate father-daughter incest.[73] But one way to understand their interest is to examine the questions and ideas that animated the case histories themselves.[74] Whatever appealed to psychoanalysts about the subject, the studies of incest that appeared in the 1940s and 1950s assumed that the precipitating factor was the normal recrudescence of Oedipal desire on the part of the adolescent girl. Indeed, female Oedipal desire became a way of understanding, coming to terms with, and, in some striking cases, even normalizing instances of incest between a father and an adolescent daughter.

Though Freud speculated on the role of the incest prohibition in the founding of early human culture in *Totem and Taboo* (1913), the problem of the actual practice of incest, particularly father-daughter incest, became somewhat of a moot point within psychoanalytic thought when he famously claimed that a "disproportionately large" number of women had reported childhood sexual abuse and thus much of what he had been hearing from his female patients must have been "falsifications" of experience.[75] He perceived in these fabrications the traces of childhood fantasy; and it was on this fundamental insight that he based his theory of the Oedipus complex. This outlook, it has been argued, contributed to a general emphasis in early psychoanalysis on the nature of fantasy rather than on the impact of actual trauma, or "childhood experiences," sexual or otherwise, on the human psyche.[76] It is in part Freud's famous "rejection of the seduction theory"—his conclusion that memories of childhood incestuous seduction were based on childhood fantasy—that has led historians to assume that psychoanalysts dismissed girls' claims of incestuous abuse throughout the postwar period—a moment when Freudian orthodoxy was ascendant.[77]

Addressing the subject of father-daughter incest did represent a challenge to the status quo, and an air of defensiveness pervades some of the earlier analyses. Several authors felt they must explain why a particular case was "not all fantasy."[78] The anxiety was justified. One group of authors, presenting a study of eleven cases of father-daughter incest at the annual meeting of orthopsychiatry in 1953, was sharply criticized by a respondent who began her comments with the observation, "Most of us have trained ourselves to skepticism toward the claims of young girls who maintain that they have been seduced by their fathers, since we recognize the strength and reality value such fantasies can assume particularly in adolescence." Hence, it was unfortunate, she continued, that the authors "say little about the evidence on which they base their impression that incest actually occurred."[79]

This kind of critique, however, was rare, and, more important, missed the point of these analyses, which did not seek to discredit the notion of adolescent incestuous fantasy so much as to reinterpret its effects in a new way. They did so by describing incest as an event that grew out of, rather than negated, the fact of Oedipal fantasy. In instances where sex occurred between a father and daughter, the act represented a less common, albeit more kinetic, trajectory of Oedipal desire: the transformation of fantasy into reality, rather than the transformation of fantasy into falsification. Hence, in these case histories incest was referred to as the "acting out of the Oedipal wish" or "manifest Oedipal behavior," designations that located the genesis and trajectory of incest firmly within the developmental fantasies and desires of the adolescent girl herself.[80] In a sense, these authors were trying to show that fabrication and consummation were not mutually exclusive possibilities—at least when it came to the question of the Oedipal imagination. In both cases, an incestuous desire that was taboo was transformed into an act: in one case it was transformed into "pseudologia," or a lie, through the act of speech, and, in the other, it was consciously pursued through sexual "acting out."[81] These girls, according to this postwar perspective, had managed to take their incestuous fantasies and transform them into a conscious and deliberate form of experience.

Case histories of incest held much in common with descriptions of normal female adolescent development: the girls struggled to disengage from their mothers, succumbed to Oedipal desire with the onset of puberty, and indulged in Oedipal fantasy. Indeed, the question that informed case histories of father-daughter incest was not "Why does incest happen?" but, instead, "Given the ubiquity of incestuous adolescent fantasy, why does incest not happen more often?" As one review of the literature put it in 1962, "Psychiatric studies on incest . . . have left unsolved the question of why incest occurs only in some cases, indeed in relatively few considering the prevalence of the problems described as favoring incest."[82]

Finally, while psychoanalysts necessarily located the father at the scene of the crime, they considered neither his psychology nor the impact of incest on his identity as a father. So overwhelming was the consensus that incest was evidence of a problem on the part of daughters rather than fathers that not a single mention of an incestuous father being subjected to a psychiatric interview appears in any of the articles on father-daughter incest that were published over the course of the postwar period. Indeed, there is a veritable gap in the literature on the question of incestuous fathers, one that lasted from 1938 —when Ernst Jones briefly considered the subject—until 1962, when a Canadian psychiatrist took up the question anew, having searched the recent literature in vain for clues on the subject of the psychopathology of incestuous fathers.[83] Inasmuch as the father was reflected upon at all, he appeared, contradictorily, as a threatening figure because of the established fact of having committed incest, but he was utterly innocent insofar as the etiology of the incest was concerned. Mostly, he was insignificant. He acted, but only within the context of his daughter's "acting out." The "acting out" was caused by conflicts with her mother, in combination with the mobilization of her Oedipal desires with the onset of puberty. In this way, a highly contradictory image of the father emerged: he was safe and yet threatening, mute yet transgressive, passive yet culpable. It was a perspective on fathers that served to reinforce the ultimately incomprehensible nature of the paternal over all.

From the Unconscious, to Consciousness, to Act: The Path to Incest

The interpretive leap from the adolescent Oedipus complex to incestuous sex was made with remarkable ease. In part, the notion that girls could act on what was originally defined as an unconscious, hence mentally unavailable, set of ideas or desires grew out of the dominant postwar perspective on the adolescent Oedipus complex in girls. Analysts adhered to the idea that a girl's "Oedipal strivings" not only became "louder and more conspicuous" at puberty but were also only "loosely repressed."[84] Certainly a girl's Oedipal wishes were considered to be far more integrated into her psyche than were a boy's, and occasionally an analyst would report, as Phyllis Greenacre did in "The Prepuberty Trauma in Girls," that a girl's fantasies about her father were "quite conscious," without any indication that such an assertion might be inherently noteworthy.[85] The assumption that Oedipal desire could exist at or near consciousness in girls had the effect of transforming the definition of the female Oedipus complex over the postwar period, subtly relocating what had been designated as an explicitly unconscious drive into the realm of near-conscious, and at times even conscious, desire.

Sylvan Keiser's article "A Manifest Oedipus Complex in an Adolescent Girl," published in the *Psychoanalytic Study of the Child* in 1953, did the most to further the idea that female Oedipal desire could burst into consciousness in response to fairly routine events. At the outset of his analysis, Keiser asserted that he had, over the course of his practice, run across "nonpsychotic patients who do not manifest the horror of incest that Freud . . . described as part of the prehistoric inheritance."[86] Those patients, of course, were adolescent girls. Because girls experienced a "slower and more gradual passing of the Oedipus complex," he explained, it was possible for them to bring "incestuous attachments into consciousness." In the case under review, a girl was brought into analysis by her mother. Like many of the girls presented for analysis, she suffered from shyness, a sense of inadequacy, and a tendency to isolate herself. Keiser diagnosed her problem as a defective organization of the superego, resulting from the fact that her father left the family when she was four years old. "Because of the physical separation," Keiser writes, the girl's "original sexualized Oedipal relationship could neither be fulfilled nor resolved." (As in Greenacre's case history, how an Oedipus complex could be "fulfilled" is not accounted for here; significantly, however, in other psychoanalytic case histories, the "fulfillment of Oedipus desires" refers to father-daughter incest.)[87] The situation was exacerbated by the fact that the mother was unable "to give real love and warmth."[88] Hence, the girl's feelings for her father contained a special urgency, and, with the onset of puberty, she began to develop "frank incestuous feelings for her father [which] were reported during the first few months of the analysis." Much of what she related were dreams with "manifest sexual incestuous content: she dreamed of meeting the father, being embraced by him and responding sexually."[89]

Two years later, in 1955, in the article "Incest as Revenge against the Pre-Oedipal Mother," published in the *Psychoanalytic Review*, Lillian Gordon cited Keiser's conclusions to bolster her argument that father-daughter incest could, in certain conditions, follow from a normal Oedipus complex. If, as Keiser had stated, a "manifest Oedipus complex" was "not symptomatic of a psychotic process," neither, she reasoned, was what she called "manifest Oedipal behavior."[90] In both situations, normal adolescent desires and, by extension, behavior were set into motion simply by heightened degrees of manifestation —in psychoanalytic terms, degrees of consciousness. "Acting out the Oedipal situation," according to Gordon, was an event that occurred because of an unusual apprehension of a very usual impulse.[91]

Gordon's patient, Helen, was twenty years old at the time that she was referred to her. She was working as a nude model and occasional prostitute, and she had trouble maintaining lasting, monogamous relationships with "appropriate partners."[92] Helen was, Gordon writes, "offered an Oedipal relationship to her father" from an early, unspecified age.[93] But it was during adolescence that she began to consciously pursue an incestuous relationship with him. Helen established this "pattern," according to Gordon, as a "vengeful use of the Oedipal relationship to get even" with her mother. The desire to "get even" stemmed from feelings of "oral deprivation." A brother had been born during her childhood who was delicate and needed special foods; "mother thus deprived her by feeding him better." In addition, Helen complained that her mother was "cold, unloving and 'vague.'"[94] Helen's sexual behavior reflected both the fact that her needs had not been met and a desire to communicate her feelings of frustration and longing to her mother through "shocking" or upsetting her.

Helen's sexual/romantic feelings for her father are described as having been quite powerful during adolescence. She felt that her father was "a very handsome man looking much like the King of England," and she liked "to go out with him alone, imagining him to be her boyfriend."[95] Even so, Gordon writes, the "successful affair with father . . . could not help Helen, who had remained masochistically attached to mother, feeling strongly deprived by her, with vengeful, self-destructive wishes predominating."[96] No matter the sexual allure of the relationship with the father, or the nature of her sexual experience with her father, the affective power of the relationship with her mother still prevailed. There are echoes here of Helene Deutsch's complaint about the modern father-daughter predicament: "He is accused of having failed to prevent by his love the girl's return to her mother."[97] Applying Deutsch's perspective on father-daughter relationships to incest, Gordon describes Helen's "successful affair" as an attempt to utilize her Oedipal wishes in a positive way. Gordon sees Helen's Oedipal strivings as the most attractive and proximate route for her feelings. Those feelings, however, were provoked by stronger feelings for her mother, a relationship from which Helen—like all young women—must escape through the only path available: her relationship with her father.

The relative value Gordon placed on the "Oedipal relationship" versus pre-Oedipal/maternal attachment shows just how little was believed to be at stake in the act of father-daughter incest itself: the impact of incest with the father on the psyche was described as negligible compared to the deprivation at the hands of the mother. Gordon begins by stating that, in general, "Oedipal attachment [is] a 'rescue station'" from the relationship with the mother, who in the child's fantasy has become "the dangerous 'giantess of the nursery.'"[98] In attempting to escape into the "less dangerous Oedipal relationship," she explains, some children carry over into that relationship the problems and anxieties of the earlier relationship with the mother. In Helen's case, she says, the "activity with father" was a conduit for carrying out the "revenge wishes against mother for pre-Oedipal frustrations."[99]

Because of the strength of her attachment to her mother, Helen needed to find a safe, indirect way to express her hostility. Incest was the solution. It was, in Gordon's words, an "admission of the lesser crime." That is, Helen used one impulse—the desire to have sex with her father—to ward off another, "less tolerable" impulse—her hostile feelings toward her mother.[100] Thus the Oedipal relationship remained a "refuge" from the mother, even when the father's sexual transgression irrevocably altered the terms of her relationship to him as a parent. In fact, there is no relationship between daughter and father to speak of here, only her conscious wish for sex with him. The father is the sexual object, the mother the emotional aim. In Gordon's final analysis, the act of incest was an elaboration of more ordinary mother-daughter conflicts, as well as of adolescent Oedipal drives. Father-daughter incest was comprehensible within the context of established ideas about adolescent girls, rather than an event that imposed upon the father-daughter relationship an experience that was altogether alien.

Over the course of the 1950s and early 1960s, the interpretation of father-daughter incest as an expression of normal adolescent Oedipal needs deployed in the attempt to solve fairly common mother-daughter conflicts predominated.[101] In articles such as "Incest: The Revenge Motive" (1959), "The Family Constellation and Overt Incestuous Relations Between Father and Daughter" (1954), and "Genesis of Overt Incest" (1961), father-daughter incest provided a solution to the problem of hostility toward mothers. Whether incest was an "admission of the lesser crime," or a hunt for parental interest, these girls somehow calculated, according to these analysts, that the gratification that incest offered would outweigh the guilt and anxiety that it exacted.

This logic was extended, and finally endorsed, in an article in which the authors themselves decided that this kind of trade-off was a legitimate route to psychological health. In "On Consummated Incest," published in the *International Journal of Psychoanalysis* (1950), Matilde Wencelblat De Rascovsky and Arnoldo Rascovsky presented the case of Susanna, a woman who came to them at the age of twenty-six. She had been involved in an incestuous relationship with her father since the age of ten. The incest began when her mother was away on a six-month trip to Europe, was resumed after a brief hiatus just after Susanna's marriage at the age of twenty-two, and continued on through the present day. Susanna also sought out fleeting sexual relations with doctors and teachers and was diagnosed as suffering from "a nymphomaniac compulsion." Typically enough, "her history showed as a main element an extremely frustrated relationship with the mother," who was described as "a cold woman who had not suckled her daughter, and whose influence had been preponderantly negative." The frustrated situation with the mother had led "to the oral search for the father," and then a "whole series of [father] substitutions represented by doctors and teachers." Susanna suffered a great deal, going through husbands and lovers, one after the other. Nonetheless, at the end of the article the authors concluded: "We believe that the actual consummation of the incestuous relation, which constitutes a secondary process derived from a former grave state of melancholy, diminishes the subject's chance of psychosis and allows better adjustment to the external world. In some cases in which there is an incestuous situation of great intensity, but in which consummation has not taken place, we have seen a similar constellation but with intense accentuation of manic-depressive psychotic traits." [102]

In other words, incest diminished a girl's chances of developing a psychosis. [103] Not only was father-daughter incest caused by maternal failure, it could be anodyne to it—a genuine measure of psychic relief. Keiser's description of conscious Oedipal desire, Gordon's notion of "acting out the Oedipal wish," and Rascovsky and Rascovsky's assertion that "consummation" could contribute to "adjustment to the external world"—all appeared between 1950 and 1954. The cumulative effect of such articles was to render father-daughter incest somewhat banal: it became one of any number of "acting out" behaviors that reflected upon the common Oedipal struggles of the adolescent girl.

In 1954, Talcott Parsons, the most influential sociologist of the postwar era and a student of psychoanalysis, claimed in an article on the incest taboo and the social structure that mother-son incest was the most "regressive" and "deeply pathological" form of incest because it kept boys within the matrix of infantile dependency. But the "case of the daughter vis-à-vis her father is somewhat different," he continued. "When she is forced to abandon her primary attachment to her mother, it should be clear that the next available alternative is her father."[104] Such offhand observations (Parsons did not elaborate further) are perhaps the best index of the accumulated weight of psychoanalytic investigations into the sexual identity of the adolescent girl that had begun in the early 1940s. The idea that, for girls, the Oedipus situation represents a way out of her attachment to her mother is strictly Freudian.[105] The notion that such ideas could be applied to cases of incest—that somehow father-daughter incest is conceivable within the architecture of normal relations—is very much the product of midcentury American thinking.

If Oedipal desire was the adolescent girl's only "alternative," however, the question remained: how could such desire be successfully incorporated into healthy, nonincestuous father-daughter relationships? It was a question, as we shall see, that would haunt postwar psychotherapists as they attempted to diagnose and treat the growing numbers of wayward and delinquent girls with whom they were confronted.

Chapter 2

DELINQUENT GIRLS AND THE

CRISIS OF PATERNAL AUTHORITY

IN THE POSTWAR UNITED STATES

Something about school always makes me want to say no.
It's the authority there. I know, it represents Father to me.
—*Anne, age fifteen, to her psychoanalyst, 1954*

On October 29, 1951, photographs of a group of white, middle-class girls from a suburb outside of Boston appeared in *Time* and *Newsweek*. The girls smiled for the cameras as they displayed lingerie, clothing, and pearls, a cigarette dangling from each of their gloved hands. The place was a New York City police station. The girls, ages fifteen, sixteen, and seventeen, were being arraigned for theft, running away, and "immorality": they had stolen $18,000 from a safe in the house of a family for whom they were babysitting, boarded a bus, and headed for New York. "Ravenous for excitement," they "engaged in a surrealistic shopping spree," then went to several nightclubs, picking up men and dropping outrageous tips to doormen and taxicab drivers along the way. Their plan had been to buy a car with the money and drive to Mexico, but the next day they were spotted outside their hotel by a detective. Reporters were delighted and appalled as the girls remained "unconcerned about their plight," instructing the photographers to take some "real cheesecake pictures" and tipping the cops for bringing them sandwiches. Both magazines ended their stories with what one reporter called "the curtain line of the week": as the flashbulbs went off, one of the girls admonished reporters, "Don't tell my father I've been smoking. He'd kill me if he knew." [1]

The joke was expertly aimed. Behind it was a decade of popular and academic perspectives that blamed female delinquency on paternal shortcomings. Indeed, during the postwar era, paternal failure was blamed more often than the traditional and more familiar culprits of youthful misbehavior, including poor schools, poverty, unwholesome influences, the decline in morals, and even the influence of the modern media. The father—as object of ridicule, psychological point of reference, or painfully absent party—was at the center of the public understanding of teenage girls' delinquent and destructive behavior that suddenly came to the fore during World War II. James Gilbert has shown how concern about juvenile delinquency in general (but particularly male delinquency) during the 1950s reflected the widespread apprehension that new forms of youth culture threatened traditional, middle-class social values and manifested itself in crusades against comic books and other forms of mass culture.[2] But the delinquent girl posed a different kind of challenge to postwar America: she became a site for the expression of cultural anxiety about the psychological substance of the father-daughter relationship in a modern social context where sexual mores, the prerogatives of parents, and the bounds of acceptable youthful behavior—particularly on the part of girls—were growing less clear.

The perception that female delinquency stemmed from the dynamics of a girl's relationship to her father both grew out of and helped perpetuate the postwar emphasis on the female adolescent Oedipus complex that emerged in the 1940s.[3] In order to better understand how analysts arrived at their conclusions about teenage girls—both "normal" (or, as Deutsch would have it, "feminine") and "delinquent"—it is necessary to understand the social context in which they practiced. Who were the girls that psychiatrists, psychoanalysts, and therapists were seeing in their private practices, at juvenile courts, and child guidance clinics? What crimes were they committing? What were the larger social anxieties and cultural concerns that surrounded the problem of female delinquency?

The girls discussed in this chapter are those who Helene Deutsch encountered at public institutions such as the Judge Baker Children's Center for "troubled" children in Boston, where she often worked, as well as those who appeared before juvenile judges and at children's agencies across the United States. They were the girls who joined gangs, smoked, skipped school, vandalized buildings, and committed acts of theft, large and small. Many came to the attention of juvenile authorities for promiscuity, but increasingly their crimes involved acts of aggression, defiance, and what was termed "social revolt."[4] Some were merely taking part in pranks and acts of daring, while others suffered serious behavioral disorders. Most were working class, but a growing number were middle and even upper class. Most of all, these girls—as I set out to show in the first part of this chapter—were not "invisible" during the postwar period as some have argued.[5] Indeed, in order to understand how and why fatherhood came to be seen as so important to the psychological health of adolescent girls, it is imperative to understand just how widespread and alarming the problem of female juvenile delinquency was during the 1940s and 1950s.

In the second section of this chapter I look at the history of a court created specifically for juvenile girls in New York City, known informally as "Girls' Term." I argue that the interpretation of girls' antisocial behavior at this and other juvenile courts changed dramatically in the years during and just after World War II. Assumptions of long standing in which most female delinquency was viewed as sexual in nature and economic in origin was replaced with a perspective that considered sexual behavior and other delinquencies as merely incidental to underlying psychological problems connected to girls' family experiences. Predictably, those disorders were rooted in Oedipal dysfunction—most prominently the problem of "Oedipal impasse," a diagnosis that owed much to ideas about adolescent Oedipal "frustration" and "conflict," discussed in Chapter 1. Finally, in the last section I demonstrate how thoroughly this psychoanalytic perspective came to dominate popular understandings of female juvenile delinquency in mass-circulation magazines, social commentary, and movies—especially such iconic films as *Rebel Without a Cause* (1955) and *The Wild One* (1954). Though these movies are primarily remembered for their representation of modern antiheroes—James Dean and Marlon Brando—both were heavily influenced by psychoanalytic ideas about the Oedipal disturbances of delinquent girls in postwar America and engaged with the psychological dimensions of their female characters.

The social interest in psychoanalytic ideas about female juvenile delinquency was intimately bound up with broader anxieties about paternal authority during this period. According to Robert Griswold, ideas about the place of the father in the family underwent a profound transformation at the turn of the century. Between 1900 and the onset of the Second World War, the traditional, "patriarchal father" gradually gave way to a "new" ideal father, a figure who was "imbued with a democratic, permissive, nurturing sensibility [that] could produce well-adjusted offspring."[6] Entrusted with new affective and psychological responsibilities, the American father, particularly the white middle-class father, was instructed to be friend rather than authority figure, an equal member of the family rather than a patriarch. This model, however, contributed to anxieties about the loss of authority, especially sexual authority, over adolescent girls. As one postwar pamphlet on juvenile delinquency put it: "Grandma capitalized on her innocence. Mother cherished her virginity as a requisite for marrying well. Both were protected by their fathers . . . until they were safely married. Today's young men and women face the larger responsibility of defining their roles for themselves."[7]

The Oedipal paradigm for understanding girls' delinquency, I suggest, was especially attractive during this period because it managed to express anxieties about the social meaning of female behavior that defied parental discipline while still containing the *meaning* of that behavior safely (and reassuringly) within the matrix of the psychodynamics of the family itself. Because parents and child experts were eager to maintain a tolerant attitude toward teenagers, they sought to define paternal authority as psychological rather than dictatorial in nature, based on the psychosexual dynamic of Oedipal love rather than on firm discipline.[8] Hence, at the same time that girls were given more freedom during this period, the possibility of achieving real autonomy—social, sexual, and psychological—was curtailed by the consensus that much of their behavior was rooted in their relationship to their fathers. Moreover, it seems to have been particularly important for experts to define antisocial behavior—as opposed to out-of-wedlock pregnancy, the other dominant way girls got themselves into trouble in the 1950s—as paternal in origin. As Ricky Solinger has shown, there was a "disproportionate focus on 'bad mothers' as the source of pregnant daughters."[9] With single pregnancy, however, authorities were coping with the result of a sexual delinquency that had already taken place, and the question was where to place blame. With other forms of rebellion, the desire was both to establish cause and to assert ongoing control over daughters' identity and behavior.

Questions of paternal authority and of the Oedipal relationship were rarely mentioned in the same sentence or even the same article — but the two issues circled around one another nonetheless, each complementing and refashioning the other, one stepping in where the other left off. Psychoanalysts were called upon to treat girls who had rebelled against paternal authority, even though analysts themselves rarely discussed the problem of authority per se in case histories.[10] Psychoanalysts, by explaining female delinquency in terms of a psychologically inescapable familial event—most typically the adolescent Oedipus complex—ingeniously left intact the importance of fathers to girls' social and sexual prospects, without advocating for his direct control over her day-to-day affairs. In the process, the social meaning of fatherhood was redescribed as a function of "psychosexual" development rather than of sexual surveillance and protection. This perspective on adolescent behavior implied that female rebellion was less an *act* than an "acting out" of anger directed at her father, less an autonomous form of expression than a reaction to her familial circumstances.

The effect of the application of notions of Oedipal disturbance to female delinquency was to further eroticize girls' relationship to their fathers in the minds of juvenile authorities, therapists, family experts, and the public at large. But at the same time it also aggravated the tensions that were inherent in the eroticized father-daughter relationship in the first place. While notions of "Oedipal conflict" or "Oedipal impasse" (in both their academic and popular formulations) invoked the specter of girls' unmet adolescent Oedipal needs, the solution to this type of problem remained, as we saw earlier, murky at best. Discourses on male juvenile delinquency, meanwhile, were full of suggestions for ways in which parents, school authorities, and even media censors could help set boys on the right path. Hence, while frustrated Oedipal desires came to be seen as the dominant cause of female delinquency, the most common solution to this problem—encouraging fathers to notice, encourage, and condone the growing sexual allure of their adolescent daughters—had many conceptual difficulties. The sexual tension it produced between father and daughter was as much a source of ongoing unease as it was deemed psychologically necessary.

An Epidemic of Delinquent Girls?

According to the Children's Bureau, overall juvenile delinquency rates increased markedly during the war, declined somewhat
in the years immediately following, then, beginning in the year 1949,
steadily increased each year thereafter.[11] Whether the postwar increase in juvenile delinquency warranted the sense of crisis that it engendered is unclear. For example, in New York City, the overall crime
rate for children under sixteen was significantly lower in 1950 than it
had been in 1907.[12] In contrast, however, the rate of *female* juvenile
delinquency in New York City, in relation to the rate of male delinquency, increased each year over the course of the first half of the
twentieth century.[13] In the first decade of the Children's Court in New
York, 1902–12, the ratio of delinquent boys to girls was approximately
60:1; by 1932 it had dropped to 8:1.[14] Nationally, statistics reveal a similar, though less dramatic, pattern. According to the Children's Bureau, the male-to-female delinquency ratio remained approximately
6:1 throughout the 1930s and early 1940s; after World War II, however, the ratio began to narrow. By 1949, girls represented one out of
every four juveniles in court cases, and the ratio continued to gradually decline throughout the postwar period.[15]

Female arrest and detention rates are colored by shifts in the definition of crime, the extent of surveillance, and the means of enforce-
ment, all of which, to further complicate matters, differed according to the legal and social practices of each state. Thus the national
male-to-female delinquency ratio of 4:1 included the state of Oklahoma, where girls made up half of all juvenile arrests, and Puerto Rico,
where boys' cases outnumbered girls' by 19 to 1.[16] In general, the ratio
was lower in the Midwestern states and a bit higher in cities on the
East and West Coasts. Even though the nature of female delinquency
changed over the period between 1945 and 1965, the bulk of female
crimes were "status crimes" rather than violations of the penal code;
that is, acts considered to be criminal because of the age at which
they were committed rather than the nature of the act itself. Ungov-
ernability, keeping late hours, associating with other delinquents, re-
sisting the authority of parents, running away, sex offenses, and truancy comprised the dominant acts for which girls found themselves
under the purview of the court. However, sex offenses decreased dra-

matically over the course of the postwar era, reflecting the rise of sexual liberalism more generally, especially in the realm of youthful sexual expression. In 1945, sex offenses accounted for 20 percent of all female juvenile court appearances nationwide.[17] By 1957, sex offenses had dropped by half, to 10 percent, and by 1965 they constituted just over 7 percent of all female juvenile court cases.[18]

The most important fact to keep in mind when assessing girls' juvenile delinquency is that there was, everywhere, an unstated assumption that it was better to handle female crime outside of the courtroom—no matter the infraction. Local police and social agencies had a variety of ways of "sheltering" girls from the judicial system in order to keep their misdeeds, as the saying went, "off the blotter."[19] For instance, a former chief of police from Philadelphia told the subcommittee on juvenile delinquency that girls' cases were routinely "adjusted" rather than dealt with as arrests: out of 3,077 girls that came to the attention of the local police, only 151 were actually arrested.[20] The resistance to officially charging girls was so great in one police department that one girl had eleven separate police contacts before she was ever referred to the court. "In each instance," according to a policewoman, "she had been given a 'sermon' and released."[21] In Louisiana, as in other states, female delinquents were grouped with cases of "dependency and neglect," so that the behavior, they said, would "reflect on the parents" rather than on the girl herself. The police, however, were not the only or even the most important contributors to what one sociologist called the "mirage" of male-to-female ratios of juvenile delinquency.[22] A criminologist looking at the records of all children's agencies in Washington, D.C.—including Children's Services and the Department of Attendance of the Board of Education—found that these agencies handled *five times* as many girls' cases without referral to the court as boys' in 1945.[23]

What, then, do these numbers tell us? Was there a reality of "girls' troubles"—known to parents, local authorities, and teenagers themselves yet persistently denied in the national delinquency picture? Were girls actually rebelling against postwar mores and gender roles? Against society itself? The number of girls caught in delinquent acts—from shoplifting to reckless driving to truancy—suggests that at the very least girls were engaging in behavior they knew would be considered either delinquent or threatening.[24] On the other hand, the rise in female delinquency rates could just as easily reflect an increase in attention paid to girls or an attempt to control girls' social and sexual behavior through children's agencies and, when deemed necessary, the court system.

The media seized upon the fact that girls committed fewer crimes than boys and announced that girls were naturally "good," while simultaneously reporting on "shocking" examples of blatant revolt, alienation, and disregard for the law.[25] The result, as I discuss in the next section, was a conflicting set of messages: time-worn assumptions about female passivity and family-centered "dependency" were invoked at the same time that alarm over unprecedented levels of female rebellion mounted. The result was a constant sense of incredulity about the female delinquent, a perception that effectively distanced her behavior as strange while simultaneously employing it as an occasion for a reflection upon the particular problems of postwar American culture.

The Mass Media Reports on Female Delinquents

When the media reported on female delinquency, they remained chronically disquieted by two stunning facts: girls were committing violent acts and white middle-class girls were making up an unprecedented proportion of the delinquent population. Both developments were interpreted as a sign of a generational conflict, and the search for psychological causes tended to occlude class and racial distinctions in favor of a more general perception of societal and emotional illness. Girl delinquents were clearly "emotionally sick," as James Farrell put it, and the "alarming growth of delinquency in America" reflected what he called "adult delinquency"—the failure of parents to truly "reach" their children.[26]

During the war, the girls who flocked to soldiers' camps, variously called "Victory Girls," "Khaki Wackies," and "Amateur Girls," set off a wave of alarm about promiscuity, encouraged in large part by the single-minded crusade for publicity initiated by the chief of the FBI, J. Edgar Hoover.[27] Yet when Hoover drew a general portrait of juvenile delinquency, he was equally emphatic about the concomitant rise in female lawlessness (as opposed to promiscuity) and especially liked to employ stories about girls' capacity for particularly daring crimes. "If the violence of boys is alarming, the increasing waywardness of teen-age girls is tragic," began one of his articles for *American Magazine*. A girl named Jenny, he continued, was the "apparent chief" of a gang of kids that stole a car and "set out on a wild trip to the Southwest," during which they "stole other cars, stole gasoline, slept in abandoned farms, [and] held up a liquor store."[28] Mary, another "ringleader" of a group of youngsters involved in ten burglaries, was remarkable for her ingenious methods of breaking into apartments: "She would . . . slip her light sweater under the door, push the inside key out so that it would fall on the sweater, draw the sweater (with key) out from under the door, and unlock the door."[29]

After the war, reports of teenage female violence and gang activity began to punctuate accounts of the national juvenile crime wave, enhancing the perception that an epidemic of adolescent female criminality had broken out. A favored way of dramatizing the scope of the juvenile delinquency outbreak was to simply list events and scenarios, one after the other, without giving contextual information about the girls' socioeconomic background or sometimes even their geographical location. One *Newsweek* report, under the heading "The Kids Grow Worse," contained postings of different events that had occurred across the nation, including one in which "girls were imitating their boy friends, organizing gangs of their own—uniformed in tight blue jeans and leather jackets" and another in which "a girl gang . . . overpowered other girls and cut off their hair."[30] Another issue read, "In Utah, a 14-year-old gun moll, after exchanging shots with policemen, complained: 'I hate cops; I wish I had got me one.'"[31] A similar list published in *Time* magazine included the announcement: "Student riot brimmed over into the streets . . . a harried school official could think only of keeping the news from the press. . . . And this at a girls' school . . . where the situation is described by teachers and students as a 'powder keg' with girls arming themselves with knives."[32] The stories from around the country were rarely elaborated upon, the lack of explication or context serving to highlight the violent nature and irrationality of the crimes and to mask the class and racial identity of the criminals, effectively implicating girls in general without actually specifying who was involved.

In fact, not only were questions of class and neighborhood ignored or even obfuscated, but the truism that juvenile delinquency was a "product of low socio-economic status" was often turned on its head.[33] Martha Eliot, chief of the Children's Bureau, said in testimony before the Senate Subcommittee on Juvenile Delinquency in 1954: "Gradually we have seen that it is not the neighborhood alone that causes juvenile delinquency . . . some of the most serious acts of delinquent behavior have been committed by children from so-called good families and good neighborhoods."[34] Eliot's impression was supported by a handful of studies conducted between 1945 and 1965 showing that acts of delinquency had become, in some ways, a normal part of growing up. When middle-class girls in Texas and Connecticut were asked what delinquent acts they had committed, a surprisingly high percentage admitted to an array of pranks and "acts of public annoyance," including "painting and flooding rooms" (18 percent), "breaking into locked homes or buildings" (34 percent), throwing "spitwads at others' displeasure" (30 percent), "reckless driving" (23 percent), "participating in 'drag racing'" (32 percent), and "taking something from a store without paying for it" (37 percent).[35] And, as evidence of middle- and upper-middle-class delinquency began to emerge, some sociologists and journalists theorized that juvenile delinquency was actually a product of the opportunities provided by postwar prosperity: leisure, automobiles, organized activities for youth, and a "legitimate" youth culture that easily shaded into the illegitimate.[36] By the late 1950s a new truism emerged, one that sat uneasily alongside the old: "more teenagers go wrong because of overprivelege than underprivelege."[37] But whereas the obvious solution to the social problems associated with slum life was class uplift, the indictment of middle-class youthful misbehavior could lead only to a gaze inward at the most basic values of a society that had emerged from the Great Depression determined to give American children a better life.

It was within the context of such self-searching that girls' delinquency often took center stage. In 1958, James Farrell, chronicler of the fictional sometime juvenile delinquent Studs Lonigan, wrote an article for *Coronet Magazine* comparing "the condition of youth today" to their condition in his own time, during which his book *Studs Lonigan* (1935) was set. His comparison of the two periods is predictably nostalgic: in his day, juvenile delinquency involved tough boys from tough neighborhoods who fought with their fists and stayed mostly on the right side of the law. Since his time, though, juvenile delinquency had "spread to many layers of our society," including "well-to-do neighborhoods" and girls' subcultures. It was the transformation in teenage girls that he found most surprising and most illustrative of the profundity of the historical change. "Most of the girls in my old neighborhood were what we called 'good girls,'" he said. "Violence on the part of girls, or the formation of such things as girl gangs would have created a sensational shock."[38] These "Rebelettes or Tigrettes," he said, were evidence of the emotional and spiritual poverty of postwar America, particularly among the middle and upper classes.[39] In well-to-do families, he claimed, fathers were "overworked," "passive," and either "neglectful" or thoughtlessly strict with their children. "Punishment, prosperity, sentimental coddling, none of these is enough," he concluded, for delinquency was nothing less than "a challenge and a criticism of our society."[40] Pointing to the sense of underlying psychological and social disorientation that informed youthful misbehavior, he lamented: "Questioned by a judge as to why they did certain things, [the girls] repeatedly say: 'I don't know.'"

Similarly capitalizing on the unfamiliarity of middle-class female misbehavior, articles like the one that appeared in the *Ladies Home Companion* with the title "Nice Girls Can Be Delinquent" examined the difficulty of understanding the delinquent girl. "This shockingly true story," the writer promised, "shows how young girls from good homes went terribly wrong."[41] According to the article, twenty-five teenagers from Tacoma, Washington, were implicated in a shoplifting ring, which had loose connections to a female gang called the Hellcats. (The story was later made into a film called *High School Hellcats*.) The only obvious purpose of the gang was to be identified as such: the group wore flannel leopard-skin-print scarves to school, a symbol that alluded to a notoriously tough male gang "the Cats." The principal of the high school ordered the girls to "refrain from wearing 'anything with feline connotations'" to school but otherwise dismissed them as silly. After one of the Hellcats was arrested for shoplifting, the police ferreted out the origins and activities of what turned out to be a shoplifting ring and were astounded to find out how many of the girls involved in the scheme had, at one time or another, connections to the Hellcats.

Parents and the local police repeatedly claimed that they were stunned by what these girls had done. Yet one of the girls had been called to her adviser's attention nine times over the past month. Her record read: "truancy, smoking, truancy, truancy, passing notes, Hellcats, smoking, truancy, shoplifting." The repeated statement that these were "nice girls" with "hidden" delinquencies is contradicted by the blatant gang insignia that they wore to school; the school authorities claimed to be "startled" by the girls' behavior but had extensive records on all of them. The confused nature of the response of parents and police was compounded by the girls' own mystification about the origins of their behavior: when asked why they became delinquent, one said, "I just wish I knew"; others said that it was just "a way of getting kicks." [42] These explanations only served to emphasize the pointlessness of the acts, the same (female) "I don't know" that was at the center of Farrell's exposé of adolescent emotional confusion and hostility. [43]

The difficulty social commentators had describing and coming to terms with female misbehavior in particular is elucidated by contrasting it with the relative ease with which they linked male juvenile delinquency to detectable social and familial conditions. The sociologists Sheldon and Eleanor Gluek conducted the most extensive and meticulous research on male juvenile delinquency during the 1950s. They compared characteristics of delinquents and nondelinquents, including bodily traits, home life, and personality type, and produced a composite picture of each through statistical difference: boys who tended to become delinquent had "an exceptional need for change, excitement and risk" and were less inhibited by the desire to please adults. The parents of the delinquent boys were characterized primarily as lacking ambition and, secondarily, inconsistent in applying discipline. Most mothers of delinquent boys, the Glueks found, were overly lax, and a considerable proportion of both parents swung "erratically from laxity to over strictness without apparent reason." The perception that boys needed to be handled more firmly and consistently was echoed by judges in adolescents' court who embraced the "back to the woodshed movement" and believed that middle-class fathers in particular allowed their sons too much "individualism." [44]

Samuel S. Leibowitz, senior judge of Brooklyn's Kings County Court, issued the simple edict in *America Magazine* in 1955: "PUT FATHER BACK AT THE HEAD OF THE FAMILY." A "permissive psychology," he complained, "where Johnny is rarely if ever disciplined have [*sic*] resulted in the confused, rebellious, unhappy teen-agers who flood our courts."[45] While not all authorities agreed that the problem of male juvenile delinquency could be solved so simply, finding a cure for female rebellion was always portrayed as confounding. All delinquents were considered to be "confused," but the response that female delinquency demanded, as well as the appropriate *authoritative*—thus paternal—attitude it called forth, was never fully located and only partially explained.

Consternation about the appropriate role of fathers in the lives of teenage girls was reflected in a series on juvenile delinquency published in the *Saturday Evening Post*. One anecdote was about a girl named Florence—a case study in the dire results of paternal restrictiveness. Florence's father demanded that she "be circumspect in her behavior in every way." She "wasn't permitted to attend dances even when they were sponsored by the high school" and "had been forbidden to wear lipstick." His authoritarian approach, the article explains, backfired when she eventually lashed out at him by acting out his worst fears. When the *Saturday Evening Post* caught up with her, she was in a state training school for girls. "She had been sent there as an incorrigible after she ran away from home, got involved with several men and learned about beer joints and narcotic peddlers," the article reported. The article concluded that "heavy use of the rod not only failed to keep Florence on the straight and narrow path but obviously had driven her away from it."[46]

The ills of repression, represented here by an antiquated notion of paternal duty, were obvious in the extremity of their results. Yet if traditional paternal authority was to be abandoned, what was to be put in its place? Beyond permissiveness, what was to define the substance of paternal involvement? What was the right way to behave toward girls who wanted to participate in the increasingly sexualized youth culture of the day, which included lipstick and school proms? Simply letting Florence do whatever she wanted was certainly not the recommendation of the article. "Passive" and "neglectful" fathers were, as we have already seen, regularly taken to task for abdicating their responsibilities. A constant reference point, the question of appropriate paternal involvement remained at the center of the problem of female juvenile delinquency.

Psychoanalysis and the Law: Girls' Term

The history of a juvenile court created for wayward girls in New York City serves as a useful illustration of the ways in which definitions of female delinquency were both contested and in flux during this period. The Wayward Minor Court for Girls, or "Girls' Term," as it came to be known after 1945, was (and remained for its duration) an "experimental" tribunal for teenage girls.[47] The court developed out of what was once a juvenile subsection of the Women's Night Court, which dealt primarily with prostitution. In 1936, the court set aside one day a week "to establish a new technique for handling wayward minors."[48] But one day a week proved unequal to the task of responding to the explosion of "bobby socks girls" falling under the purview of the court during the war, and a separate court was established for that sole purpose in 1944.

Girls' Term operated under the Wayward Minor Statute, which defined any person between the ages of sixteen and twenty-one who was addicted to drugs, associated with "dissolute persons," was a prostitute, or was "willfully disobedient to the reasonable and lawful commands of [a] parent" to be legally "wayward." In 1945, the New York legislature added new sections to the statute, including one that designated any teenager who "deserts his or her home . . . and is morally depraved or in danger of becoming morally depraved" as a wayward minor.[49] Girls who committed any other criminal acts appeared in other courts.[50] Girls' Term was designed to be a social court, or a "socio-legal tribunal," and it used the most up-to-date psychiatric methods to diagnose and then rehabilitate what was described in 1955 as "the sexually promiscuous girl, the runaway, the undisciplined, defiant youngster, the neglected girl."[51] Girls were brought to court by their parents in 98 percent of the cases, and the sitting magistrate decided the cases based on interviews with the girls, her relatives, and the attendant social workers. As a "socialized court," its powers were broad though ill defined, while its mission reflected the anxieties about sexuality and public deportment that were characteristic of the prewar era.

The very impulse to separate this "specialized" court from other courts serving female adolescents suggests that female status crimes had assumed a more distinct identity (as opposed to other forms of female crime like theft and vandalism). It also suggests that the dominant interpretation of female disobedience was, in a sense, split between two possible paradigms: behavior that was adjudicated alongside boys' and thus by similar criteria, and behavior that was only "illegal," or, more to the point, a threat to social order, because it was exhibited by girls of a certain age within the context of family life. Reflecting this difficulty, the court became the subject of an ongoing legal debate from its inception. Tellingly, both sides thought the purposes of the court too vague and its mission outmoded, if not anachronistic. Dorris Clarke, on one side of the debate, argued that "in light of present-day conditions and problems, the Wayward Minor Act of 1925, even with the amendments of 1945, is as inadequate as would be a Model T Ford in a B-29 age."[52] Pointing to "behavior problems engendered by the present complex social organization," Clarke complained that the court was inadequate to its task, leaving parents and social agencies with little support for dealing with "incorrigibility, disobedience, [and] revolt against parental control" that threatened to overtake them.[53] Clarke believed that the court needed more power and resources to intervene *before* girls became truly criminal, that is, at the moment that they were primarily a discipline problem to their parents.

She cited several "typical" Girls' Term decisions to buttress her arguments about the court's shortcomings. All involved filial insubordination; none was decided in the parents' favor. In each case, the parents—but much more often the girl's father—did not like the daughter's friends or boyfriend, the hours that she kept, or her attitude. In one instance, a father asked the court to compel his daughter to tell him who the father of her unborn child was. In another, a mother and father sought court assistance "because of the anti-Semitic tendencies of their sixteen-year-old daughter."[54] The girl's mother was Catholic, her father Jewish. For months the girl had refused to live at home, preferring to stay with an "anti-Semitic cousin" and expressed hatred for her father. The judge decided to let the girl sort out her religious convictions herself. Why didn't the court "force her to change her attitude and force her to return home?" Clarke asked. "She is 'willfully disobedient,' why isn't she a wayward minor?"[55]

On the other side of the debate was, among others, Paul Tappan, who criticized the range and scope of Girls' Term's discretion, maintaining that the court was unfairly using the correctional and custodial powers of a criminal court to handle social problems that required social solutions. Adjudication, Tappan complained, was based on a hazy conception of "total personality" or, in some instances, on a course of conduct, rather than any specific act, resulting in the violation of girls' rights, as well as the rules of due process.[56] Even more important, the very premise of a "morals court," as he called it, belied the informal social and sexual customs of the day: the court punished some for what was practiced by many. "What," he queried, "do we mean by 'moral depravity' in this day of conflicting ethical codes?" Citing several studies of adolescent sexual behavior that indicated a "large and increasing" amount of premarital experimentation, especially by middle-class girls, he claimed to be suspicious of a court that specialized in punishing girls for immorality. "In practical effect the result may be to subject to punishment merely those individuals among the sexually active who are so inept in their expression as to be 'trapped' by parent, police officer, or nature."[57]

Questions of equal difficulty plagued the assessment of incorrigibility. Tappan asked, "In an era of increasing emancipation of youth, to what standard of obedience should the daughter be held? In other words, what are parents' 'reasonable and lawful commands' today?"[58] Putting it yet another way, he asked, "Wherein does the 'bad bad girl' of the court or training school differ from the 'good bad girl' who is spared judicial attention?" To Tappan, the court made for a frustrating and disturbing picture: righteous, socially conservative magistrates (all men), furious parents, defiant daughters, and one of the highest known remand rates of any court in existence at the time.[59] Clarke's examples of leniency notwithstanding, in 1955, two-thirds of the girls who were "convicted" in Girls' Term were sentenced to some kind of "rehabilitation" program or reformatory institution, and one-third were placed on probation. More than four-fifths of the adolescent boys adjudged to be youthful offenders and who committed felony offenses were placed on probation, and only one-thirtieth were sent to reformatories.[60]

Harry Shulman, the author of *Juvenile Delinquency in American Society*, an exhaustive study of every aspect of the problem, made a similar point in 1961, albeit from a different point of view. As he put it, "The modern high school girl who drinks a cocktail at a dance (but who prefers a coke), who smokes cigarettes, who rebuilds her face from eyebrows to chin, who wears less to the beach than many a tribal matron, who necks or pets according to local custom . . . does not regard herself as a delinquent, is not regarded by her friends as one and is not regarded by her family as having 'gone to the dogs.' "[61] Like Tappan, Shulman asserted that all teenage girls now behaved in ways that could appear deviant. The problem, then, was to determine which girls were actually suffering from psychic distrubance, rather than to assess which girls could officially be labeled delinquent. The juvenile delinquent, he continued, was not someone who behaved in what seemed to be (from an adult perspective) an antisocial manner but someone who rejected her parents or who had been "rejected by them," and in the process had become "the reject of conventional society." And "nowhere," he concluded, "is this more clearly seen than in the situation of the delinquent girl."[62] The concept of rejection, and the resulting problem of "self-image," was the answer to Tappan's complaint about the imprecision of the definition of female delinquency in 1947 and to Shulman's own reiteration of the problem almost fifteen years later. Intervening in the decade of the 1950s was a combination of observations and fears about the meaning and content of female antisocial behavior that originated and gained near-universal credibility with the rising influence of psychoanalytic discourse within the field of juvenile justice—especially female juvenile justice.

Although many people had advocated the use of psychiatric clinics in conjunction with the juvenile court prior to the Second World War, few courts actually employed them for anything except diagnostic purposes until the late 1940s; and their founding, in many instances, was in direct response to the difficulty of disposing of female juvenile delinquency cases.[63] Hence, the use of psychoanalysis within the court system developed in a particularly gendered way. Proponents of the use of psychology or psychotherapy for interpreting male juvenile crime and rehabilitating male juvenile criminals often had to contend with accusations of "coddling" and "soft pedaling," in addition to general discomfort with the incomprehensible jargon of psychoanalysis.[64] Opponents complained that the use of psychology in the courtroom, when it came to boys, compromised the adjudication of guilt or innocence, thereby infringing upon the rights not only of parents and children but also of the community at large.[65] There were no objections, however, to the idea of bringing in psychoanalysts to help adjudicate girls' cases. The importance of the public dimension of justice to the social order as a whole in the punishment of male crime was absent altogether in discussions of female delinquency. Girls committed what were considered "private" crimes of a personal nature (no matter what the actual offense), and thus the public's ability to fully comprehend the nature of her offense or her rehabilitation did not present itself as urgent or even necessary. In fact, one could argue that in the different perspectives on the uses of psychoanalytic clinics we see the same kind of incomprehension that we saw in the article on the Hellcats: girls' delinquency is mystifying and exceptional.

Thus, when psychological treatment clinics were officially established as an arm of the juvenile courts, they were used most often in connection to certain types of female crimes.[66] In Massachusetts, all female runaways were sent to the court clinic as a matter of procedure.[67] In New York City, juvenile court clinics were originally established in 1948 with a grant from the New York City Youth Board. However, clinic service in the Adolescent Courts throughout the city was terminated almost immediately in favor of concentrating all psychiatric services in Girls' Term, where it was clear that cases could be "treated more effectively in a psychiatric clinic."[68] Thus, the authority of psychiatry, with its ability to diagnose hidden, "underlying" disturbances, was enhanced in relation to the problem of delinquency generally, but, at a state-sponsored institution, it was enhanced in relationship to female delinquency specifically. This relationship between psychiatry and the law had a major impact on the way that female delinquency was ultimately portrayed and interpreted. It was after the introduction of the court clinic that the female delinquent practically disappeared from the pages of the *American Journal of Soci-*

ology and began to appear instead in publications like the *American Journal of Orthopsychiatry.*

With the introduction of the court clinic and the rising influence of psychoanalysis, the case histories of girls brought to the attention of Girls' Term changed markedly. The concerns of psychoanalysis combined with the widespread anxiety about aggression during the postwar period to produce an interpretive framework that explained all female delinquency in terms of the psychodynamics of fear, insecurity, and defense—diagnoses that challenged fundamental prewar principles about female adolescent misbehavior.

Midcentury courts and psychiatrists were not the first to draw attention to the female delinquents. Progressive reformers, who were alarmed at shifts in the social and sexual mores of working-class girls, set up what Mary Odem has called a vast and "elaborate network of legal codes and institutions designed to control the sexuality of young women and girls."[69] These reformers—social workers, sociologists, and psychologists—made female delinquency virtually synonymous with sexual delinquency. According to Regina Kunzel, "even if a young woman's delinquency manifested itself in ways not overtly sexual, social workers believed that 'they are nearly always found associated with the instinctive urge.'"[70] Psychiatrists at the turn of the century contributed to the aims of the Progressive reformers by conceiving the category of the "hypersexual female," a girl or woman whose overwhelming sexual desire rendered her psychopathic.[71] The sexualization of female delinquency was a result of the clash between the imperatives of working-class girls and middle-class reformers, between an older set of assumptions about female chastity and newer conceptions of female sexual desire and expression. It was played out primarily in the urban environment of rapidly growing industrial cities and was, at its most basic level, a contest between one social class and another, the prize consisting of the management of the social organization of gender. In general, the concerns of the Progressive reformers combined with the growing research of sociologists in the 1920s and 1930s to create a powerful perspective on juvenile delinquency, one that would, despite the rise of psychoanalysis, never completely disappear. Sociologists emphasized the socioeconomic position of the female delinquent and the structural makeup of her home, in general ascribing female misbehavior to the impact of "unwholesome" influences, especially the experience of the working-class neighborhood.[72]

The burgeoning interest in female delinquency that began during the Second World War and lasted into the 1950s, or the second wave of anxiety about female adolescent behavior, was informed by a different set of cultural preoccupations. When courts and psychiatrists reflected on the problem of female teenage rebellion, they worried less about her libidinal urges and more about her anger toward authority figures, less about social mores and more about her psychological relationship to her family.

A comparison of case histories recorded before and after the introduction of the psychoanalytic clinic illustrates the point. In the late 1930s and early 1940s, court officials often described girls who came before them as having "behavior difficulties" but they almost never elaborated further. The vocabulary used to describe emotional problems was limited to observations such as "H. is literally about as impertinent a youngster as we have ever handled in this court and it was extremely difficult to repress her spontaneous outbursts throughout the hearing."[73] After the war, in contrast, the case histories were almost entirely preoccupied with the emotional complexion of the delinquent girl. Hence the words most often employed in case histories after 1945 were psychologically descriptive in nature: girls tended to be "infantile," "withdrawn," "violent reactors," "angry," "moody," and "unresponsive."[74]

In sum, the girl who was described in 1939 as "fresh, impudent, disrespectful, lazy or otherwise beyond control" had, by 1955, become the girl who was "defensive, hostile, provocative and challenging" and who often threw "violent temper tantrums."[75] This is not to say that the *same* behavior merited wholly different observations during the two historical periods but rather that the social meaning of delinquency underwent a transformation. "Freshness" and "impudence" represented an affront to a system of manners, a sense of the violation of propriety. In contrast, the descriptions of defensiveness and hostility in the case histories of the 1950s reflected concerns about emotional distress. The distinction is important insofar as it speaks to the particular ways in which demonstrations of antisocial behavior were felt to be threatening after the Second World War and the extent to which female *discontent*, as opposed to obvious infractions against a clearly spelled out social code, became central to the definition of delinquency itself. From this psychoanalytic point of view, all female misbehavior began to be cast in terms of aggression and revolt that was a result not of the disdain for social authority but of the feelings of rejection that were born out of a state of psychic confusion about self in relation to parents.

In a case under review in a Boston Juvenile Court in the 1950s, a psychiatrist explained that a particular girl who was brought in for fighting felt "rejected by the father" and thus began to show a "definite aggressive reaction," which was "really an overcompensation for her growing fear of insecurity" and manifested itself in "striking at children."[76] In a similar case reviewed in the 1950s by Girls' Term, a seventeen-year-old named Jerry was brought in by her father for staying out late and drinking. According to psychiatric interviews, Jerry's father was much preoccupied with his new girlfriend and thus "Jerry expressed considerable feeling around what she saw as her father's rejection of his role as father." According to the diagnosis, Jerry was "threatened seriously by adolescence and her repression of sexual content was prominent . . . [with] evident confusion in her psycho-sexual identification."[77] The most striking aspect of the analysis of Jerry's behavior and emotional state was that it involved the perception of a *repression* of sexuality as opposed to its illicit indulgence, the fact of which originally constituted the legal and moral grounds (especially in the Wayward Minor Act) for the intervention of the court in the first place. The fear here was not, as one might deduce from her activities, that Jerry was on the path to immorality but that her disturbed relationship with her father was blocking her path to sexual maturity—a goal that was Jerry's father's particular responsibility.

Psychoanalysis and the "Wayward Girl"

The Oedipal origin of female "acting-out" behavior was not, as it might seem, the foregone or universal conclusion of psycho-analytic thought. Rather, it was the particular conclusion of psycho-analysts practicing in the United States during the postwar period. Working out of court clinics and hospitals and in private practice, psychoanalysts observed what they believed to be a family dynamic disabled by psychoses brought about by Oedipal disturbance. Though the particulars differed, virtually all case histories of the period share a similar sense of disappointment in the American father, born out of a perception of his passivity and renunciation of emotional involvement with the family (concerns that echo James Farrell's assessment). Paternal failure was most often described as incapacity and was evinced by the sense or fact of his absence: emotional distance, literal neglect, or the removal of love and affection, experienced inevitably by his daughter as indifference.

This perception of paternal failure is best illustrated in an article by one of the foremost psychoanalytic experts on adolescence, Peter Blos, in the *Psychoanalytic Study of the Child*, published in 1957. Blos claimed that he was "struck by the difference" in the degree of neurosis found in the contemporary female delinquent as compared to the delinquents he worked with when he was a graduate student in the 1920s.[78] More recently, he observed, girls had become "fixated" at a pre-Oedipal level, unable to progress through and then surmount the adolescent Oedipal stage to become sexually mature young adults. "It is my impression," he said, "that this type of delinquent . . . not only experience[d] an Oedipal defeat at the hands of a—literally or figuratively—distant, cruel or absent father but also witnessed her mother's dissatisfaction with her husband; both mother and daughter share their disappointment."[79] Shared disappointments, however, contributed not to commiseration but to competition between mother and daughter, and indeed girls involved in such a competition often believed, according to Blos, "that if only they could be in their mother's place the father would show his true self, namely be transfigured by their love into the man of their oedipal wishes."[80]

Blos charted two types of possible "acting out" behaviors in reaction to paternal "disappointment," which, as a pair, formed the psychological foundation for a whole spectrum of female delinquencies. The first scenario was one in which the failure of the father to fulfill his daughter's romantic and erotic expectations impelled the girl to search for some kind of partner who served "to surmount in fantasy [her] oedipal impasse." Blos termed this behavior "pseudoheterosexuality" and included within its reach precocious sexuality and promiscuity. The alternative scenario was one in which the daughter, suffering from the "painful rejection" by her father, assumed "the masculine role" by identifying with him as opposed to her mother, therefore remaining in a pre-Oedipal relationship with the mother and failing to progress into the Oedipal situation with the father. The most prevalent form of delinquency arising from this scenario was stealing, an act considered to be aggressive and "masculine" in nature. In this schema, then, antisocial behavior in all of its guises was linked to a single adolescent Oedipal problem that had one of two possible ways of expressing itself: in the first instance, the girl circumvented her Oedipal desire by maintaining a "pseudo" or "illusory oedipal situation" through the substitution of one or many men for the Oedipal father; in the second, the girl fled the Oedipal by denying its existence and then retreated into a pre-Oedipal relationship with her mother.

The psychoanalytic account of "Oedipal impasse" was, in its description of paternal failure, rife with assumptions about the nature of the father-daughter relationship. Although a father might play various roles in his daughter's life, his presence was depicted as critical insofar as he validated and encouraged her sexual development; hence, his failings in relationship to his daughter were erotic by definition. In another case history, in which a girl was found "hobnobbing with questionable characters" and "running off to teenage clubs and bars," the culpable father was described as "blind" to his daughter's "pretty face" and unresponsive to "the girl's charm and beauty."[81] Elsewhere, fathers were described as rigid, fault-finding, suspicious of their daughters' sexual activities, and detached. Linking these cases was the assumption that paternal disinterest—specifically in a daughter's sexual allure—was particularly dangerous to her development. The causal relationship between paternal neglect and female delinquency demanded, as it was described in these case histories, not a father who was simply present (literally or emotionally) but a father who clearly recognized his daughter's sexual maturation, her developing "charm" and "beauty," and incorporated evidence of this recognition into his response to her. Just how that recognition would be manifested was never made clear—its lack simply loomed over the delinquent girl and informed her discontent. Thus the delinquent daughter was both a testimony to her father's failure and a call for his (specifically masculine) intervention. The burden of paternal responsibility, then, was not authority but eroticism, and the techniques of paternal power were sexual rather than custodial in nature. Instead of "policing and protecting," the responsible father noticed and encouraged, admired and delighted in his daughter's sexual maturation. Thus he would ensure that she did not feel "rejected" and become delinquent.[82]

This kind of recognition, as it was prescribed by psychoanalytic discourse during the period, was an unstable and precarious concept, full of potential pitfalls and missteps. Psychoanalysts were quick to define unhealthy forms of Oedipal or erotic father-daughter relationships as well, providing examples of fathers who behaved in a "seductive" manner. However, overt paternal desire was considered to be dangerous not because it was potentially incestuous but because a father's failure to cope with his own sexual impulses toward his maturing daughter easily incited in him a jealous attitude toward her boyfriends, which in turn could cause him to be restrictive about dating and antagonistic toward any sign of sexual maturity.

A good example of such an analysis involved a case referred to the Judge Baker Children's Center in Boston. Anne, the daughter of an Italian immigrant who worked in a factory, had been referred to the clinic for stealing lipstick on several occasions. At the time of the incidents, her father, according to the psychiatrist's analysis, "had been expressing his negative feeling with increasing intensity . . . [and] there was constant evidence of an underlying seductive attitude."[83] The father's "negativity" about Anne was evoked in his constant criticisms, suspiciousness about her dates, and the demand that she abstain from feminine adornment: "He demands that Anne . . . wear tailored, unfrilly clothes, and scorns lipstick and fingernail polish." The psychiatrist found his demands significant and reported that "when Anne's classmates began wearing lipstick, it took a great deal of courage on her part and much arguing before he accepted her wish to wear it." Thus the diagnosis concluded not that the father's "seductive attitude" was pathological but rather that his refusal to allow Anne to array herself with the latest fashions for girls had, as in Jerry's case, arrested her heterosexual development, resulting in "ambivalency in her sexual identification." Gender confusion presented itself in the tendency to dress boyishly ("Anne appears in slacks, her brother's jacket, and men's socks, size 11") and to steal cosmetics.[84]

The consuming interest in the role that fathers would play in sanctioning and encouraging their teenage daughters' sexual identity usually hinged on the acceptance of symbolic signs of sexual maturity, especially the use of lipstick. In every scenario—whether a popular narrative about the dangers of too much discipline or a psychoanalytic case history describing the etiology of psychosexual ambivalence —the goal was the same: the attainment of a healthy sexual identity through paternal sexual recognition. This recognition presumably existed somewhere in the middle of a continuum in which paternal sexual desire was on one end and paternal rejection was on the other. The appropriate space in the middle would allow for, or help achieve, a daughter's self-assured sexual identity. Within this context, fathers needed to realize that their authority lay not in their ability to lay down the law but in the strength of their Oedipal hold over their daughters. As girls became teenagers they would need their fathers—as opposed to their mothers, and prior to their boyfriends—to applaud their first steps toward sexual self-presentation.[85]

Betty Friedan, her finger ever firmly on the pulse of 1950s female discontent, helped to popularize these ideas in a piece she wrote in 1958 for *Coronet* magazine.[86] Her story of a typical teenager's "acting out" in Westchester County, New York, is a full-fledged rendering of the crisis of "Oedipal impasse." Friedan tells the story of Phyllis, who was brought to the Youth Consultation Service by her distraught mother for staying out late and "going steady with six boys in the last six months."[87] Through Phyllis's encounter with the therapist, recorded by Friedan, we are told that Phyllis's sexual behavior "was not really sexual" but rather anger directed at her parents because of her "discouragement about her own worth." Such girls, the psychotherapist explained to Friedan, "didn't have 'a good sure feeling about being a girl'" and felt unattractive to boys. In this case, the father was a busy man who never seemed to have any time for his daughter. As Phyllis herself put it, "No matter what I wear . . . my father doesn't look up from his papers at all." At the end of Phyllis's treatment, her father was called in for an appointment, and the diagnosis presented to him. "The realization," Friedan writes, "that if Phyllis had more affection from her father, she wouldn't be so hungry for boys' kisses now, appalled him."[88]

Friedan's project here was to bring attention to the importance of paternal involvement in girls' upbringing and to underscore the ways in which middle-class girls, like their mothers, were undervalued and ignored. However, the concepts available to Friedan for understanding the paternal relationship were limited to those offered by psychoanalysis and translated in the everyday services of psychotherapy. Though Friedan did not use the term "Oedipal impasse," she nevertheless invoked the specific demands of the Oedipal relationship when she suggested that Phyllis's father needed to show "'softness' for his daughter" in order to bolster her sexual self-confidence.[89] That "softness" was, in the family that Friedan described, a paternal form of specifically erotic acknowledgment.

Such as they were, these analyses represented an often well intended attempt on the part of adults to understand female social and sexual expression within a youth culture that was very different from their own. Indeed, the invariance with which they advised fathers to allow their daughter to wear lipstick almost seems to suggest that they were sanctioning the massive commercialization—and sexualization—of female adolescence that occurred as the United States emerged from the Depression. The effect of such advice, however, was to encase female sexuality so thoroughly within the psychodynamics of the family that the very notion of female sexual autonomy became incomprehensible. The teenage girl in the postwar period in the United States was granted unprecedented sexual freedom, yet every aspect of her sexual self was viewed in terms that reflected the primacy, power, and inescapability of her first and lasting sexual relationship with her father.

Psychoanalysis and Popular Culture

The influence of the psychoanalytic paradigm for understanding female delinquency can hardly be overstated. Its reach crossed boundaries of disciplines and institutions, affecting the interpretation and treatment of girls across race and class and serving to define "girlhood" in a way that superseded other forms of classification. Yet, despite their general currency, psychoanalytic explanations of female rebellion were deployed, in their popular guise, to construct and comment upon the white middle-class suburban family at mid-century. As popular articles and a whole string of films on juvenile delinquency began to take their cue from psychoanalytic theories of adolescent development, those theories became constitutive of the white middle-class father-daughter relationship, a way to evoke and flesh out the characteristics of class, as well as gender identity. This development is especially significant in light of the fact that most of the girls who came before the courts and upon whom most case histories were based were working class. Therefore, the ways in which theories of female juvenile delinquency were deployed by the media reflect assumptions—perhaps desires—about the nature of middle-class family life and its particular relationship to psychoanalytic concerns.

The middle-class psychoanalytic portrait was in part achieved through the use of contrast and elision. Sidney Poitier was the iconic black male juvenile delinquent in *Blackboard Jungle* (1955), although his character owed much more to ideas about the experience of racism in the 1950s than to those of adolescence.[90] The black female delinquent, meanwhile, was rarely portrayed at all, either in film or in the popular press. Significantly, the silence about the black female delinquent occurred at the same time that she comprised one of the fastest growing groups of juvenile delinquents. In San Francisco, for instance, black female juvenile delinquents went from making up 5 percent of the total female cases adjudicated in 1943 to comprising 27 percent of all cases in 1954; in Connecticut, cases jumped from 17 percent in 1944 to 26 percent of total female cases in 1960.[91]

Although *The Wild One* (1954) and *Rebel Without a Cause* (1955) were the most famous juvenile delinquency films, a host of low budget, quick releases attempted to capitalize on the public interest in the issue in the 1950s. A surprising number of them were about female juvenile delinquents. *Teenage Devil Dolls, Naked Youth, Girl's Town, Teenage Crime Wave, Hot Car Girl, Reform School Girl, Teenage Doll,* and *So Young So Bad,* to name just a few, were all about girl "J.D.'s."[92] Although some of the titles and promotional shots made these films look like transparent attempts to display teenage girls in provocative poses, in fact most of them were simply tales about girls who somehow got caught up in the wrong crowd or who were disillusioned, bored, or unhappy. Like the boys in delinquency films, many of these girls saw themselves as betrayed by the adult world. (As "Silver," the tough reform school girl, said resentfully to the school matron, "You created such a great world. Too bad we don't appreciate it.") Yet the pictures of female adolescent defiance that were projected on screen were in fact divided along class lines in terms of the representation of family dynamics and the kinds of Oedipal problems that working- and middle-class girls experienced. When white working-class girls appeared in these films, their fathers were invariably absent (at times through death or divorce, at others for reasons unexplained); when white middle-class girls were delinquents, fathers were present but weak, ineffectual, or somehow disappointing to their daughters. The formulas for delinquency films were inflexible on this point. And though Oedipal disturbance could be associated with paternal absence, it was only between white middle-class girls and their fathers that Oedipal struggle was dramatized.[93]

Rebel Without a Cause and *The Wild One* represent the most commercially successful depictions of paternal failure as it was understood and described by the psychoanalytic community. Indeed, both movies, though they may be remembered otherwise, had almost as much to do with restless girls and their relationships with their fathers as they did with their male antiheroes. Both used different aspects of the psychoanalytic discourse of the Oedipal but for the most part chose to concentrate on the danger of disappointment and rejection. Simply put, the father in *Rebel Without a Cause* was a caricature of the father who could not accommodate his daughter's potential sexual maturity; the father in *The Wild One* was stereotypically weak and passive—in a phrase, Oedipally disappointing. (Neither of the girls in these movies had a relationship with her mother; in *The Wild One*, the girl's mother died when she was young.) Both movies pointed to the potential for female rebellion in the instance of failed fatherhood and did so in such a way that the stories revolved more around the relationship between father and daughter than the romance budding between boyfriend and girlfriend. *Rebel Without a Cause* opens with a shot of Judy (Natalie Wood) in a police station in the middle of the night applying bright red lipstick. She begins her interview with the delinquency officer crying, "He must hate me. . . . He looks at me like I'm the ugliest thing in the world . . . my own father!" In *The Wild One*, Cathy (Mary Murphy) is drawn closer to the leader of a motorcycle gang (Marlon Brando) as her father, the local sheriff, becomes less and less capable of coping with the threat that Brando's gang poses to the town. Each example animates the film in such a way and to such an extent that the tragedies that ensue in both films appear, psycho-analytically speaking, inevitable.

Perhaps the most difficult and telling father-daughter encounter to be portrayed in popular culture occurs in the movie *Rebel Without a Cause*. Judy, arrayed in a strikingly suggestive sweater, is rebuffed by her father when she attempts to kiss him. He then exposes his own sexual difficulties by pushing her away with the self-defeating response, "You're getting too old for that, kiddo." When Judy tries to kiss him again, he slaps her. "Don't worry dear, it's just her age," observes her mother, as Judy runs out of the room, crying. "Yeah, the atomic age!" quips her little brother, shooting his toy gun: an "age," in both senses of the word, that makes this scene explosively difficult for father and daughter to navigate and, most important, for which no solution is given. The indeterminacy of Judy's problem with her father is only enhanced by the relative clarity of Jim's struggle with his. Jim (James Dean) has one demand of his father: that he stand up to his shrewish wife, that he behave "like a man." The movie closes with a tragic scene: Plato, Jim and Judy's orphaned and needy friend, has been killed by police officers who mistakenly believe him to be armed. The adults have rushed to the scene. Jim's father, clad in bathrobe and slippers, promises to change, to be as "strong" as Jim needs him to be. Gathered around are Plato's black caretaker and the perceptive police detective from the first night at the juvenile detention center. Missing are Judy's parents. What, one is left to wonder, would Judy's father offer her?

The popular suggestions and silences about female rebellion combined to produce a perspective on the father-daughter relationship that was dictated by the difficult imperatives of the Oedipus complex. The Oedipal relationship became, in effect, the tie that bound father and daughter ever more closely together during a historical moment when the authority of fathers was threatened both by the apparent social and sexual sophistication of teenage girls and by ideologies of familial egalitarianism. Yet the effect of the popular representation of Oedipal conflict, I would argue, did not so much resolve the problem of the father-daughter relationship as render its eroticism manifest, however difficult and disruptive that eroticism might have been to the postwar, middle-class American family. In the process, a girl's rebellion became tied not to an angry but nevertheless autonomous self but rather to a self-defining relationship with her father. The adolescent girl could clearly rebel from dominant, middle-class norms — but the constant invocation of the etiology of Oedipal disturbance inextricably linked the nature and meaning of that rebellion to her father, and thus brought her, full circle, back home.

Chapter 3

ADOLESCENT AUTHORITIES

> *Padded to accentuate the immature breasts, dressed tightly in*
> *provocative clothes, loaded with "grooming," tirelessly teasing and*
> *insinuating, she has assumed leadership in the Coca-Cola bacchanals of*
> *proto-adolescence. . . . The years between twelve and fifteen thus become*
> *a critical period in the sexual cycle of girls in our culture. We have made*
> *this child the prime solvent of the traditional restrictions on all that*
> *would hamper the delirious release of impulse. It is a serious*
> *responsibility, but she has hurled herself into the work with*
> *the pathetic yet joyous blindness of childhood.*
> —Jules Henry, Culture against Man, 1963

When a Philadelphia newspaper wanted to encourage retailers to advertise in its pages in 1957, it ran a picture of a teenage girl holding a dress up to her body to show her father. The caption read, "In Philadelphia, buying begins at home. . . . In Philadelphia, nearly everybody reads *The Bulletin*."[1] When *Life* magazine wanted to portray the "new $10-billion power of the U.S. teen-age consumer" in 1959, they used a picture of a father holding out a new set of suitcases to his jubilant teenage daughter.[2] And when fathers and adolescent daughters were portrayed together at all in *Parents' Magazine* after World War II, the activity in which they were invariably engaged was shopping. Images of father-daughter "companionship" achieved through other forms of shared leisure activities—tennis and music were popular in the 1920s and 1930s—all but disappeared.[3] Instead, fathers were pictured with their daughters sitting down at desks to go over expenses, discussing allowances, or admiring new clothes.[4]

These images represent the culmination of a way of characterizing the father-daughter relationship that first emerged in the early

This picture of a daughter receiving luggage from her father accompanied the article "New, $10-Billion Power: The U.S. Teen-age Consumer," in Life *magazine in 1959. Courtesy Time Life Pictures/Getty Images.*

Fathers and daughters were often shown playing tennis and working on crafts together in Parents' Magazine *in the 1930s. Such images were used to illustrate the notion of "comradeship." This photo accompanied William Henry Spence's article "Fathers and Daughters," in 1937.*

1940s—the accumulated weight of plays, advertising, advice columns, movies, and fiction that featured fathers and daughters engaged in the process of teen consumerism together. Depictions of fathers choosing and evaluating their daughters' wardrobe and accessories represented a marked departure from the prewar period. During the 1920s, the last historical moment when changing fashions and increased consumption on the part of youth prompted extensive social comment, daughters were shown consulting with their mothers in their quest to be glamorous and socially successful. Whether giving advice, sharing their own clothes, or helping a daughter dress for an important event, mothers loomed large in their daughters' efforts to appear presentable and attractive. A mother's expertise and quick judgment in these matters also served as testament to her prominence in her daughter's life and, by extension, her social authority. When fathers began to be shown supervising their daughters' clothing and accessories in the 1940s, their involvement, while less sustained, conveyed new messages about their importance to their daughters, and their social prominence as well.[5]

The desire to see fathers rather than mothers in charge of shaping daughters' wardrobes with the onset of the Second World War can be interpreted in different ways: as a collective form of post-Depression excitement over the fact that fathers could demonstrably provide for their daughters again; as a reflection of a real increase in the amount of time teenagers and their fathers spent shopping together and discussing clothes; or, perhaps, as evidence of a narrowing of the types of "companionate" activities in which fathers and daughters were engaged. However, the singular attention to consumerism that emerged in the early 1940s can be read in another way. In the popular imagination, the "teenage girl" was both a product of the father-daughter relationship and a testament to it. She stood as both reason and rationale for men's commitment to higher standards of living, which were pursued with such purpose in the postwar years, and her newfound appeal—including her sexual appeal—was owed in large part to his invigorated contribution to her self-presentation. Consumerism was a shared activity that nodded to a complicated and consequential social contract—a form of interaction that, while perhaps more limited in its scope than prewar ideals of "companionship," was actually more important to the social order.

In much the same way that technology has traditionally been credited with setting women free from much of the drudgery of housework, economic prosperity and increased consumer spending, according to historians of youth culture, lay behind the manumission of children from their parents' domestic control. Postwar abundance, as Grace Palladino put it, "was quickly translated into personal freedom and enjoyment."[6] With the boom in wartime jobs, followed by the less dramatic but steady postwar growth in part-time work, teenagers, according to James Gilbert, managed to achieve a form of "consumer independence" that led to the "rapid growth of a separate teenage culture."[7] This separate culture—innovative, mercurial, purposively incomprehensible to adults—also enhanced teenagers' status within society. As they came to be understood as a viable market, according to historians, adolescents ascended in the public eye from insignificant children to what the postwar cultural critic Dwight Macdonald called "consumer citizens."[8] This transformation was accomplished when magazines, retailers, and businessmen began to take teenagers seriously, to consider their needs and to cater to their tastes. Once children who were "seen and not heard," teenagers were now virtual adults with a strong voice both within and outside the household through their consumer/cultural power.[9]

Working mostly in sociology and media studies, scholars looking at the popular culture surrounding girls—"girls' culture," as it has been labeled—have enriched our understanding of the media's relationship to and representation of teenage girls during the postwar period.[10] Susan Douglas, for example, has persuasively argued that television situation comedies dating from the late 1950s and early 1960s like *The Patty Duke Show* and *Gidget* provided models of girls who were "spunky and aggressive."[11] In a similar vein, Jeanine Basinger has argued that the teenage film stars she grew up watching, including Jane Powell in *A Date with Judy* (1948) and Debbie Reynolds in *Tammy and the Bachelor* (1957), taught her generation that girls could be smart and authoritative; in fact, she says, these teen heroines were often portrayed as "bossy—in a cheerful sort of way."[12] Consumerism has been explored by historians from a similar perspective. Women and girls, as Kathy Peiss has shown, have used makeup as a means to create individual style and a measure of control over their public image.[13]

Without denying the subversive potential of teen films, the power inherent in rising levels of disposable income, or the possibilities of self-creation through acts of consumption, I would like to consider questions about the context in which teenage girls emerged as powerful figures in the 1940s. The nicely coiffed, domineering yet "peppy" (and, within the mainstream media, white) teenage girl did indeed play a powerful role in the cultural economy of the era. But this role was first created and fostered through pervasive images of herself in relationship to her father—a person who necessarily limited the autonomy of this market. The common understanding of teenage girls as "bossy" has, somewhat contradictorily, lent itself to the notion of female adolescent independence. But what we see when we look more closely at girls' magazines and postwar films about fathers and daughters, as well as at the marketing studies that informed this cultural production, is not a new independence born of consumer authority but a *domestic dominance* predicated on the eroticized father-daughter relationship: a reciprocal set of appeals, gifts, and attempts at mutual understanding, most of which centered around the father's response to his daughter's quest for ever more sexually alluring and adult styles of self-presentation. It was this relationship that provided a social, moral, and sexual context for a vast new array of female adolescent fashions and helped to situate those fashions as a dominant force behind both paternal breadwinning and girls' privileged place in postwar culture.

One might assume that the acceleration in the marketing of sexualized and sophisticated apparel for teenage girls—lipstick, high heels, and, later, padded bras—which was part of the overall explosion in consumer goods after the war, would have ignited anxiety among fathers, and that they might attempt to protect the sexual purity of their daughters by circumscribing their sartorial designs.[14] Such paternal intervention was indeed a staple of postwar depictions of fathers and adolescent daughters. But this is only part of the story. Fathers were called upon both to stem the tide of adolescent forms of sexualized self-presentation and to lend authoritative approval to it. At times they said "no" to certain shades of nail polish or revealing clothes, and at times they capitulated to aspects of female teen culture they found troubling or simply irritating. More often they provided the new clothes and accessories themselves, encouraging their daughters to take their first steps toward sexual adulthood. Ultimately, a father's intimate involvement in the procurement of clothes and cosmetics both allowed for and neutralized the sexual meaning of a range of colors and styles, from bright red lipstick to cocktail dresses. These things became acceptable for adolescent girls because of, rather than in spite of, the fact of paternal mediation in the 1940s and 1950s. Formerly the sole preserve of mothers and daughters, the minutiae of necklines, lipstick colors, and this year's shoe styles became the immediate and direct concern of fathers in the 1940s in a manner that was unprecedented.[15]

The message conveyed — in advertisements, plays, films, and mass-circulation magazines — was that a father's opinion mattered a great deal to adolescent girls themselves; that it was customary for a father to be involved in his adolescent daughter's purchases; and, finally, that participating in a daughter's consumerism represented the most up-to-date, modern form of paternal social involvement. A father's love and attentive devotion could be expressed through shared consumerism. It was appropriate for fathers to be fully invested in the changes in wardrobe that accompanied their daughters' adolescence — changes that were by definition sexual in nature. The effect of representations of paternal involvement in female adolescent fashions was to reinforce the idea, similarly championed by psychoanalysts during this period, that the adolescent girl's relationship to her father was the defining element of her sexual identity. While rebellion against paternal power became difficult, if not impossible, with the ubiquitous diagnosis of "Oedipal conflict" (as we saw in Chapter 2), the possibility for autonomous display was also limited by the regularly announced need for paternal approval.

Junior Miss *and the Emergence of Father-Daughter Comedy*

The play that inaugurated the father-daughter dynamic that would become ubiquitous in the 1940s and 1950s is *Junior Miss*. What is most striking about the play is the way in which the original stories by Sally Benson, published in the *New Yorker* and then collected and published in book form in 1939, were transformed by the dramatists Jerome Chodorov and Joseph Fields in the 1940s. In the original version of *Junior Miss*, the chief character, Judy Graves, sees a movie about "the hysterical devotion of a curly-haired little girl for her father" and attempts to reenact that relationship with her own father.[16] Benson may have had a Shirley Temple movie in mind, or perhaps some version of the 1930s staple "Little Orphan Annie," or both.[17] Whatever the case, Judy arrives home after seeing the film determined to mend the "careless, almost indifferent way she treated her own father."[18] She sets out to spend the afternoon with him, walking in a park, arm in arm. Mr. Graves, however, finds her clumsy attentions so tiresome that by the end of the day he takes the unusual step of mixing a drink before dinner. Judy also finds it difficult and is finally exhausted by the effort. Observing Judy yawn, Mr. Graves says with relief, "Well, well . . . that must mean somebody's hungry."[19] With the restoration of de-romanticized paternal nurturance the chapter ends, and thus this brief episode.

Five years after the publication of these stories, and simultaneous with the play's run on Broadway, Helene Deutsch introduced *The Psychology of Women* with a discussion of the psychological truths about adolescent girls and their fathers set forth in Benson's "sensitive" stories.[20] What is so illuminating about these wartime texts—*The Psychology of Women* and Chodorov's adaptation of *Junior Miss*—is that they both, in different ways, extravagantly elaborated upon what Benson had originally treated as a transitory whim. We have already seen how Deutsch wove together a theory of the father-adolescent daughter Oedipal relationship. The Broadway version of *Junior Miss* similarly concentrated on the sexual dynamic between father and adolescent daughter, but, perhaps unsurprisingly, the play had much more to say about the commercial and sartorial elements of the thirteen-year-old girl's relationship to her father.

Studies of girls' culture have concentrated on film and television. But the Broadway play, though not the force it was in the 1920s, remained a dominant cultural form in the early 1940s and a more innovative medium than film, at least when it came to representing adolescent girls.[21] Many of the most well known movies about girls began as Broadway plays. Most toured cities across the United States or were staged by local high school drama clubs before they were made into films. Hit plays were still a major happening, especially before the rise of television at the end of the 1940s, and Broadway stars were regularly featured in mainstream magazines. Broadway was one of the top reasons that people visited New York in the 1940s, and those from out of town made up about one-third of the total audience.[22]

Junior Miss was a particularly successful and influential play. In 1943 only *Oklahoma!* and *The Zigfield Follies* surpassed *Junior Miss* in ticket sales—though these titles are much more familiar than the largely forgotten *Junior Miss*. A light-hearted play, described as a veritable "typhoon of merriment" with the most "enchanting heroine," *Junior Miss* met with as much success in high school performances (the Dramatists Play Service received thousands of requests to perform the play) as it did with the U.S. Army, where it was one of the most popular plays on the United Service Organization (USO) circuit tour during World War II.[23] Over the course of its seven-year run across the United States, *Junior Miss* inspired more plays about teenage girls than at any other time in the history of American theater—*Janie* (1942), *Kiss and Tell* (1943), *A Kiss for Corliss* (1948), *The Member of the Wedding* (1950), *The Pleasure of His Company* (1958)—and spawned countless "Junior Miss" clothing lines, jewelry boxes, and even its own cologne.[24] Most important, its approach to female adolescence proved durable: every female teen movie, from *A Date with Judy* (1947) to *The Bachelor and the Bobby Soxer* (1948) to *The Reluctant Debutante* (1958), borrowed some aspect of the *Junior Miss* story line: some sort of misunderstanding, usually caused by female adolescent hyperimagination; a sudden and dramatic cosmetic transformation that startles the family; and, invariably, the intersection of the adolescent girl's love interest with her father's (or at times that of a father substitute), usually in the form of ill-advised meddling or matchmaking.[25] These conventions governed popular representations of the female teenager, ordering complicated issues surrounding sexual maturity, self-presentation, and the sartorial transformations that were increasingly at the heart of the public discussion of female adolescence.

The stage version of *Junior Miss* revolved around the antics of the thirteen-year-old Judy Graves, whose head was filled with Hollywood films and whose chubby figure announced the dreaded "awkward age." The plot was based on Judy's (inaccurate) belief that she has witnessed a passionate kiss between her father and his secretary—a scene she interprets through the prism of the movie *Wife vs. Secretary*, starring Myrna Loy and Clark Gable.[26] When her uncle, whose long absence she attributes to a "ten-year stretch" (like Tyrone Power in *Criminal Code*), arrives for a Christmas visit, Judy attempts to pair the secretary with the supposed ex-con in order to save her parents' marriage.[27] Comedy ensues: family ties are broken and restored, her father's job is lost and regained, and the uncle and the secretary fall, inevitably, in love. The most touching scenes to critics, however, were those that involved Judy's highly emotional relationship to her Christmas gifts, all of which signify the difficult transition she is making from child to adult: her wobbly encounter with her first pair of high heels, her excitement over a new "Junior Miss" coat, and her contempt for a doll given to her by her father's boss. Indeed, the real substance of the play is encapsulated in the contrast between the child who opens the play and the elegantly arrayed adult who emerges at the end. Clearly, the emotional appeal to wartime audiences lay in the experience of watching a winsome and awkward thirteen-year-old make such a stark and irrevocable leap into maturity.[28]

The somber, even reverential, response of critics to *Junior Miss*, given the farcical nature of the plot and the amount of attention paid to new "cosmetic kits" and "first ever eye-brow pluckers," is striking. What was it about Judy's encounter with these objects that spoke so well to audiences? On the one hand, the play must have simply captured for audiences some of the excitement and loss that becoming an adult involved. According to the producer of the USO tour, it was while watching a scene in which Judy takes off her new high heels, looks around to make sure she is alone, then crosses the stage to cradle the rejected doll that he knew "they had a hit." The "tenderness of the scene held them. . . . Judy was singing a lullaby to the doll, and the theater was still, still as a church." That hundreds of (male) soldiers about to go to war sat silently still and watched a thirteen-year-old girl struggle to give up a doll in favor of a pair of high heels suggests that, quite simply, the scene said something profound to them about their own (in many cases young) lives.

On the other hand, the sentimental celebration of Judy's adolescent "adorableness" — "darling" was the word most often used in reviews — also suggests that *Junior Miss* played so well because it comforted adult audiences about the nature of female adolescent coming-of-age during wartime and consequent social upheaval. "Now that *Junior Miss* has arrived . . . everything is for the best in the best of all possible worlds," proclaimed Brooks Atkinson at the play's opening.[29] And indeed it was. For *Junior Miss* managed to depict female adolescence as a process that unfolded within the safe arms of the family. As we have seen, many adults were alarmed at the appearance, if not the fact, of sexual sophistication among youth, generational conflict, and sensational accounts of rising rates of female juvenile delinquency. Recall also that, in the case of girls, most experts ascribed teenage precocity and delinquency to unmet Oedipal needs.[30] Doubtless what endeared *Junior Miss* to many audiences, then, was the fact that it managed to domesticate the socially frightening fact of a girl's sexual maturation. *Junior Miss* portrayed the process of coming-of-age as one that was realized in the intersection between children and adults, but, most important, between a girl and her father. Thus it helped assuage anxieties surrounding female sexuality and social sophistication by situating Judy's coming-of-age within the small and reassuring world of the drawing-room comedy and locating her father at the center of her romantic (or movie-saturated) imagination.

Hints at Judy's Oedipal interest in her father's love life, however, composed only one aspect of her relationship to her father. The other important aspect of this relationship emerges from those moments of the play that appealed so well to drama critics and soldiers alike.[31] On Christmas day it is Judy's father, over his wife's anxious objections, who gives Judy her first pair of high heels. When Judy finally makes her grand entrance, having transformed herself from duckling to swan for her first dance, it is her father who sanctions her sudden metamorphosis by transforming *himself* from a harassed and distracted father into a gentleman and admirer. If this is Judy's "big moment," it is also her father's: his role is to validate the importance of her transformation by looking first stunned, then pleased. In the final scene Judy's father stands "with his mouth agape" and then dashes downstage to help his daughter on with her coat as a final symbolic gesture — "allow me," he says, as her date stands motionless and the curtain falls.[32]

Wartime Girls and the "Discovery" of a New Market

Junior Miss inaugurated what became a preoccupation with adolescent girls during World War II. *Life* in particular liked to report on the multiform social developments that seemed to be blooming in

Patricia Peardon starred as the teenage girl who wins the admiration of her father with her transformed appearance at the end of the play Junior Miss, *1941.*

the world of America's teenage girls. Articles such as "Sub-Deb Clubs: The Midwest is Full of Them" and "Teen-Age Girls: They Live in a Wonderful World of Their Own" reported on the new fashions, fads, and clubs created by teenage girls. "Sub-Deb" clubs, with "sparkling and snappy" names like WITCH (We in This Club Are Hellcats) and SWAMI (Subtle Women Are Most Intriguing) were portrayed as the invisible hands that molded high school social life. As small, secret clubs with only eight or nine members, they arranged suppers, hayrides, moonlight wiener roasts, "hen parties," and barn dances.[33] The clubs were judged to be on the whole less sanctimonious and more "fun" than sororities, and many girls were in several clubs at once.[34] Boys, *Life* reported, formed "Squire Clubs," which were part of the "Sub-Deb Men's Auxiliary."

Boys were depicted, in the main, as auxiliary in nature: they were shown standing around in an unorganized group, watching girls play cards at the local "Sub-Deb lounge," attempting to "crash" the girls' slumber party, or waiting patiently while their girlfriends listened to the latest popular song at a record store. When *Life* devoted a special section to high school fads, it complained that the only contribution boys made to the spirit of experimentation was the "deliberately sloppy way" they wore their shirts untucked. Girls, on the other hand, had introduced loafers, quantities of Indian jewelry, the appropriation of men's clothing, and identification bands, just to name a few, to their repertoire.[35] *Life*'s complaint about boys, however, characterized an equally important agenda for boys as well as girls. When *Life* finally profiled teenage boys in 1945, it reported the rather unnewsworthy news that boys were "behaving exactly as they have always behaved." Even boys' fads hadn't changed, the magazine claimed (thus calling into question whether boys had "fads").[36] The constant invocation of such contrasts between boys' and girls' cultures served to reinforce a sense of boyhood as fixed and timeless and girlhood as more mutable. Girls were an ever-changing barometer of the times, guiding and being guided by the engine of consumer trends. In the 1940s, commentary on this aspect of girlhood was not, it should be noted, intended as criticism. Nor was the assertion of boys' alienation from it. Rather, girls' culture was observed with a fascination born out of a sense of its newness and a genuine appreciation for the leavening effect of its playful qualities during wartime.

Girls, as Richard Ugland has said, were the "first American teen-agers."[37] The creation of the modern "teenager" began as an out-growth of the "Sub-Deb," a social designation for the adolescent girl that had existed since the First World War ("bobby-soxer" was an-other, less common, term).[38] By 1945, the "Sub-Deb" appellation had been thoroughly superseded in common usage by the term "teen-ager."[39] The most important reason why the term "Sub-Deb" became so abruptly outmoded was that it referred solely to girls who were upper class. They were usually enrolled in private school, had enough money to buy new clothes on a regular basis, and did not work dur-ing the summer months. As more students entered high school—between 1946 and 1960 the average number of students enrolled in secondary public schools increased by nearly one-half—and began to have access to larger incomes, the class connotations inherent in the social category of the "Sub-Deb" proved inappropriate to the emergent female youth culture.[40] The word "teenager" also began to be used when the age cohort itself took on enhanced status: "Sub" was simply not the prefix that girls or the media felt was appropri-ate anymore. "By their energy, originality and good looks they have brought public attention down from debutantes and college girls to themselves," *Life* reported in 1944—and thus the teenager was born.[41] College students, as Paula Fass has written, "were the fashion and fad pacesetters whose behavior, interests, and amusements, caught the national imagination" after the First World War, but, after World War II, teenage girls took their place.[42]

Girls were called "teenagers" more often and more easily in the early 1940s because of their association with trinkets, junk-jewelry, record collecting, clothing, "malteds," and popular culture in gen-eral. The activity that *Life* used to define boys as teenagers in 1945 was "marking time." Doing nothing, "skylarking," or wasting time were oppositional to adult notions of productivity and indicative of a period of life that was separated from both childhood and adulthood.[43] Thus when *Life* reported on teenage boys, it described them as spending a great deal of time "fooling around," which entailed hours of "thumb-ing through magazines on the rack outside the drugstore." "Boys never buy any," the article hastened to add, they just "look."[44] As late as 1945, none of the attributes that applied to female teenagers and would come to define teenagers as a group in the 1950s were associated with boys. Even slang, which came to be the sine qua non of teenage ir-reverence during the postwar years, was originally referred to in *Life* as "Sub-Debese."[45] Hence, for a brief period from the early to the late 1940s, teenage girls were ascendant in the public eye.[46]

That adolescent girls were depicted as fun-loving and leisure-oriented is particularly striking because such images suggest a cul-tural ideal that was increasingly at odds with the reality of girls' lives at the outbreak of the Second World War. In 1944, the U.S. Bureau of Labor reported that between 1940 and 1944, the overall employment of fourteen- to seventeen-year-olds had increased by 189 percent. Al-though significantly more boys than girls worked, the increase in the employment of girls during this period was much greater: while the number of boys working rose by 169 percent, girls increased their ranks in the workforce by 243 percent. The percentage of girls working at the ages of fourteen and fifteen expanded by a staggering 361 per-cent between 1940 and 1944.[47] This surge reversed a century-long de-cline in child labor and upset predictions of its continued downward progress. By April 1944, approximately one out of every five girls be-tween the ages of fourteen and seventeen worked; in 1940, the figure had been one out of thirteen. Moreover, the *range* of jobs open to girls widened considerably over the course of the war. In 1940, nearly 90 percent of the fourteen- and fifteen-year-old girls who received regu-lar work certificates were employed in domestic service. By 1943, the majority of jobs were in wholesale and retail, with domestic service making up only 20 percent of the total. Girls worked in ten-cent stores, drugstores, and groceries, doing everything from working behind the counter to running errands.[48]

Youth employment never garnered the support (much less the offi-cial fanfare) that accompanied women into the war industries.[49] There were worries about industrial accidents, violations of hard-won child labor laws, and the "de-skilling" of jobs.[50] Anxieties about girls in par-ticular, however, were characteristically rooted in the association of the public sphere with sexual danger. School, for girls, was prized as a rein on socially premature expeditions. "Every mother knows," claimed Edith Stern in an article in *Woman's Home Companion*, "that girls twelve to sixteen, serving midnight lunches, are . . . more exposed to propositions than girls of the same age doing their homework in the living-room."[51]

As the war neared its end, the U.S. Department of Labor's Children's Bureau launched what it called a "Back-to-School Campaign." Employers were told to hire only adult workers, and unions were urged to "persuade" young people to choose school over "*any*" job.[52] Employers, parents, and civic groups, however, did not need much pushing to reestablish the adolescent as student rather than worker. Although girls' participation in the workforce increased modestly as the economy expanded, the vast majority of girls did not retain the kinds of jobs they had during the war. After 1946, middle-class female employment was restricted almost entirely to babysitting—a job that paid half the minimum wage in 1945.[53] Between 1940 and 1946, there was a larger explosion and collapse in the number of girls—both middle class and working class—in the workforce than there was in the numbers of either boys or married women.[54] In a postwar follow-up article examining teenagers who had lost their jobs, Edith Stern reported that many of them were unhappy about the independence they had given up but that their parents were glad they were no longer working. The article was illustrated on the cover of the *Woman's Home Companion* with a classic image of the "Sub-Deb": a pretty girl in a sweater sits next to a haphazard stack of records, clutching one of them to her chest. In a near contradiction in terms, the Sub-Deb looks thoughtfully and a bit wistfully off into the distance, rendering one of the few postwar images of the teenage girl in serious repose. The title was "Our New Lost Generation," and the image revealed some of the rarely expressed anxieties about coping with female adolescents who had been given a great deal of responsibility and a certain degree of autonomy during the war and were now expected to stay in their living rooms and do their homework.

During the war years the attributes that would express the social values inherent in the construction of the teenager were anything but inevitable. Such a social transformation would depend on the success of the "Back-to-School Campaign," the increasing affluence of both teenagers and their parents, and the celebration of "Sub Deb," or female teen, frivolity in *Seventeen* magazine, as well as in *Life*, *Ladies Home Journal*, *Harper's Bazaar*, and even *Parents' Magazine*.[55] The success of *Junior Miss*, and the role of fathers that it announced, must be viewed within the context of a wartime desire to resituate girls as dependents in their fathers' homes. As *Life* put it in 1944, "American businessmen, many of whom have teen-age daughters, have only recently begun to realize that teen-agers make up a big and special market."[56]

By situating American fathers as businessmen who suddenly discover their consumer daughters, *Life* expanded upon the role of the father that was so successfully portrayed in *Junior Miss* and helped shape what was, at the end of the war, a momentarily open-ended economic family structure. The Depression-weary cultural formula that equated fatherhood with breadwinning had suffered an additional blow when young people entered the workforce en masse during the war.[57] Before servicemen returned home, and before the full-blown domestic ideology of the 1950s emerged, the ways in which higher wages and increased consumption would intersect with family life were not entirely clear.[58] The preoccupation with teenage girls at the end of the war was thus both symptom and symbol of an emerging consensus about the way in which the family and the economy were to be structured in the postwar years. Eventually, adolescent boys would be celebrated as "consumer citizens," too, but for the moment, girls were a familiar and thus immediately available site for the construction of a formula by which adolescents were explicit consumers and fathers implicit breadwinners.[59] Fathers and fatherhood, in this context, were equated with the capitalist economy, and daughters and girlhood were equated with those who would be controlled by it—consumers.[60] Yet capitalists and consumers each have a kind of lopsided leverage in relationship to the other, and it would be in those terms that the popular representation of the father-daughter relationship would emerge.

"There Are 8 Million Girls Coming of Age, Cosmetically Speaking"[61]

As the war was coming to an end in 1945, the March of Time newsreel series aired a film called "Teenage Girls." The short film explored the phenomenon of the teenage girl and interpreted it for an implicit audience of mystified adults. The film begins with a group of gray, bearded men sitting around a table staring inquisitively at a lone girl. The voice-over announces: "Sociologists, psychologists, and students of human behavior find the teenage girl a stimulating and almost limitless field of study." One of the men then turns to the camera and says, "We are endeavoring to evaluate the teenage American girl in terms of her likes and dislikes." The girl responds by taking the men on an odyssey through the typical activities of the white middle-class girl's life of the mid-1940s. With accompanying images, the girl explains the appropriate amount of lipstick and powder to wear, how to cheer on the high school team, how much the telephone means to girls, and the fact that, "if you are not in a club, you are a hopeless drip." In short, the film showed all of the preoccupations that *Life* had so enthusiastically reported during the war. There are many humorous moments, all of which occur at the expense of older men—brothers, fathers, or innocent passersby—and, by extension, of the tweedy researchers (and marketers?) who would try to understand these girls. A man attempting to purchase a record is hopelessly pushed around by a swarm of girls invading a record shop after school; a father and then a brother bang on the bathroom door while the teenage girl of the household, chocolate bar and movie magazine in hand, lounges in a bubble bath and yells "go away." The voice-over demurs, "I admit—we may be a little thoughtless at times." The whole effect is of an overwhelming tide of "hep" feminine adolescence, so thoroughly and literally consumed with itself that everything in its path is either dismissed or mowed down. It was, in fact, a "world of their own."

The basic device used in the March of Time film, as in most portrayals of female teen life (in the consumerist mode), was to invite the viewer into the home of the adolescent girl, where the audience witnessed her "monopolizing the whole household."[62] The figure at her mercy, invariably, was her father. The classic scenes involved the telephone: in the March of Time film a frustrated father waits impatiently while his daughter lies on an overstuffed chair, gossiping with a friend. "How much longer?" he inquires; "I've just simply got to use that phone." (Ignored, he finally retreats.) Other images of the life of the avid adolescent female consumer included "cutting off her father's news to follow the fictional adventures of a contemporary," interrupting her father's peace and quiet with the blare of her record player, and sending feathers flying into his newspaper during one of her slumber party pillow fights.[63] In these scenarios mothers were rarely present and fathers were a kind of background: ruffled, taxed, and eventually utterly defeated. The last shot in the March of Time newsreel is of a party being thrown at the house of the same teenage girl seen earlier on the phone. The house shakes as the kids dance in boy-girl/girl-girl couples in the living room. Upstairs, mother puts cotton in her ears and goes to bed with equanimity. Father, frowning and grumbling to himself, sits up reading a book titled *Do You Know Your Daughter?* — which brings the film back to the mystified male gaze with which it opened.

The book was real. Published in 1944 by Alice Barr Grayson, the author of the "Let's Talk It Over" department of the magazine *Calling All Girls*, it analyzed over 3,000 letters from girls between the ages of twelve and fifteen. Grayson found that teenage girls were consumed by their insecurities, felt a constant sense of inadequacy, and suspected that their parents did not approve of them.[64] She encouraged parents to give their daughters more freedom — advice we saw in discussions on juvenile delinquency — while also providing "good settings for pleasant, normal associations."[65] The adolescent girl, she claimed, also wanted a "vote of confidence" from her parents: "more outward expression of affection, smiles and loving glances, words or gestures of praise and encouragement."[66] The producers and director of the March of Time film may or may not have been familiar with the contents of the book, but much information was conveyed in the father's reading of *Do You Know Your Daughter* (the title to which Vladimir Nabokov would later allude in *Lolita*, pointing out its salacious double entendre). Researching a daughter's psyche was an act that fulfilled Grayson's injunction to fathers to pay attention to their daughters. It was a form of parental observation, however, that was meant not for the purposes of surveillance and control but rather for conveying love and emotional interest. The father's love for his daughter inhered in his absorption with her sexual struggles, a love that translated into providing a "good setting" (what Helene Deutsch might call "environment"), understanding her insecurities, and providing a certain measure of freedom at the same time.

Depictions of the buoyancy of the teenage girl, expressed in terms of her blithe sense of entitlement and her energetically creative relationship to music, fashions, and fads, as well as (or in combination with) the humorous depiction of her father as the displaced head of the household, can be attributed to other developments as well. One is that the depictions reflected the bewildered response of adults to transformations in youth culture. As James Gilbert has described the process, after 1945, teenagers began to put up "barriers of fashion and custom around adolescence," which intensified the traditional social alienation of adolescents from adults.[67] That is, teenage girls formed a new subculture that was genuinely and unprecedentedly exclusive. Such depictions of fathers and daughters might also have reflected the simultaneous rise of professional child experts and of adolescent affluence, thus marking the waning of parental power and producing anxieties about paternal authority.[68] However, the conventions the mass media used to narrate girls' lives did not simply reflect a semi-autonomous girls' culture; rather, I would argue, they translated girls' culture in such a way that it was conceived of as a transformation in girls' relationship to the domestic scene. Domestic dominance was what the media *showed* (girls commandeering the phone, the bathroom, the living room) when it *talked* about cultural autonomy; household control became, ironically, a separate teenage feminine subculture. This was the message used to sell the new teenage girls' market to advertisers and businessmen, and it was a formula that would prove to be definitive of the teenage girl over the course of the postwar era.

This market was allegedly "discovered," and was certainly most adoringly pursued, by the editors and managers of *Seventeen* magazine. The "dazzling success" of *Seventeen* was so thorough that it is difficult to imagine the teenage girl as postwar "phenom" without it.[69] When *Seventeen* was launched in September of 1944, it sold out of its first run of 400,000 copies in several days; by its fifth issue it carried more advertising than any of the women's service magazines of the day; in 1949, circulation exceeded 2.5 million.[70] The editors claimed that the magazine reached another six million girls through sharing with friends and family members.[71]

In its early years, *Seventeen*'s marketing goal was to establish the teenage girl as a serious consumer rather than simply a bobby-soxer interested in trinkets. The promotional department circulated the ecstatic letters received from retailers and hired a marketing firm to research the average *Seventeen* reader's tastes, income, and social life. Using questionnaires returned by 1,075 readers, the magazine developed a prototype of their typical consumer: "Teena." The Teena promotional material reveals much about the way that teenage girls were situated as social actors. In fact, the lineaments of the Teena character subsequently appeared in so many popular postwar renditions of the teenage girl that the editorial construction of Teena looks like an early map of the postwar social ideal.[72] Teena, according to the promotional flyers, was many things: she was a large segment of the population (8 million), she had an allowance and often worked as a babysitter, and she was serious about shopping. Of the subscribers interviewed, almost all used lipstick regularly (93 percent), and over half wore nail polish (65 percent) and face powder (61 percent). On average, readers of *Seventeen* bought two school dresses, two skirts, four sweaters, and one party dress over the course of the year. Teena had a "will and a mind of her own" but was "attentive and receptive to new ideas," especially if they came from her favorite magazine.[73] Above all, the editors claimed, Teena was a "homebody," and this is where her true value as a consumer lay.[74] Teena's importance was not simply that her first love required new soap, or that her first junior prom required a new gown, but that *all* of her needs were encompassed within a shared domestic life. As a consumer, *Seventeen* suggested, the middle-class teenage girl stood at the crossroads of several intersecting paths. The magazine located her in this central position by establishing her foremost identity as daughter rather than high school student, Sub-Deb, or even potential bride.[75]

"Teena," the first volume of *Seventeen*'s statistical guide began, "is sixteen years old," and "her father is a professional man, a business man, a white collar worker."[76] Teenage girls, the study went on to state, helped mother with menu planning, shopped for the family groceries three times a week, selected their own brands of goods, cooked the family dinner once a week, threw parties and lunches at their houses, and collected recipes.[77] They also had a great deal of influence on decisions about home furnishings and decorated their own rooms themselves. Girls, the study attempted to prove, played an instrumental role in almost every household purchase.[78] In a pamphlet titled "You and Your Home," intended for school distribution, the editors provided ways for their readers to contribute to the beautification of their parents' houses. The pamphlet conjectured that if girls acted "mature" and offered "willing hands," they would/should be allotted "responsibility" in running the house.[79] The value of the teenage girl, according to *Seventeen*, was that she was more up-to-date than her mother—hence it behooved her to gently shepherd her mother

In 1945, "Teena" was the character chosen to embody the characteristics of the average reader of Seventeen *magazine for marketers and advertisers. Estelle Ellis Collection, Smithsonian Institution, Washington, D.C.*

through the process of staying modern. "Mother has been pretty busy running the house and she probably doesn't know all the latest developments in the field," the pamphlet gently suggested. Perhaps you could figure out "a more pleasing arrangement of the furniture," or, if the dining room table is too crowded, "suggest a serving wagon." [80]

The tension created between mothers and daughters by the teenage girl's critical invasion into her mother's domestic preserve was heightened by the marital tone accorded her relationship with her father. In similar pamphlets, girls were introduced to their fathers' troubles and needs. "Do you realize," girls were asked, "that he, like you, has fears, too—that he isn't as successful as he might be, that he isn't handling affairs right." [81] Knowledge of paternal insecurity put girls in a position of responsibility, and hence they were advised: "When he comes home at night, he often needs soothing down and building up as much as you do." [82] Addressing the teenage girl in such a manner elevated her to a place of unofficial family leadership and bestowed upon her a precocious emotional maturity. Meanwhile, "Teena," as "the strong new influence in family affairs," acted as a conduit for a contemporary lifestyle—she helped establish a way for her parents to approach their own domestic consumption. [83] The brilliance of the characterization, however, was that *Seventeen* simultaneously maintained the image of the teenage girl as childishly single-minded about her own consumer needs: "Teena the high school girl is always agitating for something new to wear. Count on her to convince her parents she needs a new hat, a new dress, a complete spring wardrobe—before anyone else in her family." [84] Another promotional flyer proclaimed, "Suspect her influence when father says she's old enough for black, mother decides she's big enough to shop on her own. Our girl Teena is persistent and persuasive." [85]

What we see in *Seventeen*'s celebrated attention to the teenage girl is not so much the emergence of a powerful separate market but rather the construction of teenage girls as influential arbiters of family consumption. Framed in terms of a girl's relationship to her family, the idea of a prototypical teenage girl was something safe and easy to digest for the millions of mothers (and perhaps fathers) who read *Seventeen* along with their daughters. [86] The teenage girl did not simply purchase a black cocktail dress, *Seventeen* reassured its readers; rather, her indulgent and adoring father sanctioned and purchased one for her. The positioning of fathers within this context was essential. A black dress signified, among other things, sexual autonomy and maturity. Yet when a father became involved in such a purchase, the color and the dress took on different connotations: it kept its sexual allure but lost its references to sexual independence.

By reaffirming girls' fundamental connection to the family, *Seventeen* invented not simply a single new consumer group but a new way for the family as a whole to consume. "When she has her heart set on a trip by plane you can be sure her family will ride along with the idea. Just as when she decides on cereal for breakfast you know dad will wind up eating cereal too." Thus, by portraying the teenage girl as convincing rather than independent, knowledgeable rather than truly innovative, *Seventeen* cast her as the consummate daughter. Parents were clearly (and, in the case of fathers, humorously) manipulated in the process; but, in exchange for parents' forbearance, Teena was maintained as a member of a family. The teenage girl deserved to be taken seriously, according to *Seventeen*, not simply because she was smart, assertive, and managed to get what she wanted; she deserved to be taken seriously because she was capable of persuading her family to give her both what she wanted and what she thought they should have.

White middle-class girls, it should be noted, did not demand to be respected as "consumer adults," but Estelle Ellis, the marketing director of *Seventeen*, sought to portray them as if they did. Marketers became interested in adolescent girls both because of their increasing affluence and because they managed to be creative, even flamboyant, within a market limited by wartime shortages.[87] In the early 1940s, they appropriated men's clothing—jackets, pants, and shirts, in addition to blue jeans—and bestowed particular imagination upon what they wore in their hair: shoelaces, dish towels, colored soda straws, paper doilies, Christmas tree ornaments, bells, and colored felt.[88] They created codes based on the color and position of their bows (a yellow bow in Louisville signified a "man hater," a bow worn on the right side of the head at Highland Park High School in Dallas indicated that a girl was "in love," etc.).[89] They paraded themselves as "slick chicks" in their fathers' white Oxford cloth shirts in Ohio.[90] Certain fashions that were created in the 1940s became standard in the 1950s, and new ones certainly arrived; but, as *Seventeen* increasingly dictated the feminine teen image, girls became fashion "leaders" as opposed to fad makers, and girls' high school fashion lost some of its more whimsical qualities.[91] *Seventeen* capitalized on an extant consumerism but enlarged it by casting its readers as influential members of families rather than as temporary members of a subculture. A girl might run roughshod over her father's household as the new "family leader" — but father was good natured about it. Her appropriation of his home was a sign that he was "a professional man, a businessman, a white collar worker."

Fathers, Daughters, Clothes, and
Makeup in A Date with Judy

In 1948, Judy Graves was revisited in the character of Judy Foster (Jane Powell) in *A Date with Judy*.[92] The movie included many references to contemporary teen culture and incorporated musical numbers reminiscent of the Mickey Rooney, Judy Garland, and Deanna Durbin films of the 1930s. As Georganne Scheiner has pointed out, depictions of bobby-soxers proliferated in the films of the 1940s, and their plots, many of which revolved around fathers and daughters, were "almost interchangeable." [93] *The Youngest Profession* (1943), *Youth Runs Wild* (1944), *Kiss and Tell* (1945), *The Bachelor and the Bobby Soxer* (1947), *Cynthia* (1947), *A Kiss for Corliss* (1948), *Mickey* (1948), *Adventure in Baltimore* (1949), and *Father Was a Fullback* (1949) were some of the most popular.[94] *A Date with Judy* is a good example of the genre at its peak.[95] The conventions that governed these films were rigid: mistaken observations about the sexual practices of either father or daughter serve as the central difficulty that must be surmounted; the professional reputation and economic fortunes of the father are tied directly to the daughter's status in the eyes of the community; and the daughter's sexual identity is, in turn, linked to the father's professional success.

Unlike Judy Graves, Judy Foster had already made the transition to consumer maturity. She was, in effect, a version of the Teena prototype brought to life and projected on screen. Her father and grandfather surrounded her with indulgent goodwill, and the reciprocity between father and daughter informed all of her feminine desires and designs. The film intertwined two seemingly unrelated plots: it began with Judy developing a crush on a "college man" who worked at the local drug-store; but that pursuit is instantly pushed aside when she comes to the (mistaken) conclusion that her father, Melvin, is having an affair with a woman he hired to teach him the rumba in the privacy of his office (to surprise his wife at their wedding anniversary party). Judy Foster's tactical response to this potential rupture in her family life is telling. Rather than attempting to divert her father's supposed lover, or inter-ceding directly, she takes it upon herself to create a domestic scene attractive enough to compete with the charms of the exotic other woman (in this case, Carmen Miranda). Attempting to take charge of the threatened household, Judy spends the afternoon rearranging the living room furniture, giving her mother, Dora, a new coiffure, and transforming the house into an oasis of calm—all of which Dora en-dures with blank-faced patience. "Mother, you should spend less time in the kitchen. You should appeal more to his aesthetic sense than to his stomach," Judy admonishes. Other suggestions include using the lipstick color "flaming folly" and purchasing a black nightgown.

The film's portrayal of the precocious undertakings of adolescent girls was mostly tongue-in-cheek, light-hearted in the same vein as most comedies about female adolescence. Judy's meddling was an occasion for humor, and her wildly outsized perceptions about love, family, and romance reflected the gap between her consumption of popular cultural ideals and her own slim experience. Threats to the family are produced, on the one hand, by Judy's approaching sexual maturity (represented by the fact that a crush on a "college man" could lead her to figuratively or literally "leave home") and by her father's potential extramarital interests on the other. Each threat plays off the other, causing misunderstandings and moving the plot forward in such a way that the father-daughter bond is reasserted by withstand-ing potential assault. As Judy puts it when she finds out that her father is not having an affair, "I should have known all along that father was fatherly." Sexual fidelity to Dora is fidelity to Judy. At the same time, Judy's agreement with her father to reconsider the idea of leaving home is "daughterly": in each instance, loyalty is couched in sexual terms.

Though a comedy with many twists and turns, *A Date with Judy* is essentially a film about the social significance of paternal mediation in the process of female adolescence during the postwar era. The film opens with a shot of a small California town. "This is Santa Barbara," an assured male voice announces, "a town like any other. Old people, young people . . . and this is Pop's Soda shop. Everyone goes there . . . well, everyone except Mr. Pringle, he's too busy." Mr. Pringle, we learn later, is Carol's father. "Mr. Foster [Judy's father]," the voice continues, "is a busy man . . . but he's never too busy to spend time with *his* family, and he gets home often." The differences between Mr. Pringle and Mr. Foster unfold over the course of the film largely through contrasts in the behavior, style, and carriage of their respective daughters. Both girls are pretty, well dressed, and heavily made-up. There are minor but significant distinctions, however, in cosmetic effect. Carol is arrayed, no matter the occasion, in glossy lipstick and bright blue eye shadow; Judy wears muted colors. Carol's perilously vampish cosmetic effect, however, is not linked to actual promiscuity but rather to the idea that she is overly interested in *appearing* seductive (a fine but nevertheless important distinction). Although Carol is often conniving and competitive while Judy is open and trusting, both girls have the same consuming desire to be attractive, the same notions about what it means to be an adult, even the same crush on the "college man," Steven.

The difference lay in Judy and Carol's respective cosmetic aims, which relied, in turn, on the behavior of their fathers. According to Kathy Peiss, "by the 1930s . . . makeup had become integral to self-expression and the belief that identity was a purchasable style."[96] More important, wearing makeup during this period was not simply one of many signifiers of adulthood; it was one of the first and most preeminent.[97] The vast majority of teenage girls in the 1940s wore lipstick, probably in large part because its application had such symbolic value. The implications, however, of, say, a certain shade of red were not established solely or even primarily by the codes of a girl's peer group. In popular narratives, the meaning given to a type or amount of makeup worn by a teenage girl depended on the familial context in which it was worn. That is, if a given kind of makeup was sanctioned by a girl's father (or her parents, but much more often her father), it was considered symbolically "innocent"; if it was not sanctioned, it was, no matter how fashionable, characterized as morally suspect.[98] Of course, parental acquiescence to certain types and shades of makeup usually corresponded, at least roughly, to current social standards—but not always.

In 1945, *Seventeen* listed the right and wrong "reasons" for wearing makeup. "One day," the article began, "you're perfectly happy to face the world after simply . . . scrubbing your face. But the very next day you would rather die than face yourself in the mirror without first burying your nose in Mother's most expensive box of face powder."[99] However, such an instantaneous shift in public identity, warned *Seventeen*, could not be unilaterally borrowed, decided upon, or purchased. "Here's where the miracle usually ends. The family doesn't always congratulate you on your brilliant . . . use of makeup."[100] The "miracle" of makeup, as it was approached in this article, only worked its magic when parents approved; otherwise, makeup was simply a patina of ill-executed color—"vegetable dye." If a girl's parents were hesitant to let their daughter wear makeup, she was instructed to consider why she wanted to wear it and present a reasonable argument. One "wrong reason" to wear makeup was, oddly enough, the desire to look more attractive. "No matter . . . the wayward tendencies of your nose . . . any girl your age who is secure in the love of her parents sparkles like a champagne bubble and naturally *feels* attractive."[101] How a girl could look "secure" in the event that she did not feel loved by her parents was apparently beside the point. "Our thumb is down, too," *Seventeen* continued, "on make-up when used as the means of declaring your independence—of giving notice to your parents and the world that you've come of age."[102]

Using *Seventeen*'s rules as a compass, Carol's failure in *A Date with Judy* is not that she applies makeup in the wrong way—all of the high school girls in the film are heavily made up and often wear bright lipstick. Carol, however, uses it for the wrong reasons: she invests makeup with the wrong set of attributes and uses it to satisfy inappropriate desires. Carol uses makeup as a way to win flattery and attention in order to assuage feelings of insecurity. Carol's mother is absent, and Carol and her brother live in a strangely autonomous world of servants and friends. Left to her own devices, Carol not only makes all of her decisions about makeup by herself, but, as the film also makes clear, her desire to look attractive is fueled by her father's absence. On the other hand, this simple, direct connection between cosmetic effect and personal confidence is undermined by Judy's comparable cosmetic pursuits. Judy, the film makes clear, is equally acquisitive about cosmetics—a fact that complicates the potentially obvious emotional meaning of the evident abundance of Carol's makeup. "Father, can I wear false eyelashes tonight? Mitsy wears them," Judy asks and wheedles before a dance. "No!" is the booming response, "No to the false eye-lashes and no to the ox-blood nail polish." Judy's reasons for wanting the false eyelashes and ox-blood nail polish are not accounted for in the film. However, she consults her father and she follows his dictates. Though she is not permitted some accoutrements, she is allowed a full supply of others, and it is not always clear from her appearance—in the absence of pronouncements from Mr. Foster—where, exactly, the line is being drawn.

Carol's outward appearance is viewed from the outset in light of the announcement that her father does not make time for his family, and it takes on more substance when we find that she lives a life entirely independent of parental oversight. There is no loving, authoritative figure to condemn or condone her, and thus her makeup choices are bound up with her independence—one of the wrong reasons for wearing makeup. Carol does not have the "look" inspired by parental attention. This point, however, is communicated less by the colors and textures that Carol chooses than by the fact that those choices have been made in a paternal vacuum. The way in which the cosmetic effect of each character is conveyed has less to do with systems of meaning inherent in the cosmetics themselves than in the context in which they have been applied. Carol's problem is that there is no acceptable form of autonomous display available—whether "vampish," "tasteful," or otherwise.

By dictating the kind of makeup girls could wear, families gained control over a potentially chaotic consumer culture where the signifiers of age and sexual maturity could be purchased. In doing so, fathers accounted for their daughters, and daughters had no accessible route out of their relationships with their fathers. If Carol was sanctioned, so certainly was her father. What the use of makeup required for teenage girls was an exchange, a context. That context was provided first by parents and then by peers. The interest in such fine distinctions about makeup and its relationship to family in *A Date with Judy* is testament to the threatening quality of the use of modern forms of consumption in the process of coming-of-age.

At the same time, however, the emphasis on clothes and makeup also reflected the positive role of teenage consumption in the construction of the postwar family. Girls were not simply a drain or threat to their parents; they were part of the connective tissue of consumerism at large. Discussions of cosmetics and clothes were a platform upon which familial reciprocity could be built and a method through which it could be sustained. Moreover, these familial efforts were perceived as an important element in the fabric of the 1940s economy. Judy kept her mother up to date and, in this instance, literally helped keep her father in business when she agrees to sing jingles about his products on the local radio station for him.

This last point would seem a minor detail if it did not appear so often in the father-daughter films of the 1940s. In *Father Was a Fullback*, for instance, a daughter's success with the local high school star quarterback was facilitated, at least initially, by her father's attempts to help her attract boys. He buys her a new dress, gives her voluble encouragement, and arranges various blind dates. On the afternoon of her first date with the high school quarterback, her father, the coach of the State University football team, has just lost the last game of a losing season. However, when the quarterback is "drafted" by father and daughter together, a winning lineup is assured for the fall. The quarterback will go to State University and not to Notre Dame after all, and father will not have to go back to coaching high school football. His daughter has warded off social embarrassment and downward mobility for the whole family by attracting the right boy. The intersection between paternal professional success and a girl's sexual success are too pervasive in these films to ignore. Their interconnectedness suggests that much was at stake in a teenage daughter's sexual status: she served as both cause and effect of men's professional aspirations and at the same time was a vital component of family harmony in the popular imagination—a mix worthy of the kind of attention it received.

By the early 1950s, girls' dependence on their fathers had become obvious to social commentators. In a 1951 profile on a girl named Cynthia Barnes, "one of the most popular girls" in a Dallas high school, the *Ladies Home Journal* columnist Maureen Daly asked, "Why

does any seventeen-year-old girl add up to the buoyant, satisfying personality that is Cynthia Barnes?" The answer, Daly believed, was that
"she has been given, accidentally or deliberately, all of the possible
props that make any girl attractive and confident. Her home . . . is a
comfortable, happy place [and] Mr. Barnes . . . earns $150 a week."[103]
Similarly, in the late 1950s, the sociologist James Coleman observed
that girls listed "parents having money" and "expensive clothes," as
well as a "good house," as the most important attributes that a girl
needed to break into the "right crowd." He concluded that it was "considerably easier for a boy than for a girl from the wrong side of the
tracks to break into the crowd" and that girls were in general far more
defined by their fathers' educational and financial position. At the
same time, he complained that in giving girls "all the advantages,"
by bestowing on them the social confidence and precocious maturity
that he believed inhered in the material gifts, parents gave their teenage daughters too much power. Giving girls all the advantages did just
that—and left parents operating at a loss.[104]

This perception of female adolescent dominance, however, does
not take into consideration at what cost girls' privileged position was
bought. Girls' social power derived from their relationships to their
fathers, who were both breadwinners for and the ultimate arbiters
of their quest for wholesome good looks, a "suitable setting," and a
respectable reputation. Such a recasting of the father-daughter relationship was culturally established in the early 1940s, commensurate
with the emergence of teen culture itself, and it calls into question
whether a "separate," or independent, middle-class teenage girls' culture was born at this time.[105] It also calls into question the extent to
which individual autonomy was possible. Persuasive, knowledgeable,
and entitled, the American teenage girl certainly gained new power
and cultural prestige during World War II. The outer limits of this
power, however, were defined by her father, whose active involvement
in her clothes and cosmetics was the condition upon which his generosity was based.

Chapter 4

COMING-OF-AGE

When Edward Streeter published his novel about the engagement and wedding of Kay Banks to Buckley Dunstan, *Father of the
Bride*, in 1948, no one had ever seen anything quite like it. It was a 250-
page book of humor about the minutia of planning a single wedding—
the family's stunned reaction to "the news," the meeting between the
bride's and groom's parents, decisions about the wording of the announcement in the local newspaper, the preparing of the guest list,
the procurement of a caterer, the seating arrangements at the church,
the dress rehearsal, the "apprehensions, doubts and bewilderments,"
and, finally, "the big day" itself—all described from the point of view
of the bride's father.[1] It was a perspective the public found fascinating.
The novel was the fourth best-selling book of the year, and the movie,
starring Spencer Tracy and Elizabeth Taylor, was a box-office success
in 1950 and eventually an enduring classic. Indeed, it is largely because of *Father of the Bride* that the wedding, couched as a paternal,
as well as young woman's, rite of passage, has become entrenched
in our national culture, a defining trope of family, masculinity, and
the attainment of womanhood. There is by now a seemingly timeless
quality about the particular sufferings of the father in the event of his
daughter's wedding: the "private sadness" of watching her officially
take leave of the family, his barely submerged jealousy of the groom,
the anxiety of how to pay for the mounting costs of the ceremony, and,
not insignificantly, the dread of having to play a major role in a public
pageant.[2] Dating back to at least the eighteenth century, the ritual of
the father walking with the bride to meet her groom was, by 1948, well
established.[3] However, the singular attention to the various responsibilities and emotional quandaries of the *father* associated with the
ceremony itself represented a new point of interest in the wedding,

one that emerged virtually overnight with the publication of Streeter's book.

Streeter, the author of several books of humor on the daily experiences of suburban men, had perfect timing. *Father of the Bride* fit a niche in the growing market of cultural representations of fathers and daughters, particularly within the context of dramatic moments in girls' coming-of-age. By "coming-of-age," I mean a complex and extended process that was represented in popular culture by a single event, realization, or transformation in the life of a girl or young woman. Such abrupt passages, designated "rites of passage" by anthropologists, are ceremonial rites that, as Arnold Van Gennep put it, "allow the individual to pass from one fixed situation to another, equally fixed." [4] The compression of the transition from child to adult into a single, ritualized moment tended to be applied to girls far more often than boys in the United States at midcentury (as it had since at least the nineteenth century). Enduring examples include weddings and the debutante ball. [5] In this chapter I will look at the popular representation of these social institutions and at celebrated instances in which a father's sudden—and most often public—realization of his daughter's physical maturity served as rites of passage. [6] These moments of recognition were presented—in plays, photographs, advertisements, and fiction—as rituals of long standing. But, in fact, they were new forms of family celebration that established themselves with great rapidity. They are an example of what historian Eric Hobsbawm has called an "invented tradition." [7] Invented traditions, according to Hobsbawm, are "a set of practices . . . of a ritual or symbolic nature, which seek to inculcate certain values and norms of behavior by repetition, which automatically implies continuity with the past." [8] The object of traditions, including invented ones, is invariance: to fix meaning, especially within the context of rapid change. [9]

The ritualistic presentation of paternal recognition emerged alongside a shift in the late 1940s and 1950s toward more explicit renderings of the eroticized father–adolescent daughter relationship. In the first section of this chapter I examine how elements of a father's contributions to his daughter's sexual maturation established in the early 1940s—economic indulgence, sexual approval, and an uncritical complicity in her quest for allure—became more pronounced, unambiguous, and ubiquitous in the late 1940s and the 1950s. The more overt nature of father-daughter eroticism of this later period, at least in white, mainstream culture, was accompanied by steeply rising expenditures on adolescent girls. A 1959 article in *Harper's Magazine* claimed that boys and girls in high school were likely to have about four times as much money to spend as their counterparts in 1945—average expenditures increased from $2.50 per week to about $10.00.[10] My argument, however, is not that increasing financial support of men for women (or fathers for daughters) necessarily leads, in all historical situations, to the sexualization of the relations between them but, rather, that after World War II, financial and erotic bonds became increasingly pronounced. These connections were of significance not only to the adolescent girl but also to the status of her father and the image of paternal power within the social order.

Whereas in Chapter 3 I look at how teenage girls were defined and circumscribed by the constant presence of their father, in this chapter I consider more closely the impact of the father-daughter relationship on middle-class male identity. In white female adolescent coming-of-age narratives, fathers were, as we saw in previous chapters, portrayed as passive and somewhat ineffectual. As we have also seen, girls were depicted as assertive, manipulative, and even domineering. These kinds of portrayals contributed to the conclusion, on the part of contemporary observers and historians alike, that there was a "postwar masculinity crisis," one that particularly applied to the "domestication of the American male."[11] However, here I argue that, at least within the context of the father's relationship with his daughter, a certain weakness was actually an inherent part of the celebration of a his economic indulgence, while his often dazed quality was deployed as a way to render his sexual attention to his daughter seemingly benign. Both of these traits pointed to a father's economic power and his *unaggressive* influence over his daughter's sexual identity. Paternal helplessness, so often seen as proof of the lack of respect accorded family men during this period, actually reflected a transformation in the guise of paternal power rather than its simple diminution—for when a father succumbed to his daughter's beauty, it was, in the end, a spell of his own making.

The popular depiction of the dazed but doting father, and the teenage girl's attachment to him, emerged at the same time that advice books and sociological studies began to reimagine female adolescence. As the postwar period wore on, experts increasingly described adolescence as a time when a girl's relationship with her parents would grow in complexity rather than as a moment characterized by her desire for greater independence. In the second part of this chapter, I examine the messages put forward by teen "experts" and argue that they stand in sharp contrast to the prewar didactic literature on adolescent girls that stressed the acquisition of independent judgment and self-reliance as the preeminent goals of both female and male adolescence.

In stories about white working-class girls, such as the movie *The Catered Affair* (1956), about a daughter's conflicts with her parents over the planning of her wedding, or *A Tree Grows in Brooklyn* (1945), fathers, though sometimes romanticized in childhood, were not sexually relevant to their daughters when they became adolescents.[12] Images of middle-class black father-daughter relationships have more significant similarities to and differences from those of the white middle class. In the last section of this chapter I examine postwar images of the black father-daughter relationship. In the late 1940s and 1950s, the black press regularly reported on and celebrated the links — mostly social and economic — between fathers and adolescent daughters. At the same time, the popular image of the black father-daughter relationship was influenced — one might say constrained — by the portrayal of a father's incestuous desire for his adolescent daughter in the Broadway play *Anna Lucasta* (1945). As Glenda Gilmore has shown, ideologies of family life and sexuality — self-consciously deployed by the black middle class and inextricably bound up with the norms of the white middle class — have played a defining role in the history of black social and political activism in the United States.[13] In this chapter I use the father-daughter relationship as a lens through which we can view black middle-class aspirations for achieving social status. From this point of view we can approach larger questions about the construction of race and the social order in the United States in the late 1940s and the 1950s. By concentrating on a single and heretofore overlooked relationship, a constellation of interrelated racial issues comes to the fore. Such an undertaking adds to the scholarship on the black middle class a different view of relations between the sexes (other than that between husband and wife or mother and son) that played a powerful role in the shaping of the image of black middle-class society.[14] Moreover, by comparing assumptions governing representations of father–adolescent daughter relationships in white and black middle-class culture, aspects of both are refracted and illuminated, contextualized, and, insofar as the fabled white middle-class family of the 1950s is concerned, made a little less familiar.[15]

Kay Banks and Mr. Banks:
The Making of the Perfect Bride

The popularity of *Father of the Bride* reflects, in part, the social reality of a steep spike in weddings among young women between the ages of eighteen and twenty-one just after World War II.[16] The book, however, concentrated not on the anxieties and aspirations of the marrying couple themselves but instead on those of the bride's father, Stanley Banks. Once again, an event of defining sexual import to a young woman is understood in terms of its effects on the sexual identity of a father who is acting as a spectator.

Mr. Banks of *Father of the Bride* was a version of a running character in Edward Streeter's stories about middle-class corporate manhood, including *Daily Except Sundays* (1938), *Merry Christmas, Mr. Baxter* (1956), and *Chairman of the Bored* (1961).[17] Supporting a family, and the endless drudgery involved, was at the center of all of Streeter's books. Like Streeter's other characters, Banks lives in the middling suburb of Fairview Manor, on the New Haven train line from New York. His daily routine—up at 7:00 A.M. to catch the 8:42, into Manhattan by 9:00, a series of clients and files to be dispensed with, back again by 6:00 P.M. for drinks, dinner, and the newspaper—is reprised in detail. It is all recounted, comically, as a low-stakes sport full of uncalled-for tension and the accumulation of minor frustrations. At home he is catered to by his wife but often ignored by his children. Streeter's particular talent is to transform the monotonous into the momentous, primarily through his use of outsized metaphors in the description of mundane events. The effect is both absurd and celebratory.

Like Streeter's other characters, the aptly named Banks must countenance endless demands for frivolous purchases from his wife and children, a position that gives him a befuddled, beleaguered air that is, however, ultimately trumped by the stature achieved by the fact that he is easily able to provide them with what they desire. In essence, what was symbolized through the act of giving a single gift in *Junior Miss* is, in *Father of the Bride*, extended to the substance of the entire narrative. Each purchase in *Father of the Bride* is simultaneously a defeat for and a tribute to Mr. Banks. As wedding expenses mount and arguments develop, the situation invariably ends with him deciding that "perhaps it was just better to let the matter drop."[18] Such passivity is, however, not a reflection upon his status as "poor old pop" but rather a recognition of his ability to "let the matter drop" in the first place. The more passive Mr. Banks is in the face of feminine expense and frivolity, the more powerful he becomes. The more he capitulates, the more obviously capacious are both father and daughter. Like Mr. Graves in *Junior Miss*, Mr. Banks is his daughter's foil. That position was appealing because it announced his financial power, his good intentions, and his sexual identity as a man.

As in *Junior Miss*, *Father of the Bride* reaches its climax when Mr. Banks presides successfully over his daughter's dramatic transformation. "The groom," as the church sexton informs him at the rehearsal, at which Buckley has failed to arrive, "don't do nothing in weddings."[19] Here, the father's role is (in a humorous way) much more grand and official than in *Junior Miss*. At the wedding, as he walked down the aisle with Kay, "a feeling of elation spread through Mr. Banks as he watched his wife's straight, slender back . . . being led humbly to her place in a front pew. For once he had stolen the show." Then he glances at Kay: "She was no longer his little daughter, but a beautiful, serene woman into whom all wisdom had suddenly and mysteriously flowed. She stood, poised . . . her face lit with understanding and confidence. . . . It would be a terrible thing to betray that expression in Kay's eyes. They were fixed far beyond Buckley, on an ideal which perhaps no mortal could hope to achieve."[20] This moment of admiring recognition on the part of Mr. Banks and Kay's sudden professionalism (she stood, throughout the ceremony, "with the calmness of a general watching his forces deploy into battle") are linked less to her feelings for Buckley ("her eyes were fixed beyond Buckley") than to that indeterminate, "mystic moment" as bride or wife-to-be — a ceremonial moment that Mr. Banks, rather than Buckley, has achieved for her.

Where *Father of the Bride* departed most markedly from *Junior Miss*,

Illustration from Edward Streeter's book Father of the Bride *(1948). Kay Banks, the main character, triumphant during the planning of her wedding, happily entertains a group of friends. Mr. Banks has just returned home from work. ("As he entered the room . . . Kay would embrace him dramatically, one foot raised slightly behind her, and say, 'Pops! We were waiting for you to make us a cocktail.'")*

however, was in Kay's maturity (she is around eighteen), her already acquired beauty, her manipulativeness with Mr. Banks, and, most important, Mr. Banks's ongoing susceptibility to Kay's charms. We see in *Father of the Bride* a glimmer of the kind of sexual bargaining that was quite pronounced in F. Hugh Herbert's immensely popular father-daughter book and play *Kiss and Tell* (see Chapter 5). When attempting to procure a favor or additional funds from her father, Kay is apt to run her fingers through his hair or "embrace him dramatically."[21] Kay's coquettishness with her father is matched by his helpless adoration of her and his unceasing jealousy of her fiancé, Buckley.

Kay is never depicted with any close girlfriends, is unaccountably living at home when it would seem she should be off at college (given her parents' financial means), and has no interest in the kinds of popular culture that defined the characters in other Broadway plays or films, like *A Date with Judy*. The book gestures at modern forms of sexual freedom—"It had never been very clear to Mr. Banks just where Kay spent her time, but wherever it was Buckley evidently spent his there also." Moreover, what Streeter refers to at one point as Kay's "unleashed" social and implicitly sexual behavior, as well as Kay's failure to ask her father for permission to marry (and Buckley's failure to do the same), all situate Kay within the context of postwar liberal sexual values.[22] Still, Kay's enclosed social world remains out of step with the celebrated youth culture that was coming into its own during the same historical moment. The dynamic between Kay and her parents, however, was emblematic of the increasing emphasis on the adolescent girl's ongoing ties—economic, social, emotional, and sexual—to her parents, particularly her father. This emphasis is evident not only in the cultural arena—plays, movies, magazines—but in the sociological and didactic literature of the late 1940s and 1950s as well.

Experts and the Shifting Ideas about the Meaning of Adolescence for Girls in the 1950s

Postwar books of advice, while becoming more frank and forward-thinking on matters of sexuality, nonetheless increasingly situated girls within the structure of their parents' homes and family relationships—indeed, markedly more so than their prewar counterparts had. The most popular advice book of the 1950s, *Facts of Life and Love for Teen-Agers* (1956) by Evelyn Millis Duvall, was directed at teens alone—a publication that signified the excision of parents from the sexual doings of teenagers altogether.[23] The chapter headings reveal the dominant postwar concerns about adolescence: "When Girls Mature," "Where Babies Come From," "Sex Problems and Promises," "Ready for Dating," "Your Parents and Your Dates," "Going Steady," "That Question of Petting," and "Getting Married."[24] The forthrightness on sexual matters, as well as the presumed sexual autonomy of girls, however, were iterated within the context of a decline, even a disappearance, of a broader notion of independence as a major goal of female adolescence.

The question of independence was often a dominant and dramatized point in books on female adolescence in the 1920s and 1930s. In an advice book for parents and teachers on adolescent girls published in 1925, the author admonished, "Age and authority raise barriers which at all costs she must vault. Nothing could be more unwise than the attempt at this period to thwart the girl's independence."[25] Similarly, under a section called "How to Gain More Independence" in a guide for girls published in 1939, the author exhorted, "Have no fear of what may happen to you when you venture into the world alone . . . depend on yourself."[26] In contrast, in the postwar period, writers of advice books on adolescence listed "maturity" and "adjustment" as the primary goals of the transition from childhood to adulthood.[27] When independence was mentioned at all—and it was discussed almost solely in connection with boys—it was described as a "stage" on the way to recognition of "interdependence" or as the realization that "he cannot live his own life all on his own, for what he does is all tied in with the lives of many other people."[28] Many books, without specifying the sex of the adolescent, belittled teenagers' attempts at independence and counseled parents to be patient and firm when coping with their teenagers' conflicting urges for both "emancipation" and dependence. For parents to remove themselves in any significant way from their teenagers' doings would be to "abdicate" their responsibilities to their children, a failure to take the very kind of responsibility for others that these books hoped to foster in young people.[29]

In one of the largest and most influential studies of teenage girls conducted in the 1950s, the question of independence was, for girls, declared irrelevant. Completed in 1958 under the auspices of the Institute for Social Research at the University of Michigan in collaboration with the Girl Scouts of America, the authors, Elizabeth Douvan and Joseph Adelson, summarized answers to thousands of questionnaires filled out by girls with the declaration, "The fact is that independence—in the sense of making one's own decisions about moral and emotional problems—is not a crucial issue for most adolescent girls." This statement was made in explicit contradistinction to boys.[30] Girls of all ages, they found, "consider their parents' guidance necessary and legitimate."[31] Hence, adolescent girls were explicitly *not* independent creatures. The authors of the study instead defined girls' development as entailing a progression from an "infantile dependent relationship to parents [to] a new, more mutual relationship between equals."[32]

In part, the invocation of "interdependence" can be attributed to the political project of "good citizenship" characteristic of the cold war era. Illustrated in one advice book by a sketch of children holding hands around a beach-ball-sized globe, the notion of "interdependence" was explicitly linked to the idea of international mutuality in an age of nuclear anxiety.[33] Within this context, the very word "maturity," as Barbara Ehrenreich has pointed out, took on a "weight and authority" that was unprecedented.[34] It informed the postwar embrace of early marriage, male breadwinning, and a sober commitment to the responsibilities of child rearing. Still, despite the fact that notions of maturity and interdependence had far-reaching political implications and were applied to both sexes, when applied to adolescent girls these ideas tended to replace, rather than exist alongside, a positive valuation of any form of independence.[35]

The disappearance of the ideal of independence for girls had an unsurprising effect on representations of the father-daughter relationship. In 1930, Grace Elliott, in explaining why a girl needed to "honor her own impulses and desires," declared, "If she has always been Mary's sister or John Dale's daughter . . . she may never have come into possession of herself in any way that will enable her to make a creative contribution."[36] The absence of such sentiment in advice books after World War II implied that such a separation was not desirable. Hence, the way in which Kay Banks remained dependent upon her parents reflected the attitude of advice books that counseled that teenagers be allowed to "choose some things for themselves" but recommended that those decisions be circumscribed by adult wisdom and power. In coping with Kay's moments of spoiled arrogance and petulant doubt, her parents had all of the markings of the ideal of parental forbearance and patience needed in the event that immature adolescent desires for emancipation combined with insecurity and neediness. Most important, the ongoing relationship that Kay had with her parents, its primary nature, and the assumption that it would continue uninterrupted was part of a literature that advised a readjustment between parents and girls rather than an emotional, financial, moral, or social break as girls grew older.

The Dangerous Date

The substantive role of paternal sexual recognition, so central to this depiction of girls' ongoing relationship to their families, was reflected in the portrayal of fathers and daughters in the short fiction published in *Seventeen* in the 1950s and early 1960s. Over the course of the postwar period, relationships between teenage girls and their parents actually lost some the adversarial tone characteristic of *Seventeen*'s fiction of the mid-1940s and came to resemble, like those prescribed in didactic literature, a more triangular relationship among three adults.[37] A representative story published in *Seventeen* in 1959, "The Dangerous Date," was about a father who arranges a date for his fifteen-year-old daughter with a business partner's twenty-year-old son in the hopes that he can complete a real estate deal at a dinner party. On the surface, the story is an account of a father exploiting his daughter for business purposes. But the narrative, which unfolds as a series of realizations on the part of the girl's father, manages to displace the sexual "danger" from the father to the date by depicting the father as an indulgent and admiring "dad" who innocently succumbs to his daughter's disarming beauty and poise.

The story, like so many of its genre, revolves around the purchase of a first junior prom dress. Mr. Carmichael, through an improbable set of circumstances, finds himself shopping with his gawky fifteen-year-old daughter, Marybeth. He is, at that very moment, trying to figure out who he could provide as a date for his business partner's son at the dinner party to be held that evening. Meanwhile, Marybeth, confident within the familiar walls of Masons' department store, "skillfully" steers her father away from the "Junior Miss" department and into the department for college girls.[38] At a distinct disadvantage, Mr. Carmichael "meekly" follows his daughter to the dressing room, drops into the nearest chair, and closes his eyes while his daughter tries on a "chiffon affair" with a "breath-takingly low neckline." When Marybeth emerges from the dressing room, he "stared briefly, and then sat bolt upright . . . in spite of himself [he] whistled softly."[39]

The idea of the date springs into Mr. Carmichael's mind like a lightbulb suddenly being turned on. Mr. Carmichael purchases the dress, and Marybeth is accordingly transformed into a glamorous and sophisticated eighteen-year-old. Marybeth, in turn, perceives why her father has bought her the dress, and at the dinner party she performs her role perfectly. Meanwhile, Marybeth's mother, amazed at her daughter's unexpected, seemingly purchased grace on the dance floor, exclaims, "I can't understand it. At home Marybeth knocks everything over that isn't nailed down."[40] Precocious sophistication, low neckline, and "fixed face" in "The Dangerous Date" contained none of the implications that would have applied to Carol, for instance, in *A Date with Judy*.[41] In this story, the precocious appropriation of the signifiers of sexual maturity was rendered innocent, safe, even socially acceptable by the fact of paternal mediation. Moreover, even though Mr. Carmichael himself transformed his daughter into "bait" for his business deal, his own sexual relationship to his daughter was successfully recuperated in several ways. First, Mr. Carmichael's erotic interest in his daughter was based solely on the glamour she was able to appropriate (and that he was providing for her) rather than on interpersonal desire. Second, the strength of his reaction to seeing his daughter in her evening gown was predicated on his prior sexual unconsciousness. When the lightbulb goes off—when Mr. Carmichael suddenly discovers his daughter's sexual allure—it is because he has never before considered it.

Mr. Carmichael was also saved by the fact that, even though he "weakly" allowed his daughter to be escorted out of the restaurant by a twenty-year-old man who seemed less than trustworthy, Marybeth arrived home safely. "The Dangerous Date" was a significantly more sexualized and glamorized version of the female teen debut— one that represented the general direction of depictions of teenage girls at the end of the 1950s. Reflecting on stories like these, one social commentator asked: What ever happened to the innocent, "heart-warming growing pains of *Junior Miss*"?[42] But this and other stories that emerged in the 1950s were actually much more similar to *Junior Miss* than they were different: all involved paternal mediation in the acquisition of adult forms of adornment, intergenerational match-making, and a moment of profound paternal recognition.

When looking at "The Dangerous Date," which appeared eighteen years after *Junior Miss*, one feels an air of inevitability surrounding the postwar trajectory of the genre. Commercial culture was in-creasingly sexualized after the war, and the process of maturity telescoped; hence, coming-of-age stories necessarily reflected and ac-commodated that reality. But another crucial part of this story in-volves transformations in the intersection between girls' culture and the institution of fatherhood. For, if Marybeth was a more cosmeti-cally baroque version of Judy Graves, characteristics specific to Judy's father, Mr. Graves, were exaggerated in Mr. Carmichael. Mr. Graves, who was clearly no match for his overactive teenage daughter in *Junior Miss*, was described by reviewers in 1941 as a typically "be-nighted" father.[43] "Dazed, Astonished and Doting" were the words crit-ics used to describe Mr. Graves: his ice cubes were missing because his daughter has used them for a facial treatment, his commands were ignored, and he endured the most constant and ridiculous ad-vice from a thirteen-year-old girl on how to manage his affairs.[44] In-deed, just what it was that appealed so much to the (male) critics (and audiences) about Mr. Graves remains a puzzle.[45] But Mr. Carmichael of "The Dangerous Date" represented an even more passive postwar "dad" in his complete capitulation to the swirl of feminine designs going on around him, in his continuous "uncertainty," and in his hap-lessness.[46] He was the apotheosis of a typical postwar "domesticated male."[47] True to the formula that equated the decline of overt paternal authority with the phenomenon of the emasculated "poor old dad," Mr. Carmichael was a typically "ineffective but . . . lovable bungler."[48]

Historians have generally associated the transformation of the authoritative father of the prewar period into the "bungler" of the postwar years as evidence of (or related to) a general decline in pater-nal authority.[49] Postwar contemporaries certainly made the connec-tion, and public grumbling about the state of fatherhood came to take its place beside the private, "ceremonial grumbling" on the part of fathers themselves that Margaret Mead had described as definitive of American patriarchs.[50] However, the state of fatherhood after the war, particularly as it was represented in the sort of helplessness that fathers were depicted as experiencing in relationship to their daughters, can be viewed in another way. Rather than simply reflecting a net loss of power or an official decline in prestige, the transformation in fatherhood also reflected a new kind of family dynamic, one in which the sexual aspects of a daughter's identity and her consumer desires revolved around the "head" of the family in new ways. Fathers and daughters, during the postwar period, were depicted as being involved in an intricate dance, a drama of mutual seduction and manipulation. The stakes were greater than they once were, for a father not only defined the social universe in which his daughter became a consumer adult (as we saw in Chapter 3), he also mediated the sexual meaning of her coming-of-age. His passivity and dazed quality perhaps rendered him less dignified. But such qualities also informed the process of sudden sexual realization, the pliability of indulgence. His passivity signaled a lack of sexual aggression, and his ineptitude rendered sexual recognition safe by suggesting that his intentions toward his daughter were neither calculating nor particularly well considered. The confused quality of a father's response to his daughter's sexual attractiveness was what made such recognition seem so inarguably benign.

Coming-of-Age in High Society: From Ebony to Town and Country to Jet

The increasingly seductive behavior of girls toward their fathers appeared not only in narrative form but also in visual images of fathers and daughters as well. For instance, in the illustration to a short sequel to *Father of the Bride*, "Mr. Banks' Other Daughter," we see Kay's sister placing a coy yet dismissive kiss on her father's head as he slouched in an armchair. This drawing, in contrast to the fairly abstract line drawings of the original book, is fully fleshed out, and Sue is depicted as a sultry persona bestowing her affections on a suspicious and definitively more debonair looking man than the original Mr. Banks.[51] The beauty and glamour of both characters (Mr. Banks's trench coat has been replaced with smoking jacket

The illustration accompanying Edward Streeter's "Mr. Banks' Other Daughter," the sequel to Father of the Bride, *which appeared in* Good Housekeeping *in 1950. Sue, Kay's younger sister, asks her father for her own wedding. Courtesy General Research Division, The New York Public Library, Astor, Lenox and Tilden Foundations.*

and ascot) throws their status, beguilingly, into question. Because Mr. Banks looks young and his daughter looks of an indeterminate age, it is difficult to discern whether he is her father or her husband. The confusion adds to the sexual tension, as one is temporarily uncertain of their relationship to one another.

More often, when daughters and fathers were shown together—whether in advertisements, drawings, or photographs—fathers were performing ceremonial roles in the event of their daughters' coming-of-age. On the cover of the 1955 edition of *Junior Miss*, Judy is shown at the culminating moment of the play, in a strapless prom gown, her father looking on approvingly. In advertisements, fathers stood as their daughters entered the living room dressed for their high school prom or looked on as they made an appearance in their wedding gowns.

The importance of fathers' ceremonial role began to be reflected in the society pages of newspapers and magazines in the late 1940s. Before World War II, brides and debutantes in both the local and national media were regularly shown alone, either sketched or photographed. When situated with others at all, they appeared either with other debutantes or with their fiancés.[52] After World War II, formal, posed pictures of individual girls or young women in their wedding gowns remained the staple of newspaper announcements. However, in magazines, where informal (or unposed) photographs were more common, as in *Town and Country*, girls and young women were increasingly accompanied by their fathers.[53] These kinds of pictures encompassed a variety of poses: a father helps his daughter out of a car; he smiles at her as she emerges at the head of the stairs in her wedding dress; or father and daughter stand, arm in arm, at her debutante ball.[54] Most commonly, a bride or a debutante simply appeared, as the captions put it, "on the arm of her father." [55] Thus the father's ritualistic role in these kinds of proceedings (no matter the extent to which they were *organized* by mothers) was reflected and reinforced by shifts in photographic conventions in the postwar period.[56]

The advent of the "father-daughter" poses in photographs of white society events, however, accompanied the general decline in the role of the upper classes in the popular imagination of the postwar period.[57] As we saw in Chapter 3, the designation "sub-debutante" was replaced by the less class-specific word "teenager" in the mid-1940s. This change in nomenclature signified, among other things, the di-

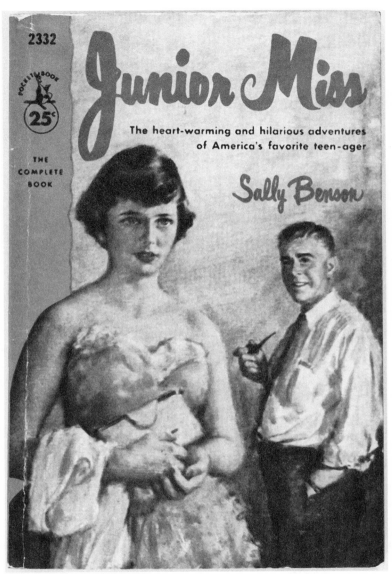

2332

POCKET BOOK
25¢

THE
COMPLETE
BOOK

Junior Miss

The heart-warming and hilarious adventures
of America's favorite teen-ager

Sally Benson

Cover of the 1959 Pocket Book edition of Sally Benson's book of short
stories, Junior Miss. *The moment illustrated here, when Judy's father
is admiring her in her first prom gown, is taken from the finale of the
Broadway play and does not occur in the book.* © 1959 Pocket Books

Advertisement for Chanel perfume in Seventeen *magazine, 1950. Courtesy General Research Division, The New York Public Library, Astor, Lenox and Tilden Foundations.*

minished social function of the white debut. In 1948, a team of white sociologists noted that in the space of two generations, between 1910 and 1945, the debutante ball had lost its social function as a means of sexual transformation and had become a conduit mostly for social ascent.[58] Moreover, as the upper classes grew to include what sociologists termed a new "lower-upper-class," "coming out" ceased to be restricted to "Assembly families."[59] Hence, "a liberalized attitude toward young girls," as James Bossard put it, in combination with the barriers to the upper classes, contributed to the decline in the social prominence of the white debutante ball. In addition, the national media, in part because of the postwar celebration of the burgeoning middle classes, was less enamored of the white upper classes or "socialites" after World War II.[60] Being the season's "No. 1 Glamour Deb" became an event that was, for the most part, confined to the local Sunday newspaper's society section.[61]

While the white, national media did not consistently cover upper-class society events, the black press did. The two major black magazines, *Ebony* and *Jet*, especially liked to report on debutante balls (much more so than weddings) and featured pictures of debutantes on their covers regularly. The black debutante was a figure of enormous cultural power and purpose in the pages of the black national press of the postwar period. Her prestige in black culture, on a national scale, certainly outstripped the attention paid to even the "most glamorous" white debutantes in the 1950s; she had enormous symbolic import among what was referred to as the "black aristocracy."[62] Because this "aristocracy" was broadcast to an encompassing, middle-class audience, the black debutante—along with the black college girl or young socialite—was a more culturally central personage in black culture than in white culture in the postwar period. Like *Life* or *Look* magazines, the black press reported on the shopping habits, musical tastes, and general spiritedness of what they more often referred to as the "bobby-soxer" than the "teenager." However, in *Ebony*, and even more so in *Jet*, such reporting was done with an emphasis on academic and, where applicable, professional achievement among upper- and middle-class girls, alongside sartorial innovativeness, consumerism, or attractiveness.

Ebony was launched in 1945 by John H. Johnson in an attempt to use "formulas and formats" that had been successful with white readers.[63]

Ebony looked most like *Life* magazine, with large black-and-white pictures and photo-essays accompanying fairly long features. By 1951, *Ebony* was selling 500,000 copies a year and by 1968 had a circulation of over one million.[64] *Jet*, a pocket-size news weekly, was first issued in 1951, sold around 100,000 copies a year in the early 1950s, lost newsstand sales in the mid-1950s, then grew steadily in the 1960s.[65] Together, *Ebony* and *Jet* overtook the national black newspapers in the 1950s and 1960s, and *Ebony* in particular arrogated to itself the role of advertising black economic and professional success.

Ebony's stated mission was to "mirror the deeds of black men" and "to help blend America's blacks and whites into interracial understanding through mutual admiration of all that is good in both."[66] To that end, the magazine highlighted the accomplishments of black individuals, recorded interracial events, as well as the doings of black colleges and social clubs, and publicized the glamorous, expensive, or aristocratic private lives of the black middle and upper classes—as long as those lives were conducted in a dignified manner. *Jet*, meanwhile, was less circumscribed in its content. This strategy was descended from turn-of-the-century black middle-class efforts to contribute to interracial cooperation through what Glenda Gilmore has called offering "testimony to convince whites to recognize class similarities across racial divides."[67] However, whereas in the early part of the twentieth century the emphasis was on celebrating and setting forward successful black marriages, in the postwar period the focus was on children and young people.[68] "World War II has come and gone," the editors proclaimed, "to prove again that our elders do not know how to run the world." Hence it is "up to youth to prove the wisdom of the Biblical passage, '. . . and a child shall lead them.'" Because children were "completely virgin as far as hates go," they had a special opportunity, and therefore responsibility, to contribute to black middle-class efforts of gradual integration.[69]

Over the course of the postwar period, the editors at *Ebony* and *Jet* remained constant in their devotion to the value of youth in the struggle for civil rights and social ascent. But, remarkably, those attentions were expended on girls to the exclusion of boys. A survey of both magazines from 1945 to 1965 found that announcements of the accomplishments of boys were almost entirely limited to the occasional athletic achievement. Moreover, when a young male athlete was featured, his parents were not listed—even if the boy was only in junior high school.[70] Black girls, meanwhile, to a degree that far outweighed that of their white counterparts, dominated the pages of the black mainstream press. In 1959, approximately 80 percent of the covers of *Jet* magazine were devoted to accomplished young women. Between January 1959 and June 1960, there was not a single black male—of any age—pictured on the cover of the magazine.

The reasons for, and the ramifications of, the attention paid to young female achievement in the black press at the expense of boys are complex and cannot be thoroughly accounted for here. But in examining the ways in which the accomplishments of girls were celebrated, pictured, embraced, and made interesting, we can begin to understand some of the logic that went into such depictions. As the objects of the photographic gaze, black girls (like white) were chosen because of their sexual desirability. As it is impossible to divorce mainstream black self-representation from white, such "cheesecake" pictures are, in certain ways, an obvious choice.[71] Indeed, part of the stated point of the large-format pictures was to emphasize black female beauty as an act of racial pride.[72] However, another way to understand the essays on black teenage girls is to see how they offered the opportunity for a mutual glory—a glory that reflected not only on the girl herself but also on the accomplishments and status of her father.

With the exception of a few stories on the student sit-ins in the early 1960s, depictions of girls were of two varieties: a celebration of her accomplishments or an announcement of her debut.[73] A representative cover picture was of a girl at a chemistry lab with the headline "Lorna Lagen: Detroiter, 16, has A's in prep subjects, takes special college course."[74] The most constant (and familiar) phrase in these articles was "daughter of" as a constant and formal invocation of the father, over and above the mother. For instance, a 1946 article on a "college girl" began, "Headed for Oberlin College in Ohio last month, the only daughter of Oscar Brown Altgeld, housing project manager and ex-NAACP executive."[75] Another article, also about a high-achieving but "typical teen," was reminiscent of the stories on white teenagers in *Life* during the war, discussed in Chapter 3: "Karen Gibson, a chestnut haired, hazel-eyed Chicagoan . . . has thoroughly 'modern' parents, international boxing club secretary Truman Gibson (and his wife Isabelle) who have given her more advantages."[76] Fathers of stature were usually referred to in this manner, whereas discussions of mothers tended to be parenthetical. Very often the fact of the girl being the daughter of a famous father made up the substance of the story itself. Sometimes the title specified the father in question: "Belafonte's Daughter Campaigns to Aid NAACP" or "Jesse Owens' Daughter Is a Campus Queen" or "Cookie Cole [daughter of Nat King Cole] Meets Society."[77] This kind of profiling of the family life of celebrities was not limited to the black press. But the sheer number of these kinds of articles, along with the near-constant invocation "daughter of," speaks to the purpose of such depictions in black, middle-class self-representation during the period.

In other important instances fathers were not named but were alluded to in terms of their professional status. In 1951, *Ebony* ran the headline "Medical Family: Two Doctor Daughters Carry On in Tradition of Famed New York Surgeon Dr. Louis T. Wright."[78] A 1962 cover of *Jet* read, "Legislator's Daughter Makes Debut."[79] There were also stories on artists' daughters and jazz musicians' daughters.[80] Another approach was to caption photographs of beauty pageant contestants with "Beauty Has Prominent Dad."[81] In *Ebony*, an article about Jane White, whose "family life had been shaped by the career of her famous father" (Walter White the president of the NAACP), was introduced with the headline "Like Father, Like Daughter."[82] Jane White was a graduate of Smith College and had recently starred in the play *Strange Fruit.* "Soon," Walter White joked, "I'll be known only as Jane White's father."[83] The reality, however, was that, as far as *Ebony* was concerned, he already was. This was *Ebony*'s first and only story that featured Walter White.[84]

Pictures of fathers reading to or talking about books with their daughters were common in *Ebony*. The emphasis on intellectual pursuit was part of a vision of higher learning as a means of racial uplift and progress that had long been part of black politics.[85] But in the case of "daughters of" important men, the project was twofold: education *and* specifically feminine privilege, the celebration of important men *and* the "advantages" they could confirm upon daughters. Pictures of girls reading books were indiscriminately mixed with pictures of socialites: " 'A' students" alongside fashion profiles, a story on a college class president in one article, followed by photographs of girls in strapless evening dresses in the next. This was because the black debutante and the serious student shared far more, in terms of both their identity and their cultural purpose, than white debutantes in the white press.

Like the white debutante, the black debutante—alongside the academically successful bobby-soxer—brought glory and prestige to her parents, particularly her father. The depiction of black debutantes obviously bolstered an image of the black middle-class family that was presided over by men, an image that reinforced not only the economic success and rectitude of fathers per se but also the implicit— and at times editorially explicit—goal of black patriarchy as a form of racial progress. In an article for *Ebony*, Lerone Bennett, following the work of sociologists E. Franklin Frazier, Abram Kardiner, and Lionel Ovesey, deplored the "role confusion," family "disorganization," and the lack of black male "self-esteem" attendant upon what he called the "tradition of female dominance." [86] Nuanced and at times contradictory, the article attempted to praise heroic female contributions to struggles for emancipation and civil rights, as well as what he called black women's "spirit of independence," while simultaneously endorsing more traditional marriages and deference to male authority. [87] Published in 1960, the article followed numerous detailed academic studies on the "Negro family," the bulk of which had emerged in the wake of E. Franklin Frazier's definitive *The Negro Family in the United States*, originally published in 1939. These studies built a case for patriarchy by critiquing the debilitating aspects of what Frazier called the "matriarchate" and celebrating the "well-organized family under the authority of the father." [88] The goal of a "well-organized" family was envisioned as progress from a pattern of paternal "indifference," precipitated by men's subordinate status under slavery, to a form of family organization where men could provide for their families and thus preside over them. These overt anxieties about fatherhood informed *Ebony*'s attempt not only to represent women as traditional wives but also to ritualistically situate girls with their fathers, much like white girls were situated with their fathers among the white middle class.

However, as a dyad, the black father-daughter relationship—from 1945 through the late 1950s—was figured differently in black culture than in white. In depictions of black debutante balls, as in white, the father was a symbolic and economic reference point: "The girls were stunning in their white lace gowns. The fathers straining against

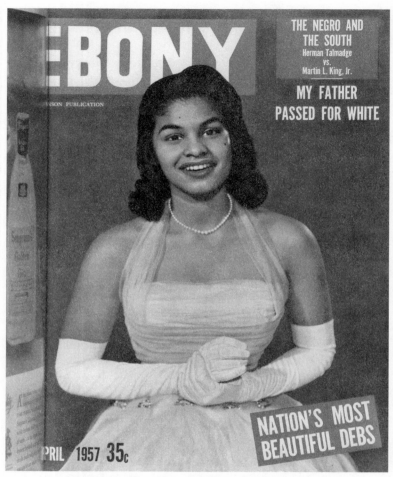

A 1957 cover of Ebony *(above) and a 1962 cover of* Jet *(opposite).
Debutantes and high-achieving girls featured on the covers of* Ebony
and Jet *magazines were almost always pictured alone. Courtesy
Photographs and Prints Division, Schomburg Center for Research in
Black Culture, The New York Public Library, Astor, Lenox and Tilden
Foundations.*

20c

JET

DEC. 27, 1962

WAR BRIDE'S TOUGH
CHOICE: HER KIDS OR
NEGRO HUSBAND

Legislator's
Daughter
Makes Debut

ELSIE RUMFORD:
Pretty daughter of
California lawmaker
is Links Cotillion deb

their vests, were proud."[89] Moreover, fathers were expected, on many occasions, to dance the "first dance" with their daughters, and then "present them to their dates."[90] Yet fathers and daughters were not *pictured* dancing together. Nor were fathers shown admiring their daughters, escorting them, or waiting for them at the foot of the stairs. Black fathers were not shown helping their daughters out of cars; girls were not pictured "on the arm of their father." Unlike in the white society pages, black debutantes were almost always pictured alone, with their escorts, or with other debutantes. Between 1945 and 1958 there were only two society pictures of girls with their fathers at social functions in *Ebony*, and in each case the girls were pictured with their mothers as well.[91] Beginning in 1958, there were a few pictures of girls with fathers and without accompanying family—most notably Cookie Cole being presented to president John F. Kennedy by her father.[92] However, the small number of pictures that began to appear at the end of the 1950s make all the more glaring their lack—especially given the high volume of reporting on balls and cotillions—in the decade before.

Moreover, when considered in light of the postwar convention of pairing white adolescent girls with their fathers, the black girls on the covers of *Ebony* and *Jet* appear strikingly alone. One reason why black girls were not shown with their fathers is because the black press exhibited less of an investment in portraying chivalric forms of assistance—moments that were often at the center of white father-daughter images. Another reason may have been that the editors of these magazines deliberately refrained from showing fathers and daughters together because they wanted to achieve a perspective on masculinity and paternity that was beyond, or at a remove from, the physical. The common textual announcement that girls were the daughters of noteworthy men, in the absence of an accompanying picture of them, rendered the fathers disembodied. *Ebony* was a self-conscious magazine; presenting an image of black men was its announced mission. Because of this self-consciousness, we can assume that the absence of pictures of fathers with adolescent daughters was a deliberate, and perhaps strongly felt, choice.[93]

The overwhelming dominance of representations of girls (and, at least textually, their fathers) must also be attributed to the integrationist goals of both *Ebony* and *Jet*. The face, so to speak, that both magazines put on integration was female: articles on peacefully integrated schools in the early 1960s, for example, tended to be illustrated most prominently with girls.[94] This reportorial strategy represented a response to white fears of integration that were framed in terms of anxieties about miscegenation. Attempts at integration were often, in the words of Glenda Gilmore, "misconstrued as a bid for sexual access to white women."[95] Moreover, the image of the sexually predatory, young black male continued to dominate the southern popular imagination in the mid-1950s.[96] On one level, girls were chosen to represent the promise of black success and integration simply because they were not young black men. They were also chosen, I would argue, because they provided an already available way to understand both glamour and achievement as an element of family life. Contextually circumscribed, they could speak to the familial, and thus sexually contained, nature of the men who were their fathers. In ways both similar to and different from girls in white culture, they helped *account for* the adult men who provided for and oversaw their social activities. Indeed, they helped account for one another.

The black press both referenced and transformed dominant white representations of father-daughter ties during the postwar period. The use of images of teenage girls as evidence of black beauty, accomplishment, and allure contributed to the objectification of women and girls, even as it helped forward the social aspirations of the black middle-class family. However, the impulse to textually conjoin yet physically separate black fathers and daughters reveals both the usefulness and limits of representations of the father-daughter relationship on the part of the black media. The lack of a particularly eroticized father-daughter relationship in *Ebony* and *Jet*, the formality of father-daughter poses, and the notable lack of paternal figuration in instances of daughters' coming-of-age were doubtless rooted in cultural tensions surrounding the sexual status of black men (and to a lesser extent black women) and the historic representation of black people as hypersexual in medical and cultural discourses.[97] But it was also, perhaps, a response to the way in which the black father-daughter relationship itself was set forth in one of the few serious portrayals of a black family in the immediate postwar period: the enormously successful, and rarely discussed, *Anna Lucasta* (1945).[98]

Race and the Universal Oedipal Dynamic

A photograph of Hilda Simms graced the cover of the second issue of *Ebony*, published in December 1945. In an elegant white suit, leaning against a lamppost, the beautiful star of *Anna Lucasta* was exactly the kind of crossover success that *Ebony* wanted to celebrate. The play, by Philip Yordan, was originally about a Polish American family called *Anna Lukasea* and was one of a spate of postwar plays about fathers and daughters that took its cues from psychoanalysis.[99] Yordan had had no success with the play before the American Negro Theatre, a Harlem-based community theater group established by Abram Hill, agreed to produce it.[100] With Yordan's permission, Hill rewrote the play. When the New York dailies raved about the show, John Wildberg, who had once been associated with the revival of *Porgy and Bess*, offered to finance its move to Broadway. Harry Wagstaff Gribble, an English-born director and playwright with an established reputation, was hired to rewrite the last act and stage the Broadway version. Gribble's stated reason for participating in such a risky venture was that he had wanted for some time to "find or write a play which includes or deals exclusively with the more brilliant facets of Negro-American society."[101] *Anna Lucasta* was an overnight success on Broadway, and by the time that Simms graced the cover of *Ebony*, 650,000 people had seen it.[102] It eventually ran for 957 performances at the Mansfield Theatre, setting a record for a play with an all-black cast.[103]

The play's chief character, Anna, is a prostitute. She works on the Brooklyn docks, having fled Philadelphia as a teenager when her father threw her out of the house when he found her "rollin' in the hay."[104] The play revolves around the dynamics of the Lucasta family: their secrets, their conniving, and their distrust and exploitation of one another. When Anna's siblings, Stella and Stanley, learn that a wealthy, recent graduate of an agricultural school from the South is in the neighborhood searching for a wife, they arrange for Anna to come back home in the hope that he will fall in love with her and they can relieve him of his recent inheritance. However, Mr. Lucasta's mysterious mental condition—his unpredictable breakdowns and seemingly unwarranted flares of temper—constantly threatens to foil Stella and Stanley's plans and provides the play with its central problem.

Within minutes of the opening scene, Anna's mother, Theresa, explains that "Pa" has a "sly-cosy" (psychosis).[105] The origins of Pa's psychosis remain unexplained for some time. He wanders in, muttering to himself. When asked to go to Brooklyn to retrieve Anna, he becomes violent in his refusal, then deeply afraid. He stutters and trembles at the mere mention of her name. When asked why Pa hates his daughter, Theresa says wistfully, "My love wasn't strong enough to hold her in this house . . . he loved her. He watched her grow up like she was the only flower in his yard."[106] How "such love could turn into such hate" remains a mystery. Once Anna appears on the scene, Pa deteriorates further. He lashes out and raves, begins drinking, and finally throws the entire family into crisis.

The narrative tension of the play does not surround Anna's prostitution but the origins of her "fall." By the middle of the second act it is clear that her father fears his own sexual desire for her.[107] He suffers, as one reviewer put it, "the reverse of an Edipus [sic] complex."[108] This reversal, however, was not merely a rarified psychoanalytic problem, it was an inversion of the popular understanding of the fundamental sexual positions of daughter and father. As we have seen, in psychoanalytic and popular narratives, girls needed sexual validation from their fathers in order to grow up; they needed their fathers to sanction their coming-of-age. Fathers were required to respond to their daughters' erotic appeal while remaining psychologically disconnected from the potential implications of such attraction (like, for instance, Mr. Carmichael in "The Dangerous Date"). As we have also seen, the line between "erotic recognition" and overt sexual desire was thin. Insofar as the father-daughter relationship in *Anna Lucasta* grew out of that peculiar—and apparently endlessly fascinating—aspect of the father-daughter relationship, this play was simply one among many such dramas of the postwar period. However, to the extent that *Anna Lucasta* attempted to look at the father-daughter relationship from the perspective of a father who was driven insane by the enormity of his desire, it was unique. (For a contrasting depiction of paternal sexual madness—or lack thereof—in Vladimir Nabokov's *Lolita* and Ralph Ellison's *Invisible Man*, see Chapter 5.)

The play employed many ideas about female adolescent Oedipal needs that were, in fact, universal in the postwar period: her mother's love was somehow not "enough"; the teenage Anna longed for her father to "see" her, with everything that that sight entailed about the adolescent longing for the paternal gaze (metaphors about the loss of sight, in reference to the original Oedipal myth, abound). But, in other ways, the popular appeal of this play should be understood as one that was grounded in racial attitudes. The play was rewritten twice — once by a black playwright and once by a white one — between its run in Harlem and its move to Broadway, so it is difficult to know how much it was changed to fit ideas about a black rather than a Polish family in the revision process. The remarkable air of warm self-congratulation that surrounded the reception of *Anna Lucasta* on Broadway on the part of the white press is telling. Virtually every reviewer believed the play to be a "historic event," because it was about a black family that was able to "transcend their race and its special problems to become human creatures, to suggest anybody's family." [109] Burton Rascoe, a regular reviewer for the *New York World-Telegram* claimed, "In my opinion *Anna Lucasta* is the most important event in our native American drama in 20 years." [110]

A play about a father's sexual obsession with his adolescent daughter seems, from a contemporary perspective, a strange way to depict "anybody's family." One way to interpret this statement is that it reflects the ubiquity of assumptions about Oedipal (or, reverse Oedipal, as the case may be) desire during this period. However, when the play is considered in light of depictions of white father–adolescent daughter relationships on Broadway during the early postwar period, it also makes a startling contrast. Compared to his fictional contemporaries, Mr. Lucasta's ungovernable sexual desire is at once pathetic and crude. Unable to acknowledge his daughter's sexual coming-of-age with equanimity, much less with the kind of delighted and sexually delicate erotic recognition that we see in white father-daughter coming-of-age stories, he not only withdraws from her, he is driven mad by the force of his desire and is unable to face her. Portrayals of incestuous fathers began to appear in literature during this period, but none of those men exhibit the lunacy and lack of comprehension that Mr. Lucasta does. This kind of sexual insanity would have most likely reinforced white assumptions about excessive black sexuality rather than challenged audiences to think differently about black families or black people as a group.

Ironically, *Anna Lucasta* portrayed exactly the kind of image of black family life that magazines like *Ebony* explicitly sought to refute. As Willard Gatewood has written about the black middle and upper classes of the prewar period, "self-control" was not simply an element of upper-class identity, it was the lynchpin of black social uplift. "Self restraint, in the parlor and on the street . . . were the prime attributes of gentility."[111] As we have seen, the commitment to decorous forms of family life, in somewhat altered form, remained after the war. Hence, as an example of a Broadway hit that took a white audience into a black home, *Anna Lucasta* violated long-established black middle-class taboos on cultural self-presentation.

Because the play decisively departed from white scripts on father–adolescent daughter relationships, it reinforced notions of racial difference by dramatizing differences in family sexual dynamics. That this difference was articulated through the father-daughter relationship speaks to the profound importance of that relationship to the construction of sexuality in general during the period. The depiction of family life in *Anna Lucasta* provided for white audiences a frame of reference, a way to interpret the white father-daughter relationship being performed contemporaneously. The editors at *Ebony*, it is safe to assume, were affected by this particular presentation of a black psychosis: better, perhaps, to steer clear of any suggestion of father-daughter eroticism at all in the pages of their magazine. The sexual explosiveness of the father-daughter relationship in *Anna Lucasta* does not fully explain the restrained formality in the images of fathers and daughters in *Ebony*, but it does help to reconstruct one important aspect of the cultural context in which editorial decisions were made.

The invocation of the sexual significance of father to daughter, and daughter to father, in the popular media defined the cultural (as opposed to simply economic) distinctions between the middle and working classes, between black and white. The cultural perspective on fathers and daughters played a major role in shaping ideas about which families could safely tolerate sexuality between family members and which families could not. It hinted at what was going on in the "parlors" of black families and the "drawing rooms" of white families. It suggested which fathers had an obligation to recognize their daughters' sexuality, which fathers were irrelevant to their daughters' sexuality, and which fathers could not be trusted to take notice of their daughters' sexuality at all.

White, middle-class fathers in the mid-twentieth century were portrayed as men who were susceptible to sexual reactions to their adolescent daughters but who were nonetheless sexually nonthreatening.[112] This somewhat precarious image was achieved primarily by describing fathers as passive or disoriented when confronted with their daughters' sexual charms. Fathers' lack of sexual sophistication was at the heart of the formula for portraying white, male, middle-class sexual innocence. Because these men were sexually unconscious, they were therefore not responsible for what audiences might infer about a father's eye-popping response to a low-cut gown. Also, the distinction between the paternal realization of a daughter's coming-of-age and simple leering was presented as self-evident in these narratives. Whatever threat that might have inhered in paternal sexual interest was safely subsumed by this ubiquitous presumption. Whereas a lack of sexual self-understanding in white culture contributed to an image of paternal sexual innocence, such a lack of self-awareness in depictions of black fathers, at least in one salient instance, was linked to an inability to come to terms with the reality of submerged lust. While Mr. Lucasta's overwhelming sexual desire for his daughter as she developed into an adolescent might have been a powerful reminder for white audiences of the possible difficulties inherent in the eroticized father-daughter relationship, it was also a reminder of their own racial distance from it. When incestuous relationships between (mostly white) fathers and adolescent daughters began to appear in print in the 1950s, they were considered, as we shall see in the next chapter, in an altogether different light.

Chapter 5

AFFECTION, IDENTIFICATION, SKEPTICISM

> *"There's nobody can stop Pa when he gets drunk and starts fighting."*
> —*Selena Cross,* Peyton Place, *1956*

F. Hugh Herbert's collection of short stories *Meet Corliss Archer* (1942) is inscribed with the dedication, "Through these pages walk the most wonderful girls in the world—my daughters, Diana and Pamela, whose endearing struggles with adolescent problems have given me most of the material for this, their book."[1] The material his daughters provided would eventually contribute to popular productions spanning many years and several different mediums, including stage, screen, and radio.[2] Indeed, forays outside the topic of adolescent daughters (and their fathers) proved mostly failures for Herbert, while the public appetite for his comic renderings of female adolescence, first exhibited in the warm reception to his short stories about Corliss Archer, appeared almost limitless. The play *Kiss and Tell* (1943), based on a short story that appeared in *Good Housekeeping* about Corliss called "Private Affair," was an enormous hit and ran for 955 performances at the Biltmore Theater in New York.[3] The play was later made into a successful film in 1945, and was followed with a sequel, *A Kiss for Corliss,* in 1948.[4] Between 1942 and 1945, *Meet Corliss Archer,* the collected stories, was reprinted several times; meanwhile, Corliss Archer could be heard on the weekly eponymous radio show, which ran for eleven consecutive years from 1943 until 1954.[5] In short, for over a decade, Corliss Archer pervaded popular culture—stage, screen, and radio—without interruption, and her character provided the makings of a lucrative career for F. Hugh Herbert.

Corliss's relationship with her father formed the substance of her characterization to a degree that surpassed that of any other fictional character of the period. Her relationship with him informed every

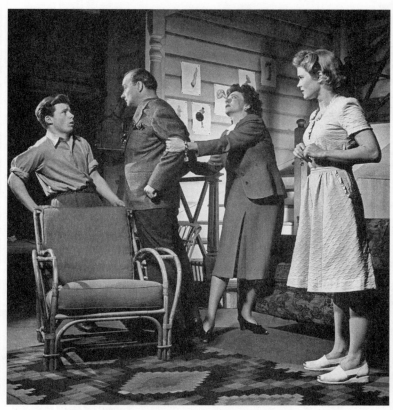

Mr. Archer queries Corliss Archer's boyfriend about what the pair have been doing together in the play Kiss and Tell, *written by F. Hugh Herbert, 1943. Courtesy Time Life Pictures/Getty Images.*

Advertisement for the film version of Kiss and Tell, *starring Shirley Temple, Columbia Pictures, 1945. Courtesy Billy Rose Theatre Collection, The New York Public Library for the Performing Arts, Astor, Lenox and Tilden Foundations.*

Photos accompanying an interview with F. Hugh Herbert on the opening night of his play The Moon Is Blue *in the* New York Post, *April 15, 1951. Courtesy Billy Rose Theatre Collection, The New York Public Library for the Performing Arts, Astor, Lenox and Tilden Foundations.*

comic scrape, every adolescent desire, every teenage quandary. Mr. Archer was drawn solely in terms of his relationship to his daughter as well. His response to her—the conscious and sustained appreciation of her beauty, skepticism about her designs on his affection, and occasional sexual hostility—would become as influential as the formula presented in *Junior Miss*. These paternal qualities, however, are vastly different from, if not incompatible with, those attributes exhibited in postwar girls' coming-of-age narratives discussed in the previous chapters. Indeed, in this chapter I argue that in celebrated plays and novels of the postwar period, the economic/erotic exchange at the heart of female adolescent coming-of-age narratives was represented in ways that deliberately undermined, or questioned, the possibility of an innocent interplay between the familial, the commercial, and the erotic (as described in Chapter 4). In some instances, fathers or stepfathers exploited popular rituals for their own pleasure; in others, they turned traditional occasions for father-daughter eroticism into opportunities for sexual transgression. These men stood as potent examples of the passive, ineffectual father's opposite and served to remind audiences of an ever-present potential for sexual transgression inherent in the modern, Oedipally inflected, and commercially oriented relationship established between fathers and adolescent daughters.

The chapter begins with an examination of the father–adolescent daughter dynamic first set forward in F. Hugh Herbert's plays, films, and radio programs about Corliss Archer, as well as one of his (failed) father-daughter plays, *For Keeps* (1944). Perhaps the most striking element of Herbert's rendition of the father–adolescent daughter relationship is the way in which it was consistently described as a combination of *mutual* identification, sexual appreciation, and light-hearted disdain. The second half of the chapter examines how Herbert's depictions influenced the manner in which incestuous father-daughter relationships were portrayed in works of fiction, including William Styron's *Lie Down in Darkness* (1951), Vladimir Nabokov's *Lolita* (1955), and Grace Metalious's *Peyton Place* (1956). These authors often referenced one another—primarily through the repetition of names—providing inescapable clues to their conceptual genesis. Following those clues, I have assembled a literary family tree of father-daughter incest novels that contains not only the best-selling books (Henry Bellamann's *King's Row* [1940] and *Peyton Place*) but also the most acclaimed (*Lie Down in Darkness, Lolita,* and Ralph Ellison's *Invisible Man* [1952]). I investigate why these works have not been considered in light of one another and examine their most salient connections. Animating all of these works is a fascination with a particular kind of relationship between father and adolescent daughter, which, by the time *Lolita* was published in Paris in 1955, had become a highly stylized—even mannered—version of father-daughter incestuous desire.

Hostility and Humor: Fathers and Daughters on Stage

Critics situated Herbert's play *Kiss and Tell* within the genre of female adolescent comedy that was becoming increasingly popular at the time, including *Junior Miss* (1941) and *Janie* (1942), both of which had long runs on Broadway. However, it was also compared to older staples: *Vogue* praised "its Andy Hardy Humours and its adolescent wit," and a review in the *New Yorker* introduced the play with the headline "Tarkington Revisited," referring to Booth Tarkington's immensely popular book about adolescence, *Seventeen* (1915), and perhaps also his Pulitzer Prize–winning book about a young woman's coming-of-age, *Alice Adams* (1921).[6] Comparisons to older comedies, including Eugene O'Neill's *Ah, Wilderness!* (play, 1933; film, 1938), were made affectionately and reflected a desire to situate the play within a venerable tradition of American comedies about coming-of-age. However, Herbert's plays represented a departure from *Ah, Wilderness!* and the Andy Hardy films from which they were believed to be descended.[7]

In *Ah, Wilderness!* and *Seventeen*, fathers provided a running commentary on their sons' immature activities.[8] They observed the various entanglements and mishaps of their progeny with responses that alternated between bemusement and flares of temper, with the balance resting on the side of bemusement. The father's temper was usually exposed but then repressed and then very often transformed again into a "chuckle," a "twinkle in his eye," or a smile, "hiding ... behind his hand."[9] For instance, in Booth Tarkington's *Seventeen*, which remained in print through the 1930s, William Baxter played supplicant to his father's wallet in much the same way that girls did in female adolescent coming-of-age narratives of the 1940s and 1950s. The item that William believes will transform him into an adult and win his girl's heart is his first dress suit. When he first approaches Mr. Baxter on the subject, he is "denied by his father with a jocularity more crushing than rigor." After William's second attempt, Mr. Baxter fumes to his wife, "Think of his coming out here and starting a regular debating society declamation before his mother and father! . . . What's the world getting to be like? Seventeen years old and throws a fit because he can't have a dress-suit! . . . He's got to learn some hard sense!"[10]

The complex relationship between anger and humor—anger portrayed as humor, anger as humorousness itself—remained in the comedies about white middle-class female adolescence that proliferated in the 1940s. However, the tone and intentions of such fathers' reactions underwent a significant transformation. First, fathers began to condemn their adolescent daughters' behavior primarily through the use of sarcasm rather than displays of temper. For instance, in *Junior Miss*, Judy Graves's pretty, sixteen-year-old sister, Lois, is besieged by boys asking for dates. For the most part, Mr. Graves ignores Lois. But when the doorbell rings yet another time, and yet another date arrives for her, Mr. Graves turns to his wife and says, "I wonder if our little Lois is going to turn out to be a tramp?"[11]

The same perceptions, and sarcastic rebukes, occur in both *Janie* and *Kiss and Tell*, plays that appeared one after the other and had much in common. Janie's father claims that the locally encamped soldiers need to be protected from his daughter rather than vice versa because "the child has no inhibitions."[12] In *Kiss and Tell*, Mr. Archer, observing his daughter's attempt to seduce a soldier in plain view of her high school boyfriend, Dexter, claims, "I'm beginning to suspect that our dear little daughter has a streak of bitchiness in her that's all wool and yard wide."[13] Later, he responds to various observations of his daughter's flirtatiousness by murmuring "all wool and yard wide . . ." under his breath. The fathers in these situations ultimately accept their daughters' behavior: the girls' interest in boys and soldiers is considered normal for their age, and the girls are not punished. Instead, the fathers respond sardonically, with a self-conscious, blasé, or knowing weariness. They accept their daughters' "trampiness" or "bitchiness" as an unfortunate part of modern mores.[14]

Kiss and Tell's Mr. Archer is sly and reserved, hence he reveals his personal feelings about his daughter's behavior indirectly. Observing her taunt Dexter, he says to the boy confidentially, "If you ever want to throttle her with your bare hands, I'll defend you free of charge."[15] The kind of humorous hostility Corliss's father directs at Corliss is characteristic of F. Hugh Herbert's rendition of the father–adolescent daughter relationship in all of his material. The hostility, however, is mixed with a constant invocation of adoring affection, and it is at the odd intersection of these two paternal reactions that the father-daughter relationship takes shape.

Affection and Affectation: Fathers Observe Their Adolescent Daughters

When Mr. Archer claims in *Kiss and Tell* that he suspects Corliss has a streak of pure "bitchiness" in her, his wife responds, "You needn't sound so proud of it."[16] Although Mr. Archer's pride in his daughter was only hinted at here in his wife's response, admiration of a very specific kind was evident throughout Herbert's collection of short stories about Corliss. For instance, when Mr. Archer finds out that Corliss has fooled him into allowing her to participate in a kissing booth at a bazaar for the war effort, his exclamation of surprise "was not entirely devoid of pride."[17] Moreover, Mr. Archer brags to the Franklins, his next-door neighbors, and Dexter's parents that Corliss can win any argument with their son. He compliments her on her lovely hands, her effective poses, and her ability to win people over with her flirtatiousness. Furthermore, Mr. Archer's compliments match the author's specific observations of Corliss, and the two men's interest in Corliss overlap. Herbert makes no effort to mask himself as Mr. Archer, and the father's observations of his daughter flow seamlessly into the narrator's omniscient view.

Herbert's stories, unlike Susan Benson's stories about Judy Graves, which formed the basis for *Junior Miss* (1939), were meant to provide us not with character development but with comedy. Therefore, Corliss's personality, or any transformation in it, was really of little consequence; the point was to enjoy Corliss rather than understand her. Corliss shared a great deal with other characters of earlier adolescent comedies: self-aggrandizement, fickleness, preening vanity, a robust imperviousness to others, and an ongoing search for cash in the absence of a job. In these ways, Corliss was a typical female teen-age character. Herbert seems to be attempting to save Corliss from a complete lack of moral dimension when he bestows upon her an energetic patriotism and an express affection for her family. Neverthe-less, the attributes most in evidence are physical: Corliss is "pretty," "slim," "deeply tanned," and the proud possessor of "lovely" hands. She is secondarily seductive and supremely self-confident, "a superb actress." [18] When she feels wronged or wrongly denied something she wants, she is petulant and vengeful. Her affection for her parents is simultaneously exaggerated ("I think all mothers are simply super") and condescending ("you're both very cute"). [19]

Her constant attempts at manipulation provide most of the situa-tion for comedy. In the story "Private Affair" she tries to convince a soldier that she is eighteen (she is fifteen) and to persuade her par-ents to go along with her dissembling. In other stories, she sets out to persuade the maid to let her wear her mother's sweater; to ratio-nalize taking money from the household expenses to buy clothes for herself; and to trick Dexter into believing that she is dying after a stay in the hospital for an appendectomy (she wants to see how he will re-act). She "purrs," "smooches," and "coos" at almost everyone. But she reserves her most potent and sensuous behavior for her father: she kisses him, throws him kisses, hugs him, looks up at him with "soul-ful" eyes, and wriggles onto his lap when he is trying to read the paper on a Sunday morning.

The first story in the collection, "Meet Corliss Archer," is represen-tative. It is a chronology of Corliss's attempts to convince her parents of the legitimacy of various expensive activities. One request is to send her brother, who is in fighting in Italy, a cable informing him of their dog's newborn puppies. Her mother gives her a tentative "We'll see, dear." At this, writes Herbert, "Corliss walked to her father, put slim arms around him, and strained him to her childishly. 'Angel,' she said, '*make* her say yes.'" [20] What follows reflects both Corliss's effective-ness with her father and Archer's adoration of Corliss: "Mr. Archer, who felt himself weakening, shoved her away, chuckling. 'Save that smooch,' he advised, 'for that unhappy youth next door. It doesn't cut any ice with me.' He brushed the soft dark hair out of her face and rubbed his knuckles against her smooth, cool young cheek. He knew that he lied through his teeth. It cut a lot of ice. Corliss could generally smooch him out of almost anything."[21] The eroticism of Corliss's approach clearly pleases Mr. Archer, and such scenes repeat themselves in almost every one of Herbert's vignettes. What is distinctive about this moment of paternal capitulation is that Mr. Archer, unlike fathers in other comedies about teenage girls, is fully aware of the effect his daughter is having on him, as well as his daughter's scheme to have such an effect. He is both a party to and an actor in Corliss's seductive designs. He "knew" what kind of effect Corliss aimed to have at the same time that he felt himself "weakening" in response. The unconscious or dazed quality of the paternal response to adolescent sexual maturation that we saw in Chapter 4—the lack of paternal observation that allowed for sudden recognition—plays no role here. For Mr. Archer, his daughter's seductiveness represents the substance of his relationship to her and the source of his ongoing affection for her.

Their relationship revolves around such moments of calculation, and what is meant to be enjoyable about watching them is the animation of Corliss's attempts to seduce her father. Archer takes pleasure in playing what he knows is a game, Corliss is triumphant in her power to attract him, and the reader is surely meant to take pleasure in witnessing their mutual enjoyment. Corliss's tone and manner (cooing and calling her father "angel") are sheer affect, and she makes no attempt to disassociate her ploys from her immediate pecuniary aims. Simultaneously, the fact that Corliss's attentions are mercenary makes no difference to Archer, who succumbs despite, or perhaps even because of, the fact that he is fully aware of her artistry.

Because Archer instrumentalizes his own affection for Corliss and assumes she is doing the same, he is never fooled by his daughter's extravagant displays. In this way Archer remains safely beyond any difficult or befuddling encounters with his daughter. Corliss herself does not consider her behavior in any terms beyond the benefit it might bring her. Any motivation underlying her activities, beyond the desire to procure cash or be thought beautiful, glamorous, or grown-up, is not in evidence.[22] The radio program offers even fewer clues about Corliss's personality. Corliss, as she was played by Janet Waldo, is even more self-serving and demanding, and Mr. Archer's tactics for bribing his daughter are more extreme (the moment she opens her mouth he begins to hand her dollar bills).[23] Moreover, Herbert's depiction of Corliss's limitless desire to consume—particularly when considered in light of the kinds of attacks that were leveled at wives for their spending habits in *Generation of Vipers* (1942), *The Crack in the Picture Window* (1957), and other popular texts—is curiously sympathetic. Indeed, her constant scheming, manipulation, and pursuit of sumptuous glamour are portrayed as substantively adorable rather than morally unattractive.

Taken as a whole, the Corliss Archer stories are a blend of sensual appeal, adolescent folly, and sarcasm. The sarcasm—expressed by both F. Hugh Herbert and his characters—is as definitive as the eroticism. "My father is a remarkable man but unfortunately has a warped sense of humor," Corliss complains.[24] Archer's teasing, which at times rankles but never hurts Corliss, is a by-product of the ongoing process of bribing and bargaining, mostly over material goods and attention. The endless teasing, wisecracking, and sarcasm in the *Meet Corliss Archer* stories reflect a degree of mutual skepticism and detachment in this father-daughter relationship. It is a detachment that coexists uneasily with their extravagant mutual affection.

Skepticism and Affection:
The Case of Fathers and Daughters

Corliss's and Archer's skepticism of one another not only lent itself to a certain degree of detachment, it also informed their mutual identification. As the relationship between fathers and daughters began to play a larger role on stage and screen during World War II, the kinds of attributes fathers began to see in their daughters came to reflect and help define certain aspects of themselves (and, to a lesser extent, vice versa). Teenage girls, as we have seen, were often depicted as demanding, opinionated, presumptuous, irreverent, discriminating, and, above all, devoted to their own needs. The attributes of the masculine, paternal self that were shared, discovered, or reflected upon through fathers' relationships to their daughters in popular culture were often similar incarnations of such qualities or related to them: a tendency to be critical, confrontational, self-indulgent, and bored by middle-class mores. That certain qualities constitutive of masculinity would be discovered through a man's connection or identification with a teenage girl appears counterintuitive (because of both the difference in ages and the fact that masculinity is most often thought of as being shared between men). Nevertheless, such mutuality was increasingly portrayed, and one can speculate upon why it might have been a useful way to think about men within the context of family life. First, when certain male/paternal traits were reflected or refracted through men's identification with teenage girls/daughters, those traits were less threatening than when men shared them with their sons or with teenage boys. With daughters, there was enough difference in their respective roles and actual identities for the specifics of identification to be masked. Identification with a daughter appeared more muted than that with a son. Second, one is a teenager for a fixed period of time. Hence, a daughter's qualities with which a father identified were confined or perhaps risible because of their assumed impermanence. Seeing himself in a teenage girl was a way for a father to identify a fleeting or only partial aspect of himself. In addition, enacting these qualities with one's teenage daughter allowed men to express and exhibit qualities—skepticism about human relationships, boredom, disenchantment—that were otherwise antithetical to family life, while still playing a successful role within it.

Despite the constant ribbing, posturing, and sarcasm undergirding the father-daughter relationship in *Meet Corliss Archer*, there exists between the two figures shared interests and attributes that crop up at strange moments. Mother is always the voice of reason, while father and daughter are often in competition with one another—over who gets to "monopolize the conversation," who is going to win a certain argument, who gets to read this month's *Esquire* first. The men's magazine to which Archer subscribes and Corliss is devoted is referred to throughout the collection of short stories.

The few odd details of personality and predilection linking father and daughter in *Meet Corliss Archer* take on added significance when viewed in light of Herbert's second father-daughter play, *For Keeps*, which premiered in 1944.[25] *For Keeps* was a critical failure, a fact that was particularly disappointing to critics after the enormous success of *Kiss and Tell*. *Kiss and Tell*, reviewers claimed, reflected the "wit" and "wisdom . . . of an understanding father" while *For Keeps*, though "well intentioned and compassionate," was "dreary" and "depressing."[26] The young heroine talked too much, there were not enough funny lines, none of the characters was particularly likable, and the ending was not satisfying.[27] In all, according to critics, it was an unamusing play. *For Keeps*, however, enlarges our understanding of Herbert's perspective on the father-daughter relationship and reflects what the mid-1940s audience wanted to see by establishing what it was they did *not* want to see. It is also representative of a group of plays like *Second Threshold* (1949) or *The Pleasure of His Company* (1958), in which girls reunited with long-departed fathers who were dissipated, world-weary, and cynical about family life.

As in almost all of Herbert's work, the entirety of the play takes place in one room—in this case the penthouse of Mr. Paul Vanda, a commercial photographer who has just married his fourth wife, a pretty twenty-three-year-old woman named Pamela. His new wife is busy attempting to make his comfortable apartment into something more modern and airy, much to the dismay of Mr. Vanda. Into this situation walks Mr. Vanda's daughter, Nancy, who has been sent to stay with her father while her mother is "globe-trotting." Nancy, who is only a few months into her fourteenth year, has lived her life in hotels, commuted back and forth between Chicago and New York since she was four, and generally has been left in charge of herself as both parents are too self-absorbed and irresponsible to have much to do with her. She drinks martinis, is purposely shocking to her elders, and is the possessor of a bored, world-weary air that is not entirely affected. At the same time, she is eager to please everyone, harbors a secret devotion to Hershey bars and longs to go ice-skating with the other children she sees in the park.[28]

Nancy also has a stepfather, Terry, whom, she tells Pamela during a singular moment of anxious self-revelation, has "taken to patting my fanny in what he calls a fond, paternal way—only I think it's more fond than paternal."[29] When Terry arrives to take Nancy back to New York, he leers at her, beckons her to sit next to him, and invites her to sit on his lap.[30] Taking sympathy, Mr. Vanda and Pamela invite her to stay with them. Nancy gratefully accepts, and the play ends with Nancy enfolded into the arms of her father's newly domesticized household. This ending, however, is neither happy nor resolved. Paul Vanda is a self-confessed failure as a father, quick-tempered, and on his way to his fourth divorce. Hence, the ending actually points to the impossibility of Nancy ever finding a father. Underscoring the point,

Herbert closes the play with this exchange between Mr. Vanda and Nancy: "Damned if I know now which you need most—a mother or a husband," Mr. Vanda says. Nancy responds, smiling, "You'll never know, Daddy, you'll never know."[31] Indeed, the original title of the play was "You'll Never Know"—an indictment of both Vanda and, potentially, male members of the audience, as well as the playwright himself. Herbert seems to have ultimately decided that this title was too depressing for a comedy.[32] Vanda thinks that Nancy, as a sophisticated fourteen-year-old, is too mature to need a mother and too immature to marry. However, it is perhaps useful to recall that it was at exactly this juncture, according to the psychoanalytic depiction of female adolescence of the period, that girls needed their fathers most. Yet Nancy is faced with sexual assault on the one hand and indifference on the other.

Part of the reason Vanda will "never know" what his daughter needs is because the paternal qualities that would enable him to discern her feelings are not only unavailable to him but also thrown into question by the play itself. When Vanda admits that he "wasn't cut out to be a fond 'Papa,'" the term "fondness" has already taken on a sexualized connotation, as just moments before Nancy used the word to describe Terry's lascivious behavior.[33] Within this context, one responds to such a pronouncement with relief. Yet if one is relieved to find out that Vanda is incapable of paternal "fondness," then what are the alternatives? If fondness is divorced from sexuality, what is the substance of the paternal? The logic of Vanda's sentiment was the problem at the center of the play: if between a mother and a husband a girl's emotional and sexual needs were met, what was there for a father to do?

Given the difficulty of this question, one wonders why Herbert paired a forty-four-year-old man who is "something of a sadist" with a precocious fourteen-year-old girl with whom he can form no substantive relationship.[34] One answer is that the two do a good job of provoking one another. He is rude, she is "fresh," and together the sparks fly—all of which produce an effect much closer to the fast-talking, screwball comedies of the 1930s than to the average domestic comedy of the postwar period.[35] The play also manages to make both Vanda and Nancy much more interesting by having each bring out in the other a kind of colorful brassiness—a quality that is all the more pleasurable to discover (at least to Herbert) within the context of a connection being made between such incongruous characters. The description of Paul Vanda evokes the classic bachelor with a lust for life (and beautiful women): He is "in his middle forties and has always lived high, wide and handsome, but, for all that, neither the years nor the dissipation show. . . . He has a violent temper which he makes little effort to control . . . [but] can be as sentimental as an adolescent girl."[36] The final attribute might seem strange but for the fact that it served to link Vanda effectively to his teenage daughter and to redeem him somewhat, even if his sentimentality was never actually exhibited. He and Nancy proclaim to one another that underneath the "cynicism" and constant "ribbing" they are both actually "sentimental slobs" who cry at the movies (meanwhile, Nancy points out that her mother never cries no matter what the occasion). Most important, Nancy understands Vanda better than his current wife for the simple reason that she shares his perspective on men. Nancy thinks "men are such swine"; he agrees and makes it clear that he would prefer to be left alone to behave in such a manner undisturbed.[37] Nancy's detachment and cynical perspective give Vanda permission to be the person he truly is: someone for whom "togetherness" is anathema; he is a bachelor to the core.

Kiss and Tell and *For Keeps* were based on the same premise — that both father and daughter were rather selfish beings who brought one another to life only in moments of sexual or cynical exchange. When their story was told in an entirely comical fashion, audiences and critics responded positively; when presented with more serious intentions, it was offensive. In both *Kiss and Tell* and *For Keeps*, the hardheadedness, sarcasm, and chemistry of mutual skepticism between father and daughter actually served to bring the two figures together and to define them both. Father and daughter were the realists in Herbert's plays, the ones who provided a running commentary on hopelessly naive young women like Pamela, who was foolish enough to attempt to reform a bachelor in his middle forties. As far as the box office was concerned, however, Herbert learned that it was dangerous to point out the implications of such depictions with statements like "you'll never know." Best to tell the audience that the kind of balance between sarcasm and affection that he managed to strike in *Meet Corliss Archer* and *Kiss and Tell* could provide a workable paradigm in which the distance of skepticism and the tenderness of family life could be reconciled.

Stepfathers, Theater, and Parody
in Vladimir Nabokov's Lolita

"The name . . . is not Humberg and not Humbug, but Herbert,
I mean Humbert, and any room will do."

The comedy and horror inherent in popular narratives of the father-daughter relationship are woven together into a coherent whole in Vladimir Nabokov's "wildly funny" and "dark" novel *Lolita*.[38] Considered one of the great novels of the twentieth century, *Lolita* is difficult to analyze in part because it has meant so much to so many.[39] Adding to this difficulty is the fact that Nabokov's image of the "nymphet" not only has become an American icon but has been re-invented in multiple, historically specific ways since the book's publication in 1955. The author himself has not helped matters; he created "the most allusive and linguistically playful novel in English" since Joyce's *Ulysses* and then refrained from disclosing much about its allusions to those enthralled scholars who would devote themselves to decoding his anagrams, following the trails of his puns, and deciphering his neologisms and verbal tricks.[40] "Satire is a lesson," claimed Nabokov; "parody is a game."[41] Rising to the challenge of the parodic in *Lolita*, Alfred Appel Jr. has engaged in the sport of allusion-chasing, much to our benefit. His *Annotated Lolita* has vastly enriched our understanding of the allusions in *Lolita* and of their thematic significance. Appel also has much to say about Nabokov's "art of assemblage"—the ways in which he combines a vast array of American popular culture and lore, including comics, movies, treatises on female adolescence, and those details of middle-class culture that Nabokov elsewhere called "poshlust," or that which is "falsely beautiful," "falsely clever," and "falsely attractive."[42]

The pastiche applies equally to the characters, who are themselves amalgams of fictional clichés: Charlotte Haze is "Woman"—the "artsy-craftsy suburban lady," the "culture-vulture"; Humbert Humbert, impersonates the hero of an "international novel"; and in the character of Lolita, according to one critic, Nabokov has perfectly realized the "external ambiance" of the mid-1940s teenage girl.[43] Critics have also commented on Humbert's emerging sense of himself as a father as he spends more time with Lolita, this sensibility growing alongside his identity as a pedophile.[44] At the same time, Lolita herself has been assessed both positively and negatively as a person, a teenager, and a daughter.[45] Almost all aspects of character (as well as literary impersonation), however, have been considered independently of one another rather than in terms of qualities that were specific to the father-daughter relationship. In the rare instances when critics have considered the representation of family life in the novel— for Charlotte, Lolita, and Humbert Humbert were a family—they have considered it in terms of Nabokov's concerns with the nature of individual family members: the typical mother, father, and child. Moreover, although aspects of individual character have been analyzed in terms of their references to mass and specifically cinematic cultural forms, none of them has been considered in light of American theater during the early postwar period. This is particularly surprising given that Clare Quilty, Humbert Humbert's doppelgänger, is a playwright; Lolita literally and Humbert Humbert figuratively find themselves "scripted" into one of Quilty's plays; and references to plays and playwrights abound. What has not been considered, then, are the ways in which the interaction or relationship between Humbert Humbert and Lolita (both within and outside of their sexual relationship) was itself a form of black parody of popular representations of the father-daughter relationship and, specifically, how that relationship parodied themes from American theater during the early postwar period.

Much has been made of the fact that Nabokov did a great deal of research on contemporary American girlhood. He visited a school principal, read studies on psychological development, listened to girls riding the school bus, and appropriated phrases from teen magazines, posters, billboards, and home decorating guides.[46] His precision is astounding, and, according to Appel, he succeeds in rendering a devastating commentary on the "Teen and Sub-Teen tyranny" of the period through the character of Lolita.[47] The verisimilitude may owe more to preexisting portraits of adolescent girls *in relationship to their fathers* than literary critics have realized. In Lolita's "first cloth coat with a fur collar" we are presented with one of the "first" objects that mark Judy Grave's coming-of-age in *Junior Miss*.[48] In the way Lolita/Dolores attempts to manipulate Humbert Humbert into changing her mother's mind ("make mother take you and me to Our Glass Lake"), there are echoes of Corliss Archer ("make her say yes").[49] In the references to the fact that Lolita is a "'juvenile delickwent,'" a "wayward girl," Nabokov is reflecting a discourse on female juvenile delinquency that was far more pervasive than historians have realized (see Chapter 3).[50] "A combination of naiveté and deception, of charm and vulgarity . . . Lolita, when she chose, could be a most exasperating brat."[51] An indictment of brattiness (or bitchiness, or trampiness), as we have seen, was a typical theme in the father/stepfather plays and comedies of the period. Within this context, then, what is most important about Lolita's character—the spoiled irreverence, the rudeness, the centrality of consumerism, and her juvenile delinquency—is that all of these attributes were aspects of female adolescence that were evoked in popular culture within the context of the father-daughter relationship. Such aspects of girlhood were rendered either as a form of connection or as a problem between fathers and daughters; they were evoked far less often in popular culture within the context of girls in school, girls on dates, girls with one another, or even girls with their mothers. Thus those specifics upon which Humbert Humbert, as narrator, dwells were contextually related to the father-daughter relationship as it was portrayed in the United States at midcentury.[52] Hence, rather than reflecting a generalized "teen tyranny," Lolita and Humbert Humbert mirrored the specifics of a relationship that was imagined as existing specifically between father and daughter rather than between teenagers and parents or teenagers and adults more broadly.

Perhaps more important, Humbert Humbert and Lolita, like so many of the (step)fathers and daughters portrayed in works of fiction, are startlingly alike—a fact that was easily disguised behind Humbert Humbert's European condescension toward and sense of incredulity about his American bobby-soxer. Of course, Lolita is unknowable outside of Humbert Humbert's self-deluding rendition of her, and thus any likeness between the two can be credited to his own self-absorption.[53] Yet the ways in which the two are alike (and not alike) follow the same pattern of similarity and difference that we saw in Corliss Archer and Mr. Archer and Nancy Vanda and Paul Vanda. Humbert Humbert's portrayal of himself, vainly, emphasizes his "movieland manhood," but he also tells us that his virility has a "sullen" cast.[54] He reveals that his most salient feature is contempt for others, that he is derisive, prickly, sarcastic, and given to profound mood swings.[55] Lolita, whose personality is recounted by others repeatedly throughout the novel, is "sullen and evasive," "rude and defiant"; Humbert describes her as "changeful" and "bad-tempered"; her mother calls her "aggressive ... critical, distrustful, irritable ... listless [and] negativistic."[56] The constant commentary on Lolita serves as a commentary on Humbert Humbert. Indeed, his obsession with Lolita reveals itself as the narcissistic impulse that it is in part because of his insistence on the likeness in their personalities—he celebrates these qualities in Lolita, and in the same way that so many readers have been won over by him, one is necessarily drawn to those "negativistic" qualities in her.[57] Her critical eye lends itself to her strongest suit, which is (occasional) wit, and her defiance is transformed into strength within the context of victimization. But, above all, Lolita is just the kind of girl who helped set the stage for a certain kind of adult masculinity. Her personality lends itself to the kind of paternal cynicism, mischievousness, and antisentimentality (despite Humbert's sentimental feelings for her) that were the hallmark of fathers or stepfathers of adolescent girls during this period. Humbert Humbert was not simply narcissistic in the act of mirroring himself in *his* Lolita but representative of the kind of masculine personality that was often *produced* through a relationship with a teenage daughter.

Nabokov laid out the first draft of Lolita in the form of a novella in Paris in 1939. The idea for the story, however, gestated for a decade, during which time he and his family emigrated to the United States (1940), and by 1949 it "had grown in secret the claws and wings of a novel."[58] Nabokov wrote that he originally abandoned the story because the little girl "possessed little 'semblance of reality,'" but the basic idea of the pedophile who marries a young girl's mother in order to be near his object of desire remained.[59] In the United States he discovered the external lineaments of an engaging personality in a culture fascinated by teenage girls (Lolita is twelve when Humbert Humbert meets her and fourteen when she escapes him). He also discovered ways of rendering the father-daughter relationship rich with double entendre and rife with suggestions that lead, in the mind of the pedophile, from eroticization to sex.

Nabokov also used to great effect the impact of Hollywood on Lolita's girlish imagination within the context of the father-daughter relationship. Moreover, the Oedipal claims that Humbert Humbert ironically states he *should* have on Lolita replicated Helene Deutsch's depiction of the female adolescent Oedipus complex, as well as its representation in popular culture. The child-development text Humbert references was one "with the unintentionally biblical title *Know Your Own Daughter.*" [60] Nabokov maintained that the title, in some form, existed, though he refused to disclose what it was; based on this claim (without being able to locate the text) Alfred Appel has argued that "Nabokov offers us a grotesque parody of a 'good relationship,' for Humbert and Lo are 'pals' with a vengeance." [61] However, the parody here was not of a didactic text on becoming "pals" with one's daughter—a kind of relationship that, as we saw in Chapter 4, was *not* prescribed for fathers and adolescent daughters during this period—but actually a reference to the text *Do you Know Your Daughter* by Alice Barr Grayson. [62] It is the book the displaced father consults on the perplexing activities of his bobby-soxer daughter in the March of Time newsreel "Teenage Girls." [63]

In his 1957 review of *Lolita*, F. W. Dupee noted that all the individual figures in the novel (except Humbert Humbert) had been portrayed in the "many . . . problem plays of modern manners." [64] Dupee was either the only reviewer who actually remembered the stuff of Broadway or the only one to connect these plays to *Lolita*, and herein lies some of the difficulty in situating the novel historically. For Nabokov was faithful specifically to the literature and popular iconography of the period in which the book took place, 1947–51. Moreover, the period in which Nabokov himself gathered information on girls and their fathers/stepfathers, between 1940 and 1949, was the period when plays about the subject were most numerous and at their most influential.

The importance of the fictional playwright Clare Quilty to the text, and the fact that Quilty is Humbert Humbert's double, has been discussed at length elsewhere. [65] The range of references in the figure of Quilty, however, can be extended to include the Broadway plays that were so popular during the period when Quilty himself was writing for the stage (he moves on to film, appropriately enough, in the late 1940s). [66] Here, again, as in the analysis of "girls' culture," scholars have not considered the impact of the theater during this period of history. Quilty's plays are produced in New York; and, more important,

Quilty's nickname is "Cue," an allusion to *Cue: The Guide to Theater and Dining in New York*.[67] Quilty, the author of the play *Fatherly Love* and the man who eventually lures Lolita away from Humbert Humbert, is also a dark parody of the playwrights who produced eroticized depictions of father-daughter relationships, like F. Hugh Herbert.[68]

Could, then, Nabokov have had F. Hugh Herbert in mind when he chose the name Humbert Humbert? Perhaps he did, given his taxonomic approach and his theoretical investment in the meaning inherent in the act of mimicry.[69] Nabokov was nothing if not deliberate, and if he had Humbert Humbert accidentally refer to himself as "Herbert," as he does in a moment of extreme irritation and anticipation, it was probably for a reason—the novel was meant, after all, to be an intellectual game.[70]

Other Links: William Styron's Lie Down in Darkness

The family relationships described in *Lolita* find their greatest precedent in William Styron's *Lie Down in Darkness*. The peculiar agony of an adult man's obsessive love for a "girl child"; a father's identification with a self-involved, cynical, and sharp-tongued daughter; the pedophile's horror of the middle-aged female body all are described in terms that are similar, in almost every detail, to Styron's portrayal of a father's agonizing love for his daughter and the eventual destruction it reaps on his family.

Lie Down in Darkness was William Styron's first book, and it made his literary reputation, which was, in the decade that it took him to publish another one, very distinguished. The book was praised as a great work of art. Critics regularly referred to Styron as one of the finest authors of a generation, and they instantly bequeathed upon him the kind of respect that often takes a lifetime of work to amass.[71] The novel was set in Styron's hometown, Newport News, Virginia, and the novel's structure was reminiscent of that of Faulkner's *As I Lay Dying*: it begins with a funeral and proceeds as a set of interior monologues. Hence the book was immediately classed as part of the "southern tradition."[72] But the thematic links to Faulkner are slight. The family exists, as Louis D. Rubin has pointed out, entirely in the present and suffers from personal rather than historical or communal sins. The book could have been set anywhere. The upper-middle-class milieu in which the family operates has no local peculiarities or odd traditions. What references there are to the larger world that do creep in, and there are only a few, are to Roosevelt and the National Recovery Act, Cezanne, Marx, and, in the final scenes, the U.S. bombing of Nagasaki.

The story is told mostly from the perspective of Milton Loftis, a middle-aged man who, much like Humbert Humbert (and Paul Vanda), still has "the appearance of a gratuitous, if somewhat dissipated youngness."[73] Loftis and his chronically ill, graying, and religiously disciplined wife, Helen, have two daughters: Maudie, who is crippled and mentally deficient (a "mystery of birth"), and Peyton.[74] Peyton is stunningly beautiful, according to everyone; "spoiled rotten," in the words of her mother; and "aggressive and argumentative," in the eyes of her father.[75] Loftis conducts an ongoing affair with Dolly, a local acquaintance, but the affair is a trifle. The only person who excites and holds his attention is Peyton.[76]

The novel is built — again, like so many father-daughter narratives — around three major coming-of-age events: Peyton's "sweet sixteen" birthday party, her college homecoming football game, and her wedding. Each event is a moment that inspires sexual longing on the part of Loftis, and each "abruptly" reminds him of his advancing age. Each is an occasion during which Loftis is called upon to protect Peyton's right to participate in events appropriate to her age in the face of Helen's jealous and controlling rage. He demands that Peyton be allowed to stay at her birthday party when she is caught drinking; he tries to convince Helen to allow Peyton to go out with friends; he protects Peyton when Helen threatens to disrupt the wedding by provoking an argument. What connects these moments most strikingly to the coming-of-age dramas examined in Chapter 4 is Loftis's pivotal role at these symbolic moments: it is he who provides for and ensures that Peyton can take her place among her peers, even when Peyton's behavior borders on delinquent. It should be noted, however, that Loftis protects Peyton from her mother's repressive interference not because he believes in giving adolescent girls some freedom but, rather, because he is enthralled with her (as Mr. Archer is with Corliss). Moreover, because he himself drinks and has affairs (like Mr. Vanda), it would be hypocritical of him to hold her to a code of social conduct he himself cannot abide.

There are several ways in which the erotic dynamics of the father-daughter relationship in *Lie Down in Darkness* mirror F. Hugh Herbert's work and anticipate *Lolita*. In the first encounter we see between Loftis and Peyton is the same mix of physical appreciation, paternal teasing, and youthful insouciance so prevalent in Herbert's stories. The encounter also involves a mock battle over "the funnies," redolent of Corliss's ongoing dispute with Archer over *Esquire*:

> [Loftis] was aroused by a tumble of feet on the grass behind him. . . . She gazed into a little mirror and said again, "I'm beautiful Daddy!" For a moment all of this crushed his heart. . . . He would always remember that moment on the lawn: picking Peyton up with a sudden, almost savage upwelling of love. . . . "Let me see the funnies" [she said]. In his lap the papers lay hopelessly crumpled, printed with small dirty footmarks. He pretended not to notice, yawning . . . "Gimme the funnies." "Don't say 'gimme.'" "Let me, then." . . . She took the funnies without a word and sprawled out on the lawn beside him, reading Jiggs, plucking grass with her toes. In a lazy voice, as if in afterthought, she said, "Thank you very much." He looked down at her. "Children," he murmured, "should respect their parents."[77]

A similar encounter in *Lolita* provides Humbert Humbert with his first pretext for physical intimacy with "his nymphet." But Nabokov's description is much more compact than Styron's:

> My heart beat like a drum as she sat down, cool skirt ballooning, subsiding. With the monkeyish nimbleness that was so typical of that American nymphet, she snatched out of my abstract grip The magazine I had opened. . . . Lo flipped violently through the pages in search of something she wished Humbert to see. Found it at last. . . . I whisked the whole obscene thing away. Next moment, in a sham effort to retrieve it, she was all over me . . . the magazine escaped to the floor like a flustered fowl. . . . Then, with perfect simplicity, the impudent child extended her legs across my lap. . . . I stroked them; there she lolled in the right-hand corner, almost asprawl, Lola the bobby-soxer. . . . Immediately afterward . . . [she] jumped to her feet. . . . There she stood and blinked . . . her eyes passing over me as lightly as they did over the furniture.[78]

The two scenes share much: the horsing around, the mock withhold-ing, the girls' "sham efforts" to grab what they want—the funnies, a popular magazine. Both scenes also contrast the intense, desperate feelings of these men and the thoughtlessness of the girls. It is not simply that the girls are, at this moment, unaware of these men's feel-ings; it is their self-confidence and their self-absorption, their physical aggressiveness and delight, combined with subsequent, total detach-ment—so crushing to the men—that makes these passages so simi-lar, that gives them their frisson above and beyond the simple fact of sexual desire.

The other driving similarity between Peyton and Lolita is their des-perate measures to distance themselves from their fathers' overbear-ing physical desire for them and, as a result of that effort, their de-tachment from sentiment altogether. Loftis is abject in his pursuit of his daughter—kissing, patting on the bottom, hugging, following, chasing ("Didn't she see, how it had been a torture for him all day: this pursuit of something which he had finally despaired of ever at-taining?")[79] There are careful, rhapsodic, florid descriptions of sexual transgression, so full of metaphor as to be too tricky to pin down: "He doesn't know why his heart pounds so nor, when he kisses her again, in an agony of love, why she should push him so violently away with her warm small hands."[80] The definitive incestuous event is at Peyton's wedding, after Loftis has spent the entire evening in a heated state of sexual desire. "*Now don't be an ass*, his conscience said, but she seemed to be fading from him, vanishing in a powder of crushed-up dreams, and he found himself beside her, kissing her in front of everyone, much more than a father."[81] Her response—"Don't *smother* me, Daddy!" is a repetition of a plea she made in private before the ceremony: "I love you but please lay off all the sentimental slop today . . . don't smother me."[82] Peyton's antisentimentalism applies not only to her father, but to the wedding ceremony itself ("look at this cir-cus") and middle-class conventions in general. She is "bored" and "unexcited" by the prospect of the party being thrown in honor of her marriage, finds it all to be fake and ridiculous. Lolita, the "cynical nymphet" is similarly bored by "wholesome" activities, and, during Humbert's more gentle "nuzzling," she tells him to "lay off" what she calls the "romantic slosh."[83]

In both books, the girls' rejection of sentiment is tied, on the one hand, to their attempt to free themselves from their fathers' physical demands, and, on the other, to what seems to be a disdain for official pieties, whether religious "rot" (Peyton) or "The Girl Scouts motto" (Lolita).[84] The girls' attitude is mirrored in Loftis's and Humbert Humbert's ongoing critiques of the largely feminine middle-class culture around them. The father and daughter's shared cynical perspective binds them together even as it excludes the possibility of a more affective relationship between them.

Would Loftis's and Humbert's "sentimental slop"—their demonstrative romanticism and affection—continue or grow in the event that Lolita or Peyton accepted such overtures? What would happen if the girls returned those feelings, and put up with their fathers' sexual demands as well? It is a scenario that is unimaginable, not only because it is taboo, but also because Peyton and Lolita are incapable of such feelings. How they got to be that way (who or what is responsible for their cynicism) is not at issue here and has been debated elsewhere.[85] The point is that the girls' disdain for (feminine) sentiment creates an unbreachable barrier between father and daughter. The father-daughter relationship thus becomes all the more starkly sexual, the feelings of tenderness on the part of the fathers all the more disconnected from the reality of the situation, superfluous and without purpose. Because Peyton and Lolita are uninterested—at times disdainful—of paternal expressions of affection, their fathers are absolved of a certain measure of emotional responsibility. If emotional needs are not evident, the question of meeting them becomes moot.

Literary Criticism and Narratives of Father-Daughter Incest

The name Peyton reappeared in 1956 in Grace Metalious's best-selling novel, *Peyton Place*, about two teenage girls, one who suffers from a romantic longing for her missing father, and another who is raped by her stepfather. Metalious's use of the name Peyton, according to Emily Toth, was a reference to a character in Henry Bellamann's *King's Row*, a novel that had gone through eighteen printings by the time Metalious read it in 1943.[86] *King's Row* is about a psychoanalyst, Dr. Tower, who moves to a small Midwestern town, and a local boy,

Parris, who becomes his student. Parris is enchanted with Dr. Tower's mysterious daughter, Cassie, but Dr. Tower refuses to allow her to see him because, as it is revealed at the end of the book, he is guilty of having committed incest with her. Peyton, Parris's boyhood friend and one of a large number of supporting characters, has an affair with and then marries a black woman, much to the dismay of town residents. Metalious's fictional town in New Hampshire is named for its founder, Samuel Peyton, an escaped slave who married a white woman, made a fortune in Europe, then returned to New England with his wife to live in a castle — imported stone by stone from Europe. Though Metalious discussed her debt to Bellamann publicly, there is no record of her mentioning Styron. This is odd, given the unusual similarities in the sexual content of their books, as well as Styron's use of the name Peyton. Styron, meanwhile, discussed his references to William Faulkner but not to Bellamann.[87] This is also odd, given the distinctiveness of the name, the books' common theme of father-daughter incest, the authors' limited and uncomfortable use of symbolic black characters, and the popularity of *King's Row* during the years leading up to the publication of *Lie Down in Darkness*.[88] The question then becomes, why did contemporary reviewers, literary critics, and journalists fail to notice these connections?

The historical record suggests some explanations. First, what most postwar critics were looking for in Nabokov and Styron, and to a lesser extent Bellamann and Metalious, were problems of moral order in the modern world. Repeatedly in the reviews of these books, in one form or another, the reviewers state that there is simply "no moral to be drawn" from them.[89] As William Graebner has said, a sense of doubt, ambivalence, and contingency pervaded postwar culture during the 1940s and early 1950s. "This doubt," he writes, "was rooted in the forebodings of an age that had witnessed a war that left sixty million persons dead; the murder of six million Jews in the Holocaust; the development and use of the atomic bomb; the Great Depression, which seemed always on the verge of reappearing."[90] It was against this backdrop that American intellectuals and critics, through the writings of Arthur Schlesinger, Reinhold Niebuhr, and Lionel Trilling, had come "to appreciate the absurdity of absolute innocence in a contingent world."[91] In the eyes of postwar intellectuals, modern America was sexually tolerant, technologically omnipotent, racially backward, and morally disoriented. Literary critics argued over whether Styron's "suspended nihilism" could offer any "life affirming purpose" or whether Nabokov's cold mimesis of American "poshlust" allowed for moral discernment.[92] We may, however, enrich these "big" questions by asking why these writers turned to the father–adolescent daughter relationship as peculiarly emblematic of their time—a time that was, as one critic described Peyton Loftis, "haunted, alienated, desolate."[93]

The second reason postwar critics failed to notice the connections between the works studied here was that they categorized books in terms of literary merit. While *Peyton Place* could legitimately be compared to *King's Row*, the immediate response to *Lie Down in Darkness* was that it was "art," and that it was part of the "Southern Tradition," hence any thematic links to Bellamann would have been not only inappropriate but detrimental to the case for Styron's greatness, of which many were convinced.[94] The same holds true for Metalious— she and Styron, in the eyes of the literary establishment, would have nothing in common. The lack of a perceived connection between Styron and Nabokov, however, is harder to account for. Nabokov, when compared to other authors at all, was likened to Gogol and Dostoyevsky. Moreover, whereas *Lie Down in Darkness* was a tragedy, *Lolita* was most often referred to as satire. Still, the similarities are so profound that we must look elsewhere in order to understand why such overt literary connections were ignored.

Another way to approach the issue of what was and was not visible to the postwar intellectual establishment is to think about these works in terms of the way Linda Nochlin has described the functioning of ideology in representations of women in the history of art. According to Nochlin, "commonsense views about the world," particularly those concerning ideologically central issues about women and gender, are usually "invisible" because they are taken for granted.[95] While father-daughter incest was not taken for granted by postwar culture, it did not especially offend the sensibilities of midcentury critics. In fact, reviewers of *Lolita* regularly reprimanded anyone who might be revolted by its sexual content. Lionel Trilling's comment on the matter was typical: "We have all become so nicely clear-eyed, so sensibly Coming-of-Age-in-Samoa. But let an adult male seriously think about the girl as a sexual object and all our sensibility is revolted."[96]

But revulsion to the sexual content of *Lolita* was the exception, and Trilling's impatience with it was preemptive. The vast majority of reviews of the novel were insistent about the acceptability of *Lolita*, and discomfort with the subject matter was regularly denounced as unsophisticated and immature.[97] Indeed, reviewers of novels that described incidents of father-daughter incest published between 1940 and 1956 were uniformly accepting of their content. None of the reviewers of *Lie Down in Darkness*, for example, condemned the depiction of an incestuous relationship between father and daughter, and reviews of *Kings Row* and *Peyton Place* simply put incest on a long list of uglinesses that were part of such exposés of rural or small-town life.

In "Two Modern Incest Heroes," an article that appeared in *Partisan Review* in 1961, the psychoanalyst Selma Fraiberg made a case for the literary "incest hero" that provides us with some clues about the nature of thinking about father-daughter incest in postwar American novels. Freud's revelation about the "ubiquitous [and] universal dread of incest," she argued, had not been particularly good for novelists: in the post-Freudian mid-twentieth century the tragic nature of the discovery of the repressed wish for incest had been diminished.[98] Novels thus suffered in their capacity to surprise, having taken on a "clinical drabness."[99] Can the Oedipus complex, she asked, still be "material for tragedy?" Yes, she said, as long as it was treated with "irony" and "wit," indeed, as "comedy"—a stance that allowed for the fact that those who participated in incestuous sex already knew what they were doing, accepted it, and rose above it. "The heroic act," she wrote, was "the casting off of pretense." For this reason, she contended, one of the best incest stories of recent years was Ralph Ellison's *Invisible Man* (1947), which presents a "burlesque of the incest myth."[100]

In *Invisible Man*, Jim Trueblood is a sharecropper who has achieved local notoriety by sleeping with his daughter. Her age is not given, but she appears to be in her twenties. As Trueblood tells it, he was in a half-asleep, half-awakened state when he reached for her in the bed that he and his wife shared with their daughter. Upon discovering what has transpired, his wife attempts to kill him, but only succeeds in maiming him. Trueblood runs away; but, after taking measure of the situation, he returns, telling himself, "I ain't nobody but myself and ain't nothin' I can do but let whatever is gonna happen,

happen."[101] Though Trueblood is a disgrace to the black community, his fortunes improve when he becomes an object of fascination to the "white folks" who give him money and tobacco in return for telling and retelling his story.[102] Trueblood, according to Fraiberg, is a hero because, after pondering his "sin," he returns to his family. "In this way," Fraiberg wrote, "he reverses the classic fate of the incest hero. Instead of an Oedipus blinded we are given an Oedipus newly sighted."[103] When Trueblood decides to go home and face his crime and assume his masculine prerogatives, "God approves and rewards him by causing him to prosper." This turn of events suggested to her that "we are left to conclude that it is the myth that destroys, and the heroic act for modern man is the casting off of pretense."[104]

There are, however, a few details in Fraiberg's article that suggest that her perceptual framework applied to some incestuous situations and not others. At the outset of her article, Fraiberg claimed that the incestuous desire of an adult man for his mother was revolting. "A boy's love for his mother does not offend," she argued, "while the incestuous love of the man [for his mother] . . . sometimes repels. It's easy to see why. This love belongs to childhood." Thus the incestuous love of an adult man—and one must assume a young adult man as well—for his mother "repels," but the love of an adult man for his daughter (as in the case of Trueblood) does not.[105]

If we take Fraiberg's forthright article as an indication of postwar attitudes toward incest, it is safe to say that the idea of mother-son incest remained "repulsive," while, at the same time, psychoanalytic concepts were being deployed as a means to come to terms with father-daughter incest. And, indeed, John Hollander, using language similar to Fraiberg's, observed in his review of *Lolita* in 1956: "By parading the theme of incest with drums and banners, Mr. Nabokov makes it ridicule itself out of existence. . . . *Lolita*, far from being mythic, is anti-mythic in this respect."[106]

Lolita, when viewed in light both of what came before and of the intellectual paradigms through which it was interpreted, should be viewed as anything but a *success de scandal*. It was a reflection, an assemblage, a mimesis not only of the kitschiness of American life, or its Freudianism, or its consumerism, or its obsession with adolescent girls, but also—and I would argue that this is its most trenchant observation—of the eroticized father–adolescent daughter relationship as it was everywhere described in the 1940s and 1950s. *Lolita* was a blueprint of all contemporary works about fathers and adolescent daughters. Whether this is its particular achievement or potential limitation is an artistic rather than historical question, and I set it aside here. However, critics and reviewers failed to call attention to common themes in *King's Row*, *Lie Down in Darkness*, *Invisible Man*, the plays of F. Hugh Herbert, *Lolita*, and *Peyton Place* because they found such themes unnoteworthy. To comprehend the lack of response to father-daughter incest in these novels one must understand not simply how some critics self-consciously embraced the "casting off of pretense" but how the stage had already been set for such an intellectual endeavor by the relentless eroticization of the father-daughter relationship on all levels of culture, and thus how, when this shocking literary event occurred, everyone was prepared.

Epilogue

> *If you don't protect her it's unendurable. If you do protect her it's*
> *unendurable. It's all unendurable. The awfulness of her terrible*
> *autonomy. The worst of the world had taken his child. If only that*
> *beautifully chiseled body had never been born.*
> —Philip Roth, American Pastoral, 1997

In 1966, Marjorie Leonard, professor of psychiatry at the Albert Einstein College of Medicine, published an article with the simple title "Fathers and Daughters" in the *International Journal of Psychoanalysis*. The article claimed that the role of fathers in the emotional development of girls outside of that of "Oedipal object" remained obscure to psychoanalysts. We still, she maintained, do not know what "we mean by fathering."[1] Although she, like her predecessors, acknowledged the need for a positive Oedipal experience during adolescence, she stated that "following the Oedipal conflict, the girl must establish a *desexualized* object-relationship to her father, enabling her to . . . give love to a young man in her peer group."[2] Leonard concluded her article with the admonishment, "It takes a mature man . . . to be able to offer his daughter desexualized affection at the crucial stages in her development."[3] Leonard's article represents the first mention since the 1930s of the notion that a girl could, or should, move beyond an Oedipal relationship with her father.

A few years earlier, in 1963, *Life* magazine published a series of articles on high school life—much like those that had appeared during World War II—investigating the clubs, fads, and fashions of American teenage girls. Profiling the "most popular girl" at a California high school, Jill Dinwiddie, the article cataloged the various pressures Jill felt "to be like everybody else."[4] Adult society, the article lamented, did not provide American girls with examples of how to be "an individual."[5] Several sociologists were called upon to analyze the attitudes that Jill exhibited. One found that Jill and her friends were "exploited for external attributes only," while another complained that they had been reduced to "glistening-eyed shoppers."[6] In the photographs of the girls trying on various costumes for school activities, their facial expressions reflect joyless acquiescence rather than irreverent fun. The sense of excitement that had informed articles on teenage girl's social activities and consumer behavior in the 1940s was replaced with critique and condescension. High school society was judged to be shallow and oppressive. Marjorie Leonard's criticism of the Oedipalization of fatherhood was one part of a larger attack on the psychoanalytic interpretation of the feminine personality that had begun in the early 1960s. The condemnation of Jill Dinwiddie in the pages of *Life* coincided with the disappearance of teenage girls from stage, screen, and radio. With interest shifting away from both the Oedipus complex and teenage girls, the father–adolescent daughter relationship ceased to hold the public's interest.

After a brief, and relative, hiatus during the 1970s and 1980s, teenage girls reemerged in the 1990s as a dominant cultural concern, and they remain so at the beginning of the twenty-first century.[7] It is a cultural focus that is, as it was in the 1940s and 1950s, predominantly sexual. The suggestiveness of teen and preteen fashions; anxieties about "body image"; teen pregnancy; sexual abuse and repressed memory syndrome; how girls are designated "sluts" and "bad girls" by their peers; the extent to which menarche is arriving at earlier ages — these are the subjects of animated discussion on the part of social psychologists, journalists, and social commentators.[8] Meanwhile, advertisements, teen films, and music videos churn out an inescapable barrage of sexually provocative images of teenage girls. Some of the best contemporary social criticism has been concerned with the impact of commercial culture on girls' identity, or, as Joan Jacobs Brumberg recently put it, "the interaction between the garish commercial culture . . . and the psyches of ordinary girls."[9] Those who write more particularly about fathers and daughters believe that the sexualization of adolescent girls in popular culture has been damaging to the relationship: buffeted by an expanding commercial culture on the one hand and changes in mores amongst teenagers themselves on the other, the father-daughter relationship is anxiously diagnosed as beset with sexual discomfort. When girls reach adolescence, the father-daughter relationship becomes, to use Mary Pipher's word, "treacherous."[10] It is a relationship that remains, it would seem, a dilemma.

However, the perception that the relationship between adolescent daughter and father suffers from an onslaught of forces that originated outside itself ignores the cultural role that this relationship played in the sexualization of teenage girls in the first place. As we have seen, fathers in the 1940s and 1950s were accomplices in their adolescent daughters' sartorial designs and were major figures in the cultural project of transforming their sexual status. The father–adolescent daughter relationship was the apparatus through which the sexualization of the teenage girl was envisioned. The dictates of the adolescent Oedipus complex provided the reason for the eroticization of the teenage girl's relationship to her father, and the commercialization of youth culture provided the rationale. The eroticization of the father-daughter relationship helped transform the cultural perception of girls' sexuality in larger ways because of that relationship's inherent authority. Who more important to turn to than a girl's father when attempting to explain changes in her behavior? Who better to validate her increasingly visible sexual coming-of-age? Who more unassailable in sanctioning the transformation of her public image?

The most immediately visible effect of the depiction of fathers' intimate involvement in their daughters' sexuality was, in fact, to render her status more fully and inescapably sexual. In the 1940s and 1950s, teenage girls related as sexual beings not only to boys at school or men in public but to their fathers at home as well. With the eroticization of the father-daughter relationship, girls became sexualized in every context of their lives. Cultural perceptions of men were similarly compromised by formulas of eroticization: fathers were perceived to be on the one hand overwhelmed by their daughters' sexual allure and on the other suspicious of its aims. But by far the most insidious effect of the eroticization of the relationship between adolescent girls and fathers was to set new limits on girls' identity. The postwar depiction of the father-daughter relationship circumscribed girls' autonomy by reducing a range of behaviors to Oedipal needs and by viewing girls' expression—whether sartorial, sexual, or social acts— as bound up with parental ties rather than part of a larger encounter with the world. The eroticized father–adolescent daughter relationship contributed to a diminished vision of girlhood—its goals, personality, and public face. Amid the strides made in this period for girls—better schools, inclusion in the nation's vision of the future, cultural prominence, commercial influence, new social freedoms— the eroticization of the father-daughter relationship stands as a set-back, if not a counterweight, to an otherwise open future.

✑ Notes

INTRODUCTION

Epigraph. Lionel Trilling, "The Other Margaret," *Partisan Review* 12 (Fall 1945): 495.

1. *Life*, December 15, 1941, cover.

2. G. Stanley Hall, "Flapper Americana Novissima," *Atlantic*, June 1922, p. 779.

3. Ibid.

4. Interview with Postmaster General Robert E. Hannegan, in "Prognosis for Parents," *Seventeen*, November 1945, p. 100.

5. John Modell, *Into One's Own: From Youth to Adulthood in the United States, 1920–1975* (Berkeley: University of California Press, 1989), p. 170.

6. Thomas Hine, *The Rise and Fall of the American Teenager* (New York: Avon, 1999); Grace Palladino, *Teenagers: An American History* (New York: Basic Books, 1996).

7. On the growth of sexual liberalism in the twentieth century, see John D'Emilio and Estelle B. Freedman, *Intimate Matters: A History of Sexuality in America* (New York: Harper and Row, 1988), and Pamela Haag, *Consent: Sexual Rights and the Transformation of American Liberalism*. Ithaca: Cornell University Press, 1999.

8. Hine, *Rise and Fall of the American Teenager*, p. 228.

9. Modell, *Into One's Own*, p. 235.

10. Joseph Kett, *Rites of Passage: Adolescence in America, 1790 to the Present* (New York: Basic Books, 1977), p. 269.

11. Frances Bruce Strain, *"But You Just Don't Understand": A Dramatic Series of Teen-Age Predicaments* (New York: Appleton, 1950); Robert Paul Smith, *"Where Did You Go?" "Out" "What Did You Do?" "Nothing"* (New York: Norton, 1957); James S. Coleman, *The Adolescent Society: The Social Life of the Teenager and Its Impact on Education* (New York: Free Press, 1961); Grace Hechinger and Fred M. Hechinger, *Teen-Age Tyranny* (New York: William Morrow, 1962).

12. Christopher Lasch, *Haven in a Heartless World: The Family Besieged* (New York: Basic Books, 1977), p. 175.

13. Frank Rich, "Oh, What a Miserable Mornin'," *New York Times Magazine*, October 28, 2001, p. 58.

14. Stephen J. Whitfield, *The Culture of the Cold War* (Baltimore: Johns Hopkins University Press, 1991), p. 155.

15. Leila J. Rupp and Verta Taylor, *Survival in the Doldrums: The American Women's Rights Movement, 1945 to the 1960s* (New York: Oxford University Press, 1987).

16. Wini Breines, *Young, White and Miserable: Growing up Female in the Fifties* (Boston: Beacon Press, 1992). For an attempt to prove that housewives were "delighted" with life in the suburbs, see James T. Patterson, *Grand Expectations: The United States, 1945–1974* (New York: Oxford University Press, 1996), p. 366.

17. Susan Lynn, "Gender and Progressive Politics: A Bridge to Social Activism of the 1960s," in Joanne Meyerowitz, ed., *Not June Cleaver: Women and Gender in Postwar America, 1945–1965* (Philadelphia: Temple University Press, 1994), pp. 103–27.

18. Frederic Jameson, *Postmodernism or the Cultural Logic of Late Capitalism* (Durham: Duke University Press, 1992), p. 19.

19. Ibid.

20. William Tuttle, *"Daddy's Gone to War": The Second World War in the Lives of America's Children* (New York: Oxford University Press, 1993), p. 215.

21. Ibid., pp. 213–30.

22. Philip Wylie, *Generation of Vipers* (New York: Farrar and Rinehart, 1942); David Levy, *Maternal Overprotection* (New York: Columbia University Press, 1943); Joseph Pleck, "American Fathering in Historical Perspective," in *Changing Men: New Directions in Research on Men and Masculinity*, ed. Michel Kimmel (Newbury Park, Calif.: Sage, 1987), p. 92; Steven Mintz and Susan Kellogg, *Domestic Revolutions: A Social History of American Family Life* (New York: Free Press, 1988), p. 184.

23. Reuben Hill, "The Returning Father and His Family," *Journal of Marriage and Family Living* (Spring 1945): 31. See also Robert Griswold, *Fatherhood in America: A History* (New York: Basic Books, 1993), p. 207.

24. For a historical theory about why psychoanalysis has been more popular in the United States than anywhere else in the world, see John Demos, "Oedipus in America: Historical Perspectives on the Reception of Psychoanalysis in the United States," *Annual of Psychoanalysis* 6 (1978): 23–39.

25. Nathan G. Hale Jr., *The Rise and Crisis of Psychoanalysis in the United States: Freud and the Americans, 1917–1985* (New York: Oxford University Press, 1995). Freud graced the cover of *Time* in 1956; see "The Explorer," *Time*, April 23, 1956; see also Nancy Lynch, "A Walk in a Dark Room," *Mademoiselle*, October 1957, 98, 146–53.

26. Michael Paul Rogin, *"Ronald Reagan," the Movie: And Other Episodes in Political Demonology* (Berkeley: University of California Press, 1987), p. 252.

27. Rebecca Plant, "The Repeal of Mother-Love: Momism and the Reconstruction of Motherhood in Philip Wylie's America" (Ph.D. dissertation, Johns

Hopkins University, 2001). See also Molly Ladd-Taylor and Lauri Umansky, eds., *"Bad" Mothers: The Politics of Blame in Twentieth-Century America* (New York: New York University Press, 1998).

28. See, for instance, Margaret L. Meiss, "The Oedipal Problem of a Father-less Child," *Psychoanalytic Study of the Child* 7 (1952): 216–29. See also Tal-cott Parsons, *Social Structure and Personality* (New York: Free Press of Glencoe, 1964), pp. 72–73.

29. Mary Ryan, *The Cradle of the Middle Class: The Family in Oneida County, New York, 1790–1865* (New York: Cambridge University Press, 1981), p. 101.

30. On this transformation, see also John Demos, *Past, Present and Personal: The Family and the Life Course in American History* (New York: Oxford University Press, 1986).

31. Margaret Marsh, *Suburban Lives* (New Brunswick, N.J.: Rutgers University Press, 1990), p. 80.

32. Griswold, *Fatherhood*, p. 121.

33. Peter Gabriel Filene, *Him/Her/Self: Sex Roles in Modern America* (Baltimore: Johns Hopkins University Press, 1974); on the ways in which television was thought to be emasculating, see Lynn Spigel, *Make Room for TV: Television and the Family Ideal in Postwar America* (Chicago: University of Chicago Press, 1992), pp. 60–65.

34. Because of the obviousness of the decline of patriarchy over the course of the twentieth century, questions of power have been disconnected from discussions of fatherhood. When addressing questions about fatherhood, historians have concentrated less on power than on the ways in which ideologies of child rearing have created a deeply entrenched division of labor. In other words, how the need for sustaining the family economically (the primary definition of what it has meant to be a father) has secured the best work for men and diminished women's professional opportunities while relegating the entire burden of child rearing (in addition to household maintenance) to women. What has not been explored is the extent to which men have been constituted as powerful figures in twentieth-century American culture *as fathers*—that is, men who have a proprietary relationship to children—rather than simply as breadwinners for the sake of children. Historians of fatherhood—who are, in fairness, operating within a much younger historiography—have mostly sought to recover a lost history of paternal efforts at involvement on the one hand and of the growth of the breadwinner ethic that has so severely curtailed those efforts on the other. See Ralph LaRossa, *The Modernization of Fatherhood: A Social and Political History* (Chicago: University of Chicago Press, 1997). On the history of masculinity and power, see E. Anthony Rotundo, *American Manhood: Transformations in Masculinity from the Revolution to the Modern Era* (New York: Basic

Books, 1993); Gail Bederman, *Manliness and Civilization: A Cultural History of Gender and Race in the United States, 1880–1917* (Chicago: University of Chicago Press, 1995); Kim Townsend, *Manhood at Harvard: William James and Others* (Cambridge: Harvard University Press, 1996); and Kristin L. Hoganson, *Fighting for American Manhood: How Gender Politics Provoked the Spanish-American and Philippine-American Wars* (New Haven: Yale University Press, 1998).

35. Geoffrey Gorer, *The American People: A Study in National Character* (New York: Norton, 1948), p. 54.

36. O. Spurgeon English and Constance J. Foster, *Fathers Are Parents, Too: A Constructive Guide to Successful Fatherhood* (New York: G. P. Putnam's Sons, 1951), p. ix.

37. One could refer to this form of paternal power as "patriarchy." For historians, the term "patriarchy" conjures up images of the seventeenth- and eighteenth-century family, in which a father's social and legal right to rule over his family, including his wife and all other dependent family members, was total and the subordination of the family to the father was the foundation of the social order. Alternately, "patriarchal" has been used, colloquially, as a catch-all phrase to describe systemic sexism. This use of the word is a legacy of early second-wave feminist theorists' descriptions of the historical roots of the relations between the sexes. "Patriarchy," in the late 1960s and early 1970s, was used to refer both to the historical nature of the oppression of women and to universal, political power structures based on male domination. The more exact meaning of the word, as Linda Gordon has recently pointed out, is a "subcategory of male dominance, a particular social/economic/political system of father domination, not just male dominance." See Linda Gordon and Allen Hunter, "Not All Male Dominance Is Patriarchal," *Radical History Review* 71 (Spring 1988): 72. I hesitate to use that term here, as it still carries with it connotations of more universal forms of male dominance. On patriarchy in the eighteenth century, see Kathleen M. Brown, *Good Wives, Nasty Wenches, and Anxious Patriarchs: Gender, Race, and Power in Colonial Virginia* (Chapel Hill: University of North Carolina Press, 1996), and Lawrence Stone, *The Family, Sex and Marriage in England, 1500–1800* (New York: Harper and Row, 1977). For a good example of the concept in the late 1960s, see Kate Millett, *Sexual Politics* (Garden City, N.Y.: Doubleday, 1970). She says, "If one takes patriarchal government to be the institution whereby that half of the populace which is female is controlled by that half which is male, the principles of patriarchy appear to be twofold: male shall dominate female, elder male shall dominate younger" (p. 25).

38. Jessica Weiss, *To Have and to Hold: Marriage, the Baby Boom, and Social Change* (Chicago: University of Chicago Press, 2000), p. 103. "Men remained providers, first, and buddies and sex-role models, second" (Griswold, *Father-*

hood, p. 6). It is in large part these kinds of work schedules and the pressure to provide for the ever-rising standards of the middle-class lifestyle that led Griswold to argue that, for the bulk of middle-class men in the 1950s, breadwinning *was* fatherhood—it fulfilled their most important responsibility to the family and their highest obligation as men.

39. On the relationship between class and sexuality at the turn of the century, see Glenda Gilmore, *Gender and Jim Crow: Women and the Politics of White Supremacy in North Carolina, 1896–1920* (Chapel Hill: University of North Carolina Press, 1996); on sexuality and race, see Robyn Wiegman, *American Anatomies: Theorizing Race and Gender* (Durham: Duke University Press, 1995). On the embodiment of white fears and desires in the black body, see Toni Morrison, *Playing in the Dark: Whiteness in the Literary Imagination* (New York: Vintage, 1992). On the need to interrogate "whiteness" for its racial specificity, see Hazel Carby, *Reconstructing Womanhood: The Emergence of the Afro-American Woman Novelist* (New York: Oxford University Press, 1987); David Roediger, *The Wages of Whiteness: Race and the Making of the American Working Class* (New York: Verso, 1991); and Matthew Frye Jacobson, *Whiteness of a Different Color: European Immigrants and the Alchemy of Race* (Cambridge: Harvard University Press, 1998).

40. Helen Deutsch, *The Psychology of Women*, vol. 1 (New York: Grune and Stratton, 1944), p. 89.

41. *Newsweek*, March 15, 1954, p. 2.

42. Andrea Huyssen, *After the Great Divide: Modernism, Mass Culture, Postmodernism* (Bloomington: Indiana University Press, 1986), esp. ch. 3; Victoria De Grazia, ed., *The Sex of Things: Gender and Consumption in Historical Perspective* (Berkeley: University of California Press, 1996); William Leach, "Transformations in a Culture of Consumption: Women and Department Stores, 1890–1925," *Journal of American History* 71 (September 1984): 319–42.

43. For diatribes against wives' spending, see Philip Wylie, *Generation of Vipers* (New York: Farrar and Rinehart, 1942), and Barbara Ehrenreich's discussion of Hugh Hefner in her *The Hearts of Men: American Dreams and the Flight from Commitment* (New York: Anchor, 1983).

44. This study does not discuss television. This is largely because none of the family shows that portrayed fathers and their children, most of which did not appear until the late 1950s, were among the top twenty-five in the Nielsen ratings. As Ralph LaRossa points out, we are familiar with *The Adventures of Ozzie and Harriet* and *Father Knows Best* because they have been popular as reruns. Also, fathers and sons were much more prevalent on television than fathers and daughters. See Ralph LaRossa, "The Culture of Fatherhood in the Fifties: A Closer Look," *Journal of Family History* 29 (January 2004): 47–70.

45. Foundational texts on the history of sexuality include Michel Foucault,

The History of Sexuality, vol. 1 (New York: Random House, 1978); Ann Snitow, Chirstine Stansell, and Sharon Thompson, *Powers of Desire: The Politics of Sexuality* (New York: Monthly Review Press, 1983); and Irene Diamond and Lee Quinby, *Feminism and Foucault: Reflections on Resistance* (Boston: Northeastern University Press, 1988).

46. Keith Thomas, "History and Literature" (Swansea: University College of Swansea, 1988), p. 19.

47. William H. Prescott, "Irving's *Conquest of Granada*," cited in David A. Boruchoff, ed., *Isabel La Catolica, Queen of Castile: Critical Essays* (New York: Palgrave, 2003), p. 1.

48. On contradiction and contestation in the ideological construction of gender in general, and the nineteenth century in particular, see Mary Poovey, *Uneven Developments: The Ideological Work of Gender in Mid-Victorian England* (Chicago: University of Chicago Press, 1988).

CHAPTER ONE

1. Kata Levy, "Simultaneous Analysis of a Mother and Her Adolescent Daughter: The Mother's Contribution to the Loosening of the Infantile Object Tie," *Psychoanalytic Study of the Child* 15 (1960): 384.

2. Ibid.

3. Rose W. Coleman, Ernst Kris, and Sally Provence, "The Study of Variations of Early Parental Attitudes," *Psychoanalytic Study of the Child* 8 (1953): 20–47. See also Ernst Kris, "Notes on the Development and on Some Current Problems of Psychoanalytic Child Psychology," *Psychoanalytic Study of the Child* 5 (1950): 24–46.

4. David Levy, *Maternal Overprotection* (New York: Columbia University Press, 1943), pp. 20–37.

5. Joel Pfister, "Glamorizing the Psychological: The Politics of the Performances of Modern Psychological Identities," in Joel Pfister and Nancy Schnog, eds., *Inventing the Psychological: Toward a Cultural History of Emotional Life in America* (New Haven: Yale University Press, 1997), p. 186.

6. Nathan G. Hale Jr., *The Rise and Crisis of Psychoanalysis in the United States: Freud and the Americans, 1917–1985* (New York: Oxford University Press, 1995), p. 205.

7. David Wilbern, "Filia Oedipi: Father and Daughter in Freudian Theory," in Lynda E. Boose and Betty S. Flowers, eds., *Daughters and Fathers* (Baltimore: Johns Hopkins University Press, 1989).

8. Hale, *Rise and Crisis of Psychoanalysis*, p. 276.

9. John Burnham, *Paths into American Culture: Psychology, Medicine, and Morals* (Philadelphia: Temple University Press, 1988), p. 100.

10. Ibid.

11. Mari Jo Buhle, *Feminism and Its Discontents: A Century of Struggle with Psychoanalysis* (Cambridge: Harvard University Press, 1998), p. 169.

12. Peter Blos, *On Adolescence: A Psychoanalytic Interpretation* (New York: Free Press of Glencoe, 1962), p. 69.

13. Buhle, *Feminism and Its Discontents*, p. 77.

14. Paul Roazen, *Helene Deutsch: A Psychoanalyst's Life* (New York: Anchor/ Doubleday, 1985), pp. 271–90.

15. Ralph P. Truitt, M.D., *The Child Guidance Clinic and the Community: A Group of Papers Written from the Viewpoints of the Clinic, the Juvenile Court, the School, the Child Welfare Agency, and the Parent* (New York: Commonwealth Fund, 1928).

16. On the mushrooming of studies on adolescence in the United States after the war, see Leo A. Spiegel, "A Review of the Contributions to a Psychoanalytic Theory of Adolescence," *Psychoanalytic Study of the Child* 6 (1951): 375–93; Irene Josselyn, "The Ego in Adolescence," *American Journal of Orthopsychiatry* 24 (April 1954): 223–37; Elisabeth R. Geleerd, "Some Aspects of Psychoanalytic Technique in Adolescence," *Psychoanalytic Study of the Child* 12 (1957): 394–405; Leo Spiegel, "Comments on the Psychoanalytic Psychology of Adolescence," *Psychoanalytic Study of the Child* 13 (1958): 296–308; Edith Buxbaum, "Panel Reports: The Psychology of Adolescence," *Journal of the American Psychoanalytic Association* 6 (1958): 111–20; Anna Freud, "Adolescence," *Psychoanalytic Study of the Child* 13 (1958): 255–78; Elisabeth Geleerd, "Some Aspects of Ego Vicissitudes in Adolescence," *Journal of the American Psychoanalytic Association* 9 (1961): 394–405; and Blos, *On Adolescence*.

17. John D'Emilio and Estelle B. Freedman, *Intimate Matters: A History of Sexuality in America* (New York: Harper and Row, 1988), p. 261. See also Kathleen W. Jones, *Taming the Troublesome Child: American Families, Child Guidance, and the Limits of Psychiatric Authority* (Cambridge: Harvard University Press, 1999), ch. 2.

18. On early dating and marriage practices, see Beth Bailey, *From Front Porch to Back Seat: Courtship in Twentieth-Century America* (Baltimore: Johns Hopkins University Press, 1988), and Elaine Tyler May, *Homeward Bound: American Families in the Cold War Era* (New York: Basic Books, 1988).

19. In the psychoanalytic literature of the postwar period, the number of articles specifically on female adolescence outnumbered those on boys (this finding based on a survey of the following journals, 1945–65: *Psychoanalytic Study of the Child, Journal of the American Psychoanalytic Association, American Journal of Orthopsychiatry*, and *American Journal of Psychiatry*).

20. Helene Deutsch, *The Psychology of Women*, vol. 1 (New York: Grune and Stratton, 1944), p. 117.

21. Sigmund Freud, "Three Essays on the Theory of Sexuality" (1905), in

James Strachey, trans. and ed., *Standard Edition of the Complete Psychological Works of Sigmund Freud* (London: Hogarth Press, 1953); "Femininity" (1933), in James Strachey, trans. and ed., *Introductory Lectures on Psycho-Analysis* (New York: Norton, 1989), p. 47.

22. Sigmund Freud, *A General Introduction to Psychoanalysis* (New York: Washington Square Press, 1952), pp. 341–42.

23. Ibid., p. 335.

24. Deutsch, *Psychology of Women*, p. 89.

25. Josselyn, "Ego in Adolescence," p. 229. On boys and the repression of the adolescent Oedipus complex, see also Blos, *On Adolescence*, p. 108.

26. Anna Freud, *The Ego and the Mechanisms of Defense* (New York: International Universities Press, 1946), pp. 150–83.

27. Erik Homburger Erikson, "The Problem of Ego Identity," *Journal of the American Psychoanalytic Association* 4 (1956): 56–121.

28. From information gathered in the *Social Science Citation Index: 1956–1965* (Philadelphia: Institute for Scientific Information, c. 1978–c. 1989).

29. Deutsch is conspicuously left out of major reference works on the history of psychology and psychoanalysis. There is no mention of Deutsch in Leonard Zusne, ed., *The Biographical Dictionary of Psychology* (Westport, Conn.: Greenwood Press, 1984), or in Agnes N. O'Connell, ed., *Women in Psychology: A Bio-Bibliographic Sourcebook* (New York: Greenwood, 1990). Both reference books include, among other psychoanalysts, Karen Horney.

30. Roazen, *Helene Deutsch*, p. 246.

31. Ferdinand Lundberg and Marynia F. Farnham, *Modern Woman: The Lost Sex* (New York: Harper, 1947), p. 237. For a discussion of the relationship between Deutsch's work and Lundberg and Farnham, see Buhle, *Feminism and Its Discontents*, pp. 178–83.

32. Roazen, *Helene Deutsch*, pp. 33–62.

33. Ibid., pp. 117–18.

34. Ibid., p. 245.

35. Deutsch, *Psychology of Women*, p. 217.

36. Ibid., p. 275.

37. Buhle, *Feminism and Its Discontents*, p. 182.

38. See James Gilbert, *A Cycle of Outrage: America's Reaction to the Juvenile Delinquent in the 1950s* (New York: Oxford University Press, 1986); William Graebner, *The Age of Doubt: American Thought and Culture in the 1940s* (Boston: Twayne, 1991). For an analysis of the ways in which U.S. culture and society were threatened by and hostile to teenagers in the 1950s, see Edgar Z. Friedenberg, *The Vanishing Adolescent* (Boston: Beacon Press, 1959).

39. Deutsch, *Psychology of Women*, p. 53.

40. Phyllis Blanchard and Carlyn Manasses, *New Girls for Old* (New York: Macaulay, 1930), p. xii.

41. What image we have of Deutsch's perspective on the mother-daughter relationship has been shaped by Nancy Chodorow's vastly influential book, *The Reproduction of Mothering: Psychoanalysis and the Sociology of Gender* (Berkeley: University of California Press, 1978). Chodorow uses Deutsch's assertion that girls are often unable to complete a shift in attachment from the mother to the father as evidence for her theory that girls do not disengage from their mothers at all. According to Chodorow, a girl's relationship with her mother is so strong that she retains an identification and emotional involvement with her rather than simply transferring affection to the father when entering the Oedipus complex. The fact that girls remain "attached" to their mothers undergirded Chodorow's thesis that women maintain throughout their lives a pre-Oedipal or nonboundaried form of attachment that produces a lifelong ability and desire for connectedness—a desire that is satisfied upon reproducing the mother-child relationship with their own children. However, in Chodorow's account, Deutsch's deep anxieties about the intensity of the mother-daughter bond is elided, and in the process Chodorow obscures the salvific quality that Deutsch explicitly ascribed to the father-daughter relationship (Chodorow, *Reproduction of Mothering*, p. 140).

42. Deutsch, *Psychology of Women*, pp. 8–12.

43. Ibid., p. 116.

44. Ibid., p. 107.

45. Ibid., p. 9.

46. Ibid., p. 92.

47. On attempts to prescribe normality within psychoanalysis, see Elizabeth Lunbeck, *The Psychiatric Persuasion: Knowledge, Gender, and Power in Modern America* (Princeton: Princeton University Press, 1994).

48. Deutsch, *Psychology of Women*, p. 191.

49. Ibid., p. 129.

50. Ibid., p. 125.

51. Ibid., p. 98.

52. Ibid., p. 200.

53. Sigmund Freud, "The Dissolution of the Oedipus Complex" (1924), in Strachey, ed., *Standard Edition of the Complete Psychological Works of Sigmund Freud*, 9:173.

54. Ernest Jones, "The Early Development of Female Sexuality," *International Journal or Psycho-Analysis* 8 (1927): 459–72; Melanie Klein, "Early Stages of the Oedipus Conflict," *International Journal of Psycho-Analysis* 9 (1928): 167–80; J. Lampl–De Groot, "The Evolution of the Oedipus Complex in Women," in

The Psychoanalytic Reader: An Anthology of Essential Papers, with Critical Introductions, ed. Robert Fleiss (New York: International Universities Press, 1962), pp. 207–22.

55. According to Freud, the developmental process works something like this: the girl starts out loving her mother in the same aggressive way that a little boy does. She is at this point "a little man." Once she realizes that she cannot offer her mother what the boy can, that is, that she is castrated, she begins to renounce her aggressive feelings in favor of more passive desires. The wish for a penis is replaced by a wish for a baby—and at this point she turns to the person who is available to give her a baby—her father. Hence, "the girl's turning to her father is accomplished principally with the help of passive instinctual impulses" (Freud, "Femininity," p. 159).

56. Deutsch, *Psychology of Women*, p. 250.

57. Ibid., p. 251.

58. Ibid., pp. 253–54.

59. Phyllis Blanchard, *The Adolescent Girl: A Study from the Psychoanalytic Viewpoint* (New York: Dodd, Mead, 1930), p. 108.

60. Lucille Dooley, "Analysis of a Case of Manic-Depressive Psychosis Showing Well-Marked Regressive Stages," *Psychoanalytic Review* 5 (1918): 1–46.

61. Winifred Richmond, *The Adolescent Girl: A Book for Parents and Teachers* (New York: Macmillan, 1925), p. 57.

62. For a case history of maternal forestallment of a daughter's adolescent Oedipus complex, see Kata Levy, "Simultaneous Analysis of a Mother and Her Adolescent Daughter," p. 385.

63. American Psychiatric Association, *Biographical Dictionary of Fellows and Members of the American Psychiatric Association* (New York: American Psychiatric Association, 1977), pp. 778–79; Gale Literary Data Bases, *Contemporary Authors* (New York: Gale Group, 1999).

64. See especially Spiegel, "Comments on the Psychoanalytic Psychology of Adolescence"; Blos, *On Adolescence*, pp. 47–49; and Geleerd, "Some Aspects of Ego Vicissitudes in Adolescence."

65. Phyllis Greenacre, "The Prepuberty Trauma in Girls," *Psychoanalytic Quarterly* 19 (July 1950): 298.

66. Ibid., p. 301.

67. Ibid., pp. 305–17.

68. Ibid., p. 310.

69. Ibid., p. 305.

70. Ibid., p. 306.

71. Melanie Klein, "Early Stages of the Oedipus Conflict," *International Journal of Psycho-Analysis* 9 (1928): 176. On this point, see also Ernest Jones, "Early Development of Female Sexuality."

72. Prewar studies mostly concentrated on the question of mother-son incest. See especially Karl Abraham, "Neurotic Exogamy," *Psychoanalytic Review* 8 (1921): 101–20; and Otto Rank, *Inzest Motiv in Dichtung und Saga* (Leipzig: F. Deuticke, 1926), cited in Blanchard, *Adolescent Girl*, p. 123.

73. The "sex crime panic" of the postwar period, as Estelle Freedman has shown, inspired many social scientists to study the problem of "sex psychopaths," and psychoanalysts' interest in father-daughter incest might have been inspired by the frequent and electrifying headlines in the national media about pedophiles and sexual predators. See Estelle Freedman, "'Uncontrolled Desires': The Response to the Sexual Psychopath, 1920–1960," in Kathy Peiss and Christina Simmons, eds., *Passion and Power* (Philadelphia: Temple University Press, 1987), pp. 199–225.

74. For a discussion of some of the larger social, statistical, and legal questions surrounding father-daughter incest during this period, see Rachel Devlin, "Acting Out the Oedipal Wish: Father-Daughter Incest and the Sexuality of Adolescent Girls in the United States, 1941–1965," *Journal of Social History* (forthcoming, 2005).

75. Interestingly, the authors of some studies of father-daughter incest begin with a re-telling of Freud's abandonment of the seduction theory—probably as a way to let the audience know that they were already aware of the questions the study of father-daughter incest could raise. See especially Hector Cavallin, "Incestuous Fathers: A Clinical Report," *American Journal of Psychiatry* 122 (April 1966): 1132–38; Irving B. Weiner, "Father-Daughter Incest: A Clinical Report," *Psychiatric Quarterly* 36 (1962): 607–32; John H. Gagnon, "Female Child Victims of Sex Offenses," *Social Problems* 13 (1965): 176–92; and Jeffrey Moussaieff Masson, *The Assault on Truth: Freud's Suppression of the Seduction Theory* (New York: Pocket, 1984), p. 129.

76. Masson, *Assault on Truth*, p. 133. For a discussion of Freud's emphasis on "instincts and constitutional factors" as opposed to the "social environment" or "external influences," which became important to psychoanalysts and psychoanalytically influenced intellectuals in the United States in the 1930s, see Buhle, *Feminism and Its Discontents*, ch. 3. Many scholars have disputed how and to what extent Freud actually did abandon this theory. For example, David Wilbern ("Filia Oedipi: Father and Daughter in Freudian Theory," in Lynda Boose and Betty S. Flowers, eds., *Daughters and Fathers* [Baltimore: Johns Hopkins University Press, 1989]) argues that Freud continued to employ ideas about abuse and psychic trauma but that he did so selectively. See also Elizabeth Pleck on this question in *Domestic Tyranny: The Making of American Social Policy against Family Violence from Colonial Times to the Present* (New York: Oxford University Press, 1987), p. 153.

77. Hale, *Rise and Crisis of Psychoanalysis*, pp. 231–44, 133, 284.

78. J. Butler Tompkins, "Penis Envy and Incest: A Case Report," *Psychoanalytic Review* 27 (1940): 319–25.

79. Irving Kaufman, Alice L. Peck, and Consuelo K. Tagiuri, "The Family Constellation and Overt Incestuous Relations between Father and Daughter," *American Journal of Orthopsychiatry* 24 (April 1954): 266–78.

80. Kaufman, "Family Constellation," p. 277; Lillian Gordon, "Incest as Revenge against the Pre-Oedipal Mother," *Psychoanalytic Review* 42 (1955): 291.

81. On the tendency for adolescent girls to resort to "pseudology," see Deutsch, *Psychology of Women*, p. 125; and Greenacre, "Prepuberty Trauma," p. 308.

82. Bruno Cormier, "Psychodynamics of Father-Daughter Incest," *Canadian Psychiatric Association Journal* 7 (October 1962): 205. The sense that these analysts failed to see incest as an extraordinary event is reinforced by the fact that none of the analyses described the experience of father-daughter incest as traumatic for the daughter. Several authors asserted that the guilt and anxiety aroused by the incest did not occur until after the sexual activity had been terminated, and thus they deduced that any psychological disturbance was motivated by the fact of having violated a social taboo rather than the impact of the sexual transgression itself. The fact that the incest often continued over a course of several years suggested to many analysts that the daughters were "gratified" by the experience (Paul Sloan and Eva Karpinski, "Effects of Incest on the Participants," *American Journal of Orthopsychiatry* 12 [October 1942]: 666–73). This perspective on incest owed something to the psychoanalytic consensus on childhood sexual trauma first put forward by Karl Abraham in 1907. According to Abraham, it was only the guilt about having done something wrong, rather than the experience of sexual attack itself, that gave rise to the psychological disorders that followed childhood sexual abuse. It was believed that some children simply desired sexual contact with adults. However, it is worth noting that the articles on incest produced between 1940 and 1965 contributed to this perspective, and even further entrenched the sense that sexual experience with adults could be counted as a social problem involving girls rather than adult men, and thus could not be counted as a type of uninvited assault that damaged the psyche. Psychoanalytic studies of incest contributed to the notion that sexual abuse was not traumatic primarily by linking it to normal Oedipal desires. Hence these studies of incest did affect the larger question of the impact of sexual abuse on children and adolescents. See Karl Abraham, "The Experiencing of Sexual Traumas as a Form of Sexual Activity," in *The Selected Papers of Karl Abraham*, ed. Ernest Jones (London: Hogarth, 1965), pp. 47–63.

83. Ernest Jones, *Papers on Psychoanalysis*, 4th ed. (Baltimore: William Wood, 1938); Cormier, "Psychodynamics of Father-Daughter Incest."

84. Blos, *On Adolescence*, pp. 69, 107–8.

85. Greenacre, "Prepuberty Trauma," p. 308.

86. Sylvan Keiser, "A Manifest Oedipus Complex in an Adolescent Girl," *Psychoanalytic Study of the Child* 8 (1953): 99–106.

87. Ibid., p. 106. On incest as Oedipal fulfillment, see Kate Friedlander, *The Psycho-Analytical Approach to Juvenile Delinquency* (London: Keegan Paul, 1947), pp. 174–75.

88. Friedlander, *Psycho-Analytical Approach*, p. 101.

89. Keiser, "Manifest Oedipus Complex," p. 102.

90. Ibid., p. 99; Lillian Gordon, "Incest as Revenge," p. 292.

91. Lillian Gordon, "Incest as Revenge," p. 284.

92. Ibid., p. 206.

93. Ibid., p. 287.

94. Ibid.

95. Ibid., p. 288.

96. Ibid.

97. Deutsch, *Psychology of Women*, pp. 253–54.

98. Lillian Gordon, "Incest as Revenge," p. 284.

99. Ibid.

100. Ibid., pp. 291–92.

101. See especially Harry S. Howard, "Incest: The Revenge Motive," *Delaware State Medical Journal* 31 (1959): 223–25; and John W. Rhinehart, "Genesis of Overt Incest," *Comprehensive Psychiatry* 2 (December 1961): 338–49.

102. Matilde Wencelblat De Rascovsky and Arnaldo De Rascovsky, "On Consummated Incest," *International Journal of Psychoanalysis* 31 (1950): 45–46.

103. De Rascovsky and De Rascovsky's conclusions were, it is perhaps worth noting, cited elsewhere. See Cormier, "Psychodynamics of Father-Daughter Incest," and Irving B. Weiner, "Father-Daughter Incest."

104. Talcott Parsons, *Social Structure and Personality* (New York: Free Press, 1964), pp. 72–73.

105. Freud, "Femininity," p. 160.

CHAPTER TWO

Epigraph. John C. Coolidge, "Brother Identification in an Adolescent Girl," *American Journal of Orthopsychiatry* 24 (July 1954): 630.

1. "Youth," *Time*, October 29, 1951, p. 24; "Three Smart Girls," *Newsweek*, October 29, 1955, p. 38.

2. James Gilbert, *A Cycle of Outrage: America's Reaction to the Juvenile Delinquent in the 1950s* (New York: Oxford University Press, 1986), p. 15.

3. For an analysis of the ways in which gender roles were perceived to be converging in the 1950s, see Joanne Meyerowitz, ed., *Not June Cleaver: Women and*

Gender in Postwar America, 1945–1965 (Philadelphia: Temple University Press, 1994). For accounts of the kinds of anxieties that changes in gender roles produced, see Rickie Solinger, "The Smutty Side of Life: Picturing Babes as Icons of Gender Difference in the Early 1950's," in Erika Doss, ed., *Looking at Life Magazine* (Washington, D.C.: Smithsonian Institution Press, 2001); and Wini Breines, *Young, White, and Miserable: Growing up Female in the Fifties* (Boston: Beacon Press, 1992), esp. ch. 1. On changes in conventions of dating and sexual codes of youth, see Beth Bailey, *From Front Porch to Back Seat: Courtship in Twentieth-Century America* (Baltimore: Johns Hopkins University Press, 1988). For juvenile delinquency statistics, see United States Department of Health, Education and Welfare, Children's Bureau, *Juvenile Court Statistics* (Washington, D.C.: Government Printing Office, 1927–65).

4. James Farrell, "What Makes Them That Way?" *Coronet*, January 1958, pp. 68–77.

5. Breines, *Young, White, and Miserable*, p. 127.

6. Robert Griswold, *Fatherhood in America: A History* (New York: Basic Books, 1993), p. 186.

7. Evelyn Millis Duvall, "Keeping Up with Teenagers," Public Affairs Pamphlet No. 127, The National Council on Family Relations (1947), p. 26.

8. Griswold, *Fatherhood in America*.

9. Rickie Solinger, *Wake up Little Susie: Single Pregnancy and Race before Roe v. Wade* (New York: Routledge, 1992), p. 93.

10. A 1965 survey of sociological literature on juvenile delinquency found that sociologists had minimized the incidence of female delinquency and ignored its role in American society generally. See Nancy Jo Barton, "Disregarded Delinquency: A Study of Self-Reported Middle-Class Female Delinquency in a Suburb" (Ph.D. dissertation, Indiana University, 1965). Although there were few articles that dealt with female delinquency in the *American Journal of Sociology*, there were more articles specifically on female delinquency than on male delinquency between 1945 and 1965 in the *American Journal of Orthopsychiatry*.

11. U.S. Department of Health, Education and Welfare, Children's Bureau, *Juvenile Court Statistics, 1946–1949*, Statistical Series Number 8 (Washington, D.C.: Government Printing Office, 1951). All national statistics referred to in this chapter are from Children's Bureau data. *The Uniform Crime Reports of the United States*, published by the Federal Bureau of Investigation, provides statistics on annual rates of juvenile arrests; however, those reports do not differentiate between male and female crime.

12. James Gilbert, *Cycle of Outrage*, p. 68.

13. In general, the ratio of the girls who were classified as delinquents in relation to the general population was not stated by either the Federal Bureau of Investigation or the Children's Bureau.

14. J. B. Maller, "The Trend of Juvenile Delinquency in New York City," *Journal of Juvenile Research* 17 (January 1933): 10–18. The statistics for New York reflect, at least in part, the growth of a juvenile justice system prepared to handle adolescent girls. In Chicago, for example, where the juvenile justice system was older, the male to female delinquency ratios were less uneven at the turn of the century and therefore underwent less change over time. See Sophinisba Breckinridge and Edith Abbott, *The Delinquent Child and the Home* (New York: Charities Publication, 1912).

15. U.S. Department of Health, Education and Welfare, Children's Bureau, *Juvenile Court Statistics*.

16. U.S. Department of Health, Education and Welfare, Children's Bureau, *Juvenile Court Statistics, 1946–49*, p. 4.

17. Harry Shulman, *Juvenile Delinquency in American Society* (New York: Harper, 1961), p. 70.

18. For an in-depth discussion of the difficulty of legally classifying a girl as a sex offender, see Paul Tappan, *Delinquent Girls in Court* (New York: Columbia University Press, 1947). On the difficulty of legally classifying a juvenile as delinquent, see Sol Rubin, "The Legal Character of Juvenile Delinquency," *Annals of the American Academy of Political and Social Science* 261 (January 1949): 1–18; and Paul Tappan, "Children and Youth in the Criminal Court," *Annals of the American Academy of Political and Social Science* 261 (January 1949): 128–36.

19. Fred Murphy, "Delinquency Off the Record," in *Year Book of the National Probation Association* (New York: National Probation Association, 1946), pp. 184–85.

20. United States Congress, Senate, *Hearings before the Senate Subcommittee to Investigate Juvenile Delinquency*, "National, Federal and Youth Serving Agencies: Philadelphia," 83rd Cong., 1954, pp. 35–36, Statement of Norma B. Carson, representing the Juvenile Aid Bureau of Philadelphia, Pa.

21. Murphy, "Delinquency Off the Record," p. 185.

22. Barton, "Disregarded Delinquency," p. 20. The proportion of girls found in clinics as opposed to courts was much higher. See Richard I. Perlman, "Delinquency: The Size of the Problem," in *Reference Papers on Children and Youth* (Washington, D.C.: Government Printing Office, 1960), pp. 243–49; Lester E. Hewitt and Richard L. Jenkins, *Fundamental Patterns of Maladjustment* (Illinois: n.p., 1946); and A. E. Wood and J. B. Waite, *Crime and Its Treatment: Social and Legal Aspects of Criminology* (New York: American Book Company, 1941).

23. Edward E. Schwartz, "A Community Experiment in the Measurement of Juvenile Delinquency," in *Yearbook of the National Probation Association* (New York: National Probation Association, 1946), pp. 157–81.

24. On the question of the extent to which teenagers were behaving against expected norms on purpose, see James Gilbert, *Cycle of Outrage*, pp. 63–78.

25. Jhan Robbins and June Robbins, "Why Girls Are So Good," *Popular Science Monthly* 172 (January 1958): 158–61.

25. Farrell, "What Makes Them That Way?" pp. 71–80.

26. John D'Emilio and Estelle B. Freedman, *Intimate Matters: A History of Sexuality in America* (New York: Harper and Row, 1988), p. 261; J. Edgar Hoover, "Major Crime Wave Due," *New York Times*, December 11, 1945.

27. J. Edgar Hoover, "Wild Children," *American Magazine* 136 (July 1943): 39–41, 103–5.

28. Ibid., p. 103.

29. "The Kids Grow Worse," *Newsweek*, December 6, 1954, pp. 31–33.

30. "All Our Children," *Newsweek*, November 9, 1953, p. 28.

31. "The New Three R's," *Time*, March 15, 1954, pp. 68–69. The *New York Daily News* dubbed the three R's "rowdyism, riot and revolt."

32. Robert H. Bohlke, "Social Mobility, Stratification Inconsistency and Middle Class Delinquency," *Social Problems* 8 (Spring 1961): 351–63.

33. United States Congress, Senate, *Hearings before the Senate Subcommittee to Investigate Juvenile Delinquency*, "National, Federal and Youth-Serving Agencies," 1954, p. 33.

34. Austin L. Porterfield, *Youth in Trouble: Studies in Delinquency and Despair* (Fort Worth: Leo Potishman Foundation, 1946), pp. 39–41; Nancy Barton Wise, "Juvenile Delinquency among Middle-Class Girls," in *Middle-Class Juvenile Delinquency*, ed. Edmund Vaz (New York: Harper and Row, 1967), pp. 179–88. Original percentages included decimal figures. Figures listed have been rounded off at plus or minus .5 percent.

35. Joseph W. Scott and Edmund W. Vaz, "A Perspective on Middle-Class Delinquency," reprinted in Vaz, ed., *Middle-Class Juvenile Delinquency*. See also Farrell, "What Makes Them That Way?" pp. 71–80.

36. William Allan Brooks, *Girl Gangs* (New York: Padell, 1952), p. 10.

37. Farrell, "What Makes Them That Way?" p. 73.

38. Ibid., p. 77.

39. Ibid., p. 79.

40. Murray Morgan, "Nice Girls Can Be Delinquent," *Woman's Home Companion*, April 1955, pp. 48–64.

41. Ibid., p. 63.

42. Maud Merrill, *Problems of Child Delinquency* (New York: Houghton Mifflin, 1947), p. 5.

43. "All Our Children," p. 28.

44. "Put Father Back," *America*, March 15, 1958, 682.

45. Richard Clenenden, "The Shame of America," *Saturday Evening Post*, January 8, 1955, 18.

46. For history and philosophy of the Girls' Term court, see Anna M. Kross,

"Procedures for Dealing with Wayward Minors in New York City," 1936, New York City Magistrates Courts, U.S. Works Progress Administration for the City of New York, New York Public Library; Patrick J. Shelly, "The Wayward Minors' Court: An Evaluative Review of Procedures and Purposes, 1936–1941," 1942, New York City Magistrates Courts, New York Public Library; New York City Probation Bureau, "Justice for the Wayward Minor Girl in the City Magistrates' Courts: Facts and Figures for 1939," 1941, New York Public Library; Bernard C. Fisher, *Justice for Youth: The Courts for Wayward Youth in New York City* (New York: Community Service Society, Bureau of Public Affairs, 1955); and Tappan, *Delinquent Girls*, p. 1.

47. Tappan, *Delinquent Girls*, p. 42.

48. Laws of 1923, chap. 868, As Amended by Laws of 1925, chap. 389; "Youthful Offender Act," Title VII-A and Title VII-B, New York State (Fisher, *Justice for Youth*, p. 137).

49. Fisher, *Justice for Youth*, p. 21.

50. Ibid.

51. Dorris Clarke, "Treatment of the Delinquent Adolescent Girls: By Court or Administrative Tribunal?" *New York University Law Quarterly Review* (January and April 1946): 99.

52. Ibid., p. 100.

53. Ibid., p. 103.

54. Ibid.

55. Tappan, *Delinquent Girls*, ch. 3.

56. Ibid., p. 35. On changing sexual mores, Tappan cites Willard Waller, *The Family: A Dynamic Interpretation* (New York: The Cordon Company, 1938), which discusses the "moral confusion" of the era, and Lewis Terman, *Psychological Factors in Marital Happiness* (New York: McGraw-Hill, 1938). Terman's study of 792 couples found that only 31.7 percent of the women were virgins at marriage.

57. Tappan, *Delinquent Girls*, p. 36.

58. Tappan describes all of the sitting magistrates for the year 1946. Most are described as strict, some retaliatory, and others religiously motivated. See ibid., pp. 161–64.

59. Fisher, *Justice for Youth*, pp. 27–29. Statistics in 1946 were similar. See Tappan, *Delinquent Girls*, p. 153.

60. Shulman, *Juvenile Delinquency*, pp. 486–87.

61. Ibid.

62. The first child guidance clinic was set up in connection with the Chicago Juvenile Court in 1908. In Boston, the Judge Baker Guidance Center had been providing psychiatric diagnoses and services to the juvenile court since 1917. However, such clinics, on the forefront of psychoanalytic treatment, were the exception. On the Judge Baker Guidance Center, see Linda Gordon, *Heroes*

of *Their Own Lives: The Politics and History of Family Violence, Boston, 1880–1960* (New York: Viking Press, 1988), and Kathleen Jones, *Taming the Troublesome Child: American Families, Child Guidance, and the Limits of Psychiatric Authority* (Cambridge: Harvard University Press, 1999). On the demand for clinics in New York, see Kross, "Procedures for Dealing with Wayward Minors," and Paul Blanshard and Edwin J. Lukas, *Probation and Psychiatric Care for Adolescent Offenders in New York City* (New York: Society for the Prevention of Crime, 1942). In 1947, Tappan (*Delinquent Girls in Court*, p. 102) argued that "prolonged case work and psychological and/or psychiatric treatment" was the answer to the problem of female delinquency, as opposed to the "patently absurd" method of judicial adjudication.

63. Blanshard and Lukas, "Probation and Psychiatric Care for Adolescent Offenders," p. 60; Juvenile Court for the State of Connecticut, "Annual Report," 1943 and 1955, pp. 5–6, Mudd Library, Yale University Library, New Haven, Conn.

64. Juvenile Court for the State of Connecticut, "Annual Report," 1949, p. 4, Mudd Library, Yale University Library, New Haven, Conn.

65. In Connecticut, the need for establishing a court clinic was argued for on the anecdotal evidence of a case in which two girls, during the course of a quarrel in the school locker room, stabbed each other with pen knives. In this case, one of the girls was belatedly discovered to be psychotic. The girl's "true nature" had gone undetected until a court psychiatrist stepped in to diagnose and then treat the girl. The need for a psychiatric interpretation of a stabbing was, in this case, as in many others, clearly motivated by an inability to connect the motivation for such a crime with the gender of its perpetrator (Juvenile Court for the State of Connecticut, "Annual Report," 1955, p. 7).

66. In Framingham, Massachusetts, females who came before the court for running away were "usually" sent to the court clinic for treatment (Ames Robey, "The Runaway Girl," in *Family Dynamics and Female Sexual Delinquency*, ed. Otto Pollak and Alfred S. Friedman [Palo Alto: Science and Behavior Books, 1969]). Robey's article was originally presented as a paper at the seminar on family counseling for sexual behavior problems of adolescent girls, conducted in January 1963–June 1965. See also Ames Robey, "The Runaway Girl: A Reaction to Family Stress," *American Journal of Orthopsychiatry* 34 (July 1964): 762–67.

67. New York City Youth Board, "Reaching Adolescents Through a Court Clinic," Monograph Number 3, 1955, p. 32, New York Public Library.

68. Mary Odem, *Delinquent Daughters: Protecting and Policing Adolescent Female Sexuality in the United States, 1885–1920* (Chapel Hill: University of North Carolina Press, 1995), p. 1. See also Ruth M. Alexander, *The Girl Problem: Female Sexual Delinquency in New York, 1900–1930* (Ithaca: Cornell University Press, 1995).

69. Regina Kunzel, *Fallen Women, Problem Girls: Unmarried Mothers and the Professionalization of Social Work, 1890–1945* (New Haven: Yale University Press, 1993), p. 55; see also Pamela S. Haag, "In Search of 'The Real Thing': Ideologies of Love, Modern Romance, and Women's Sexual Subjectivity in the United States, 1920–1940," *Journal of the History of Sexuality* 2 (1992): 558.

70. Elizabeth Lunbeck, "'A New Generation of Women': Progressive Psychiatrists and the Hypersexual Female," *Feminist Studies* 13 (Fall 1987): 513–39.

71. See Katherine Du Pre Lumpkin, "Parental Conditions of Wisconsin Girl Delinquents," *American Journal of Sociology* 38 (September 1932): 232–39.

72. In a review of cases between 1936 and 1941, twelve of the twenty-six cases listed evidence of either a sexually transmitted disease or pregnancy, whereas in cases reviewed after 1945, such conditions, for whatever reason, were not mentioned. See Shelly, "Wayward Minors' Court."

73. Case histories drawn from New York City Youth Board, "Pattern for Prevention," ca. 1955; "Reaching the Unreached Family: A Study of Service to Families and Children," Monograph No. 5, 1957; "Reaching Adolescents through a Court Clinic"; "Police and Children: A Study of the Juvenile Aid Bureau," 1951, all at New York City Public Library; and *New York Youth Board News*, 1957–59.

74. Shelly, "Wayward Minors' Court," p. 21; New York Youth Board, "Reaching Adolescents through a Court Clinic," p. 55.

75. Shelly, "Wayward Minor's Court."

76. S. Harvard Kaufman, "Aggression in the Girl Delinquent," *American Journal of Orthopsychiatry* 15 (January 1945): 167–71. See also Oscar B. Markey, "A Study of Aggressive Sex Misbehavior in Adolescents Brought to Juvenile Court," *American Journal of Orthopsychiatry* 20 (October 1950): 719–31.

77. New York City Youth Board, "Reaching Adolescents through a Court Clinic," p. 36.

78. Peter Blos, "Preoedipal Factors in the Etiology of Female Delinquency," *Psychoanalytic Study of the Child* 12 (1957): 229–49.

79. Ibid., p. 237.

80. Ibid.

81. Nathan W. Ackerman, "Sexual Delinquency among Middle-Class Girls," in Pollak and Friedman, eds., *Family Dynamics*.

82. I am referring to Mary Odem's conceptualization of the ways in which young female sexuality was controlled by the family and state together in *Delinquent Daughters*.

83. John C. Coolidge, "Brother Identification in an Adolescent Girl," *American Journal of Orthopsychiatry* 24 (July 1954): 611–45.

84. Ibid., p. 616.

85. The provenance of even "sexual" acting out was not considered to be sexual desire itself but, as many psychoanalysts saw it, revenge against one or

both parents brought about because of "Oedipal impasse." In fact, many girls charged with promiscuity were believed to be frigid. "A teenage girl of this type," according to the prominent psychoanalyst Nathan Ackerman, "is not yet awakened sexually . . . carries a secret prejudice against sex . . . and does not enjoy the experience." Frigidity was linked to revenge against not only fathers but, in some cases, all men (Ackerman, "Sexual Delinquency"). In his description of "pseudoheterosexuality" in response to Oedipal disappointment, Peter Blos claimed that a girl who indulged in such a "display" had "no relationship to nor interest in her sexual partner, in fact her hostility to the male is severe" (Blos, "Preoedipal Factors").

86. Betty Friedan, "Teenage Girl in Trouble," *Coronet*, March 1958, pp. 163–68.

87. Ibid., p. 163.

88. Ibid., pp. 164–66.

89. Ibid., p. 168.

90. Black delinquency, both male and female, tended to be linked either to the fact of racial prejudice or to activity in the civil rights movement in the South. See Hans von Henting, "The Criminality of Colored Women," *University of Colorado Studies, Series C: Studies in the Social Sciences* 1 (November 1946); Joseph S. Himes, "Negro Teen-Age Culture," *Annals of the American Academy of Political and Social Science* 338 (November 1961); and Walter Chivers, "The Negro Delinquent," in *Yearbook of the National Probation Association* (New York: National Probation Association, 1942), pp. 46–59. Alternatively, in the sociological imagination, black female delinquency was linked to the problem of the "matriarchal family." See E. Franklin Frazier, *The Negro Family in the United States* (New York: Citadel, 1948), ch. 7; and Shulman, *Juvenile Delinquency*, pp. 480–81. See also Robin D. G. Kelley, *Race Rebels: Culture, Politics, and the Black Working Class* (New York: Free Press, 1994).

91. *Hearings before the Senate Subcommittee to Investigate Juvenile Delinquency*, "Juvenile Violence in California," Citizens Advisory Committee to the Attorney General on Crime Prevention (Washington, D.C., Government Printing Office, 1958); Juvenile Court for the State of Connecticut, "Annual Report," 1944–60, Mudd Library, Yale University Library, New Haven, Conn. See also Henting, "Criminality of the Colored Woman." The Children's Bureau ceased to differentiate among races in the annual *Juvenile Court Statistics* after 1936. Douglas Sirk's *Imitation of Life* (1959) is an important exception; the movie was not, however, specifically about juvenile delinquency.

92. For discussion on many of these films, see Mark Thomas McGee and R. J. Robertson, *The J.D. Films: Juvenile Delinquency in the Movies* (Jefferson, N.C.: McFarland and Co., 1982). I would like to thank Mark McGee for helping me to locate some of the hard-to-find movies.

93. According to Georganne Scheiner (*Signifying Female Adolescence: Film Representations and Fans, 1920–1950* [Westport, Conn.: Praeger, 2000], ch. 2), in films about delinquent girls made in the 1920s the neglectful mothers were depicted as chiefly responsible for girls' delinquency.

CHAPTER THREE

Epigraph. Jules Henry, *Culture against Man* (New York: Random House, 1963), p. 219.

1. Advertisement appeared in *Sales Management* (1957).

2. "A New, $10-Billion Power: The U.S. Teen-age Consumer," *Life*, August 31, 1959, pp. 77–85.

3. Survey of *Parents' Magazine*, 1920–63. In many Deanna Durbin musicals of the 1930s, such as *Three Daughters*, fathers and daughters share musical interests. For an example of the transformation of the genre in the 1950s, see *Daddy Long Legs* (Universal, 1955).

4. Anne Alexander, "How Our Daughter Spends Her Allowance," *Parents' Magazine*, April 1954, 40–41, 133.

5. On the question of maternal direction concerning fashion in the nineteenth century, see Valerie Steele, *The Corset: Cultural History* (New Haven: Yale University Press, 2001). On mothers and daughters sharing clothing catalogs in the twentieth century, see Rhona Justice-Malloy, "Little Girl Bound: Costume and Coming of Age in the Sears Catalog 1906–1927," in Sherrie A. Inness, ed., *Delinquents and Debutantes: Twentieth Century Girls' Cultures* (New York: New York University Press, 1998), pp. 109–33; and Mary G. Hood, *For Girls and the Mothers of Girls; A Book for the Home and the School Concerning the Beginnings of Life* (Indianapolis: Bobbs-Merrill, 1914). The movie *Our Dancing Daughters* (1928) is a good example of how the mother-daughter relationship was shaped around questions of fashion in prewar film. See also Booth Tarkington, *Alice Adams* (New York: Doubleday, 1921). For a narrative that reflects the prewar assumption that fathers should not, no matter the circumstances, be involved with their daughters' wardrobe, see Robert Nathan, *Winter in April* (New York: Knopf, 1938).

The emergence of the postwar cultural ideal of paternal sartorial oversight did not necessarily reflect reality. Though a father's involvement in his daughters' wardrobe may have grown over the course of the twentieth century, mothers remained the more active party. One survey found that 60 percent of teenage girls between the ages of thirteen and seventeen agreed with the statement, "A girl my age should buy clothes which she thinks her father will like." A much larger percentage, however (90 percent), believed that they should make decisions about clothes in consultation with their mother. The emphasis in this study was on compromising with mothers and seeking paternal admiration.

See Sylvia S. Silverman, *Clothing and Personal Appearance: Their Psychological Implications for Teen-Age Girls* (New York: Teachers' College, 1945), p. 137.

6. Grace Palladino, *Teenagers: An American History* (New York: Basic Books, 1996), p. 101. So basic is consumption to our current notion of what it means to be a teenager that Palladino introduces her book with the statement, "No matter what we profess to believe about teenagers and their vital importance to the future, we tend to value them most as consumers" (p. xi).

7. James Gilbert, *A Cycle of Outrage: America's Reaction to the Juvenile Delinquent in the 1950s* (New York: Oxford University Press, 1986), p. 19.

8. Dwight Macdonald, "Profiles: A Caste, a Culture, a Market," *New Yorker*, November 22, 1958, p. 87.

9. On youth and the growth of consumer culture, see Langdon Y. Jones, *Great Expectations: America and the Baby Boom Generation* (New York: Coward, McCann and Geoghegan, 1980), and Beth Bailey, *From Front Porch to Back Seat: Courtship in Twentieth-Century America* (Baltimore: Johns Hopkins University Press, 1988). On child rearing see Robert Griswold, *Fatherhood in America: A History* (New York: Basic Books, 1993).

10. For a good guide to some of the recent scholarship on girls, see Miriam Forman-Brunell, ed., *Girlhood in America: An Encylopedia* (Santa Barbara, Calif.: ABC-CLIO, 2001). For a theoretical look at cultural production surrounding girls, see Catherine Driscoll, *Girls: Feminine Adolescence in Popular Culture and Cultural Theory* (New York: Columbia University Press, 2002).

11. Susan Douglas, *Where the Girls Are: Growing up Female with the Mass Media* (New York: Random House, 1994), p. 108.

12. Jeanine Basinger, "The Girls Next Door," *New York Times Magazine*, November 24, 1996, 64.

13. Kathy Peiss, *Hope in a Jar: The Making of America's Beauty Culture* (New York: Metropolitan Books, 1998).

14. Bailey, *From Front Porch to Back Seat*, p. 48.

15. Sally Benson, *Junior Miss* (New York: Random House, 1939), p. 45.

16. For an analysis of "Little Orphan Annie" and Shirley Temple, see Valerie Walkerdine, *Daddy's Girl: Young Girls and Popular Culture* (Cambridge: Harvard University Press, 1997).

17. Ibid., p. 50.

18. Ibid., pp. 58–59.

19. Helen Deutsch, *The Psychology of Women*, vol. 1 (New York: Grune and Stratton, 1944), p. 11.

20. For a sense of the spirit of New York theater during these years, see Moss Hart, *Act One: An Autobiography* (New York: Random House, 1959).

21. Brooks Atkinson, *Broadway* (New York: Macmillan, 1970), p. 424.

22. Richard Watts Jr., "The Theater: A Chronicle of Youth," *New York Her-*

ald Tribune, 1943; and "Publication of the Dramatists Play Service," 1943, Billy Rose Theatre Collection, Lincoln Center for the Performing Arts, New York, N.Y. (hereafter BRTC). All reviews and statistical information about the plays mentioned in this book are from the clippings files at the BRTC. Many articles are missing page numbers and other identifying information.

23. David Sievers, *Freud on Broadway* (New York: Hermitage House, 1955). Information on product lines from *Harper's Bazaar*, December 1941. Other articles from *New York Times*, dates missing, "'Junior Miss': Clippings," BRTC.

24. As Illana Nash has shown ("'Nowhere Else to Go': Gidget and the Construction of Adolescent Femininity," *Feminist Media Studies* 2 [2002]: 341–56), the structure and plots of the Gidget films and television series continued to revolve around portrayals of fathers and daughters well into the 1960s.

25. *Wife vs. Secretary*, directed by Clarence Brown (Metro-Goldwyn-Mayer, 1936).

26. Omar Ranney, "'Junior Miss' Is Hilarious, Relaxing Comedy," *Cleveland Press*, 1943, BRTC.

27. The reaction to *Junior Miss* in London provides a good perspective on the American delight taken in witnessing the coming-of-age gifts given to a thirteen-year-old girl. In *"Junior Miss* Has London Somewhat Puzzled" (*New York Times*, April 18, 1943, BRTC), one reviewer surmised that "in America, I take it, Judy Graves is an appealing figure. . . . [In London] they see a child behaving with a precocity astonishing to them and being treated by parents with forbearance still more astonishing." A less patient reviewer said merely, "Go away, little girls. Can't be bothered with little girls like you" (James Agate, in *Sunday Times*, March 28, 1943, BRTC). Both reviews claimed that the attention paid to "high heeled shoes and nail varnish" was silly and, from an English perspective, premature.

28. Brooks Atkinson, "Junior Miss," *New York Times*, November 19, 1941, p. 28.

29. On alarm over female delinquency in general, see Chapter 2. On sexual delinquency during World War II, see John D'Emilio and Estelle B. Freedman, *Intimate Matters: A History of Sexuality in America* (New York: Harper and Row, 1988), ch. 11. In *The Psychology of Woman*, Helene Deutsch discusses at length the effect of wartime sexual behavior on the psychological process of female development. She found that the wartime atmosphere encouraged sexual delinquency. See also Karen Anderson, *Wartime Women: Sex Roles, Family Relations and the Status of Women during World War II* (Westport, Conn.: Greenwood Press, 1981).

30. On the influence of the psychoanalytic concept of the Oedipus complex, particularly in representations of adolescent girls and their fathers, see Chapters 1, 2, and 4.

31. Jerome Chodorov and Joseph Fields, *Junior Miss* (New York: Random House, 1942), p. 207. The play was based on a series of short stories by Sally Benson originally published in the *New Yorker*, and then later as a book, *Junior Miss* (New York: Random House, 1939).

32. "Sub-Deb Clubs: The Midwest Is Full of Them," *Life*, April 2, 1945, pp. 87–93; "Teen-Age Girls: They Live in a Wonderful World of Their Own," *Life*, December 11, 1944, pp. 91–99; "*Life* Goes to a Slumber Party," *Life*, January 4, 1943, pp. 72–75.

33. Although *Life* portrayed "Sub-Deb" clubs as an innocent source of sociability and fun, they were also discriminatory. Clubs tended to be formed along class and religious lines (Richard Ugland, "The Adolescent Experience during World War II: Indianapolis as a Case Study" [Ph.D. dissertation, Indiana University, 1977], p. 371).

34. "High School Fads," *Life*, May 15, 1944, pp. 65–69.

35. "Teenage Boys," *Life*, June 11, 1945, 33.

36. Ugland, "Adolescent Experience," pp. 392–93.

37. On the characterization of the "Sub-Deb," see Mary Rhinehart, *Bab: A Sub-Deb* (New York: George H. Doran, 1917). The origins and growth of the word "teenager" in relationship to its reference to the lifestyle characteristic of the "Sub-Deb" or "bobby-soxer" is discussed in Ugland, "Adolescent Experience," p. 350.

38. "Bobby-soxer" had different, more saccharine connotations through the 1940s. It disappeared at about the same time as "Sub-Deb."

39. John Modell, *Into One's Own: From Youth to Adulthood in the United States, 1920–1975* (Berkeley: University of California Press, 1989), p. 225.

40. "Teen-Age Girls," p. 91.

41. Paula Fass, *The Damned and the Beautiful: American Youth in the 1920's* (New York: Oxford University Press, 1977), p. 126.

42. On masculinity, rebellion, and "marking time," see Mauricio Mazon, *The Zoot Suit Riots* (Austin: University of Texas Press, 1984). Eric Erikson's notion of adolescence as a psychosocial moratorium was informed by this socially sanctioned aspect of male adolescence. See Erik Homburger Erikson, "The Problem of Ego Identity," *Journal of the American Psychoanalytic Association* 4 (1956): 56–121.

43. "Teenage Boys."

44. Some of the most popular expressions were "stinky super" and "that curdles me," as in, "Home Ec curdles me." See "How America Lives: Meet a Sub-Deb," *Ladies Home Journal*, December 1944, 138; and "Sub-Debs: They Live in a Jolly World of Gangs, Games, Gadding, Movies, Malteds and Music," *Life*, January 27, 1941, 74–79.

45. The ascendance of the teenage girl in the media had, in part, to do with

the number and large circulation of women's magazines, which began to focus on girls. This development, however, happened in tandem with the attention from general magazines.

46. United States Department of Labor, Bureau of Labor Statistics, "Trend in Child Labor, 1940–1944," *Monthly Labor Review* 60 (1944): 760.

47. Ibid., pp. 773–74. The reversal also upset a century-long trend in women's employment generally. Over the course of the twentieth century, the "working girl," as Lynn Weiner put it, was gradually replaced with the "working mother." The trend continued after the war. When the simultaneous increase in married women workers and decrease in single women workers is plotted on a graph, the ascending and descending lines cross one another in 1945. Thus 1946 was the first year that married women workers outnumbered younger "working girls." Thereafter, married working women, particularly above the age of thirty-five, steadily replaced the young, single girl in the workplace. What is interesting about the entrance of older, white, middle-class women into the workforce in the late 1940s and 1950s is that the greatest growth was among white, middle-class wives who worked for their own personal satisfaction and to raise their family's overall standard of living. These women went to work when their children were old enough to be in school. The entrance of these women into the workforce correlated with increased expenditures as their children reached their adolescence—a time when, according to one study, family expenditures increased substantially. Expenses included an extra telephone line, more clothes, another car, entertainment, etc. Hence the dependent teenage girl who was given the privilege of ceasing work and going back to school after the war was supported not only by her father but also by her mother, who moved into those jobs in retail that many younger girls had held during the war. The stenographer's job that was held by a girl of seventeen in 1944 was more than likely held by a woman over thirty-five in the 1950s—a woman with teenagers of her own whose lifestyle she helped support. See Lynn Weiner, *From Working Girl to Working Mother: The Female Labor Force in the United States, 1820–1980* (Chapel Hill: University of North Carolina Press, 1985), p. 7. On increases in family spending as children reached adolescence, see Philip R. Cateora, "An Analysis of the Teen-Age Market," *Studies in Marketing* (Austin: Bureau of Business Research, 1963), pp. 15–19.

48. Alice Kessler-Harris, *Out to Work: A History of Wage-Earning Women in the United States* (New York: Oxford University Press, 1982); Anderson, *Wartime Women*; William H. Chafe, *The Paradox of Change: American Women in the Twentieth Century* (New York: Oxford University Press, 1991), ch. 7; Amy Kesselman, *Fleeting Opportunities: Women Shipyard Workers in Portland and Vancouver during World War II and Reconversion* (New York: State University of New York Press, 1990).

49. Department of Labor, *Annual Report of the Secretary of Labor* (Washington, D.C.: Government Printing Office, 1941–45), survey of annual reports.

50. Edith M. Stern, "Danger! Children at Work," *Woman's Home Companion*, January 1944, p. 69.

51. U.S. Department of Labor, Children's Bureau, *The National Go-to-School Drive, 1944–1945* (Washington, D.C.: Government Printing Office, 1944), pp. 4, 10; U.S. Department of Labor, Children's Bureau with the Office of Education, *Back to School! Suggestions for a Fall Campaign* (Washington, D.C.: Government Printing Office, 1943).

52. U.S. Department of Labor, Bureau of Labor Statistics, Ella Arvilla Merritt and Edith S. Gray, "Child Labor Trends in an Expanding Market," *Monthly Labor Review* 67 (December 1948).

53. United States Census of Population, *Special Reports: Employment and Personal Characteristics* (1950). The report compares statistics on employment by age, race, etc., between 1940 and 1950. On expansion in the number of girls in the workforce during the war, see U.S. Department of Labor, "Trend in Child Labor" and "Child Labor Trends in an Expanding Market."

54. *Parents' Magazine*, perceiving a need for a special magazine for the sartorial, emotional, and social problems of the teenage girl, launched *Calling All Girls* in 1941. The magazine ran for only a few years. Beginning in the late 1930s, *Ladies Home Journal* had a regular "Sub-Deb" column, written by Maureen Daly, for teenage girls, which addressed fashion, romance, school, makeup, and sports, among other issues.

55. "Teen-Age Girls," p. 91.

56. Griswold, *Fatherhood in America*, ch. 2.

57. Ibid., ch. 4.

58. On the role of the family in structuring consumption in America, see Susan Porter Benson, "Living on the Margin: Working-Class Marriages and Family Survival Strategies in the United States, 1919–1941," in *The Sex of Things: Gender and Consumption in Historical Perspective*, ed. Victoria De Grazia (Berkeley: University of California Press, 1996), pp. 212–43.

59. On masculinity and its relationship to consumption during the Great Depression, see Margaret T. McFadden, "America's Boy Friend Who Can't Get a Date: Gender, Race and the Cultural Work of the Jack Benny Program, 1932–1946," *Journal of American History* 80 (June 1993): 113–34.

60. "*Seventeen*: A Unique Case Study," *Tide: The News Magazine of Advertising and Marketing*, April 15, 1945, p. 119, in Estelle Ellis Collection, scrapbook 2, folder 8, Smithsonian Institution, Washington, D.C.

61. From *March of Time* newsreel, 1945. The girl explains, "Of course, our families get mad because they think we're monopolizing the whole house-

hold." See also "*Life* Goes to a Slumber Party," pp. 72–75; and "How America Lives," pp. 137–40.

62. "*Life* Goes to a Slumber Party," p. 75. Father-daughter tension surrounding the radio was a common theme. See also Sally Simpson, *Popularity Plus: Good Manners for Young Moderns* (New York: Pocket Books, 1950), p. 85.

63. Alice Barr Grayson [Jean Schick Grossman], *Do You Know Your Daughter?* (New York: Appleton-Century, 1944). Grossman writes, "Many of the girls who wrote these letters are the girls in bobby socks and sweaters, calling themselves 'hep cats,' swooning over Frank Sinatra, smearing themselves with lipstick. . . . And yet . . . they are not very sure of themselves . . . they want to find adults to whom they can turn, whom they can trust." See also Catherine McKenzie, "Teen-Age Daughters," *New York Times Magazine*, January 14, 1945, p. 29.

64. Grayson, *Do You Know Your Daughter?* p. 85.

65. Ibid., pp. 34 and 128.

66. Gilbert, *Cycle of Outrage*, p. 15.

67. This argument appears in, among other places, Christopher Lasch, *Haven in a Heartless World: The Family Besieged* (New York: Basic Books, 1977); Joseph Kett, *Rites of Passage: Adolescence in America, 1790 to the Present* (New York: Basic Books, 1977); Kelly Schrum, "Teena Means Business: Teenage Girls' Culture and *Seventeen* Magazine, 1944–1950," in Inness, ed., *Delinquents and Debutantes*; Griswold, *Fatherhood in America*; and Bailey, *From Front Porch to Back Seat*.

68. "*Seventeen*," p. 19.

69. Ibid.

70. Estelle Ellis Collection, Smithsonian Institution, Washington, D.C. See also Schrum, "Teena Means Business," p. 8.

71. In the late 1940s, *Seventeen* launched a comic book based on its promotional character simply called "Teena." The comic shows Teena mostly at home or in her neighborhood, dancing with girlfriends in her bedroom, coming up with schemes to get the attention of a boyfriend or money out of dad. Later Teena was folded into the more successful comic, "Kathy." In standard "Kathy" comics, Kathy was drawn on a scale larger than her parents. See Hilda Terry, "Teena," New York, 1947–50, Comics Collection, Smithsonian Institution, Washington, D.C.

72. Research conducted by Benson and Benson/Opinion Research Corp., Inc., Princeton, N.J. Results compiled in *Life with Teena*, vols. 1 and 2 (1945–46), in Estelle Ellis Collection, series 1, scrapbook 2, folder 9, Smithsonian Institution, Washington, D.C. See pp. 54, 45–50.

73. *Life with Teena*, 2:97.

74. Although advertisements for engagement rings, hope chests, silver, and other wedding-related items proliferated, the magazine's official editorial stance was to discourage early marriage. The editors refused to run copy on marriage and wedding planning. The point was to dream about marriage and learn about marital skills while staying at home. See Schrum, "Teena Means Business."

75. *Life with Teena*, 1:18.

76. Ibid., 2:13–98.

77. In *Cycle of Outrage*, James Gilbert includes *Seventeen* as an important part of the female subculture, a sort of analog to male hot-rodding magazines. Charles H. Brown's argument is similar in "Self-Portrait: The Teen-Type Magazine," *Annals of the American Academy of Political and Social Science* 338 (November 1961): 13–21.

78. "You and Your Home," pamphlet, 1949, in Estelle Ellis Collection, series 1, scrapbook 2, folder 6, Smithsonian Institution, Washington, D.C.

79. Ibid., pp. 2–7.

80. "Your Parents and You," pamphlet, 1948, in Estelle Ellis Collection, series 1, scrapbook 2, folder 6, Smithsonian Institution, Washington, D.C.

81. Ibid.

82. Promotional flyer, ca. 1947, Estelle Ellis Collection, scrapbook 1, Smithsonian Institution, Washington, D.C.

83. Ibid.

84. Ibid.

85. *Life with Teena*, vol. 1.

86. On cloth shortages during the war see Mazon, *Zoot Suit Riots*.

87. "High School Fads," p. 70.

88. Ibid.

89. Ibid., p. 67.

90. On teenage girls as merciless fashion experts, see Sumner Ahlbum, "Are You Afraid of Your Teenager?" *Cosmopolitan*, November 1957, 41.

91. *A Date with Judy* (Metro-Goldwyn-Mayer, 1948).

92. Georganne Scheiner, *Signifying Female Adolescence: Film Representations and Fans, 1920–1950* (Westport, Conn.: Praeger, 2000), p. 110.

93. For a discussion of many of these films and an analysis of their place in the history of portrayals of female adolescence in movies, see ibid., pp. 91–116.

94. In the 1950s, similar or related characterizations of teenage girls were portrayed in *Gigi*, *Daddy Long Legs*, and, most precisely, *Gidget*, which was made into a television series in 1965. On the television show, see Douglas, *Where the Girls Are*.

95. Kathy Peiss, "Making Up, Making Over: Cosmetics, Consumer Culture, and Women's Identity," in De Grazia, ed., *Sex of Things*, p. 311.

96. Peiss, *Hope in a Jar*, p. 252. The black cocktail dress and high-heeled shoes were also symbolically important but tended to be introduced at a later age and were thus represented as less of a leap. Among the upper classes, or in the Sub-Deb group, putting up one's hair was depicted as the most critical transformation in a girl's coming-of-age as late as the 1920s. See Gene Stratton-Porter, *Her Father's Daughter* (New York: Doubleday, 1921).

97. In short fiction in *Seventeen*, if an item of clothing had to be taken back to the store for reasons of age-appropriateness, it was always the father who ordered the return. In this way, fathers had official sanction over what could and could not be worn. Examples abound in short-fiction pieces in *Seventeen* between 1945 and 1965. A particularly good example is Ann Chidester, "Journey to the Heart of this Earth," May 1961, pp. 139–201. Similarly, when a girl wanted to wear black, that decision was usually made by her father. There are instances where mothers ordered their daughters to remove makeup; however, I have not found any instances where rebellion against a maternal command was linked to a girl's moral or sexual status.

98. "Handling the Make-Up Situation," *Seventeen*, January 1945, p. 112.

99. Ibid.

100. Ibid.

101. Ibid.

102. Maureen Daly, ed., *Profile of Youth* (New York: J. B. Lippincott, 1951), p. 23.

103. James Coleman's *Adolescent Society: The Social Life of the Teenager and Its Impact on Education* (New York: Free Press, 1961), pp. 38–41, is based on research conducted in 1957 and 1958.

104. A better case can be made for the use of magazines such as *Teen World* and *Hep Cats*, which devoted much more space to movie stars and teen idols. James Coleman (*Adolescent Society*, ch. 3) found that there was a direct correlation between both class and popularity and these magazines. Girls who read *Hep Cats* in the 1950s, as opposed to *Seventeen*, were more likely to be working class and less likely to be "with the crowd."

CHAPTER FOUR

Epigraph. Lionel Trilling, "The Other Margaret," *Partisan Review* 12 (Fall 1945): 494.

1. Edward Streeter, *Father of the Bride* (New York: Simon and Schuster, 1948), p. 206.

2. Ibid., p. 231.

3. John R. Gillis, *For Better, For Worse: British Marriages 1600 to the Present* (New York: Oxford University Press, 1985), pp. 135–45.

4. Arnold Van Gennep, *Les Rites de Passage* (Paris, 1909), quoted in James

H. S. Bossard and Eleanor S. Boll, "Rite of Passage: A Contemporary Study," *Social Forces* 26 (March 1948): 247.

5. Karen Halttunen, *Confidence Men and Painted Women: A Study of Middle-Class Culture in America, 1830–1870* (New Haven: Yale University Press, 1982), p. 27.

6. Interview with Postmaster General Robert E. Hannegan, "Prognosis for Parents," *Seventeen*, November 1945, p. 100.

7. Eric Hobsbawm and Terence Ranger, eds., *The Invention of Tradition* (New York: Cambridge University Press, 1983), p. 1.

8. Ibid.

9. In the fiction and films of the 1920s and 1930s, fathers were often cast as supporting characters. Good natured, dignified, usually wealthy, but most of all otherwise detained, these men looked on from a distance, occasionally facilitating their daughters' various projects, including their daughters' quest to find "true love." His aid was monetary or logistical and usually rewarded with affection and regard. Then, during World War II, fathers began to appear as *defining*—though not always larger—characters in the vast preponderance of female teenage drama. Good examples of pre–World War II narratives of female coming-of-age include Mary Rhinehart, *Bab: A Sub-Deb* (New York: George H. Doran, 1917); Gene Stratton-Porter, *Her Father's Daughter* (New York: Doubleday, 1921); and Robert Nathan, *Winter in April* (New York: Knopf, 1938). Booth Tarkington's *Alice Adams* (New York: Doubleday, 1921) provides an especially stark contrast to the postwar coming-of-age narratives: the story culminates in Alice's realization that she must give up her dreams of entering the upper classes through the support of her father and an eventual marriage to an upper-class young man and instead learn to support herself. The Deanna Durbin and Judy Garland films of the 1930s also provide a contrast to later films about girls. The fathers/father figures in Durbin and Garland films function mostly as distant if benevolent protectors or facilitators of the girls' various projects. See especially Deanna Durbin in *First Love* (Universal, 1933), *Three Smart Girls* (Universal, 1936), *Mad about Music* (Universal, 1938), and *Lady on a Train* (Universal, 1933); and Judy Garland in *Listen, Darling* (Metro-Goldwyn-Mayer, 1936).

10. Eugene Gilbert, "Why Today's Teen-Agers Seem So Different," *Harper's Magazine*, November 1959, p. 77.

11. Peter Gabriel Filene, *Him/Her/Self: Sex Roles in Modern America* (New York: Harcourt Brace Jovanovich, 1974), p. 194; Beth Bailey, *From Front Porch to Back Seat: Courtship in Twentieth-Century America* (Baltimore: Johns Hopkins University Press, 1988), pp. 101–8; Lynn Spigel, *Make Room for TV: Television and the Family Ideal* (Chicago: University of Chicago Press, 1992); Steve Cohan, *Masked Men: Masculinity and the Movies in the Fifties* (Bloomington: Indiana

University Press, 1997). See also Lawrence Frank, "How Much Do We Know about Men?" *Look*, May 17, 1955, pp. 30–34; and Arthur Schlesinger, "The Crisis of American Masculinity," *Esquire*, November 1958, p. 133.

12. The father in *A Tree Grows in Brooklyn* is highly romanticized in the mind of the main character, Frances, when she is young. Part of the process of her growing up is coming to terms with her father's alcoholism, and realizing that her mother has been the more valiant figure in her life.

13. Glenda Elizabeth Gilmore, *Gender and Jim Crow: Women and the Politics of White Supremacy in North Carolina, 1896–1920* (Chapel Hill: University of North Carolina Press, 1996). On the black upper classes at the turn of the century, see Willard B. Gatewood, *Aristocrats of Color: The Black Elite, 1880–1920* (Bloomington: Indiana University Press, 1990), and E. Franklin Frazier, *Black Bourgeoisie: The Rise of a New Middle Class* (New York: Free Press, 1957).

14. Much of the history of the black middle classes has centered on women's club efforts and social projects, which have included within them efforts at molding an image and reality of black family life. See Paula Giddings, *When and Where I Enter: The Impact of Black Women on Race and Sex in America* (New York: William Morrow, 1984); Gatewood, *Aristocrats of Color*; Jacqueline Dowd Hall, *Revolt against Chivalry: Jessie Daniel Ames and the Women's Campaign against Lynching* (New York: Columbia University Press, 1993), ch. 3; and Gilmore, *Gender and Jim Crow*.

15. Hazel Carby pointed out the need for a study of "whiteness" as it has been produced in reference to black identity in her book *Reconstructing Womanhood: The Emergence of the Afro-American Woman Novelist* (New York: Oxford University Press, 1987).

16. John Modell, *Into One's Own: From Youth to Adulthood in the United States, 1920–1975* (Berkeley: University of California Press, 1989), p. 247.

17. Edward Streeter, *Daily Except Sundays* (New York: Simon and Schuster, 1938); *Merry Christmas, Mr. Baxter* (New York: Harper, 1956); *Chairman of the Bored* (New York: Harper, 1961).

18. Streeter, *Father of the Bride*, p. 105.

19. Ibid., p. 169.

20. Ibid., pp. 199–200.

21. Ibid., p. 107.

22. Ibid., pp. 8 and 12. For an analysis of the contemporary reemergence of the "tradition" of men asking a girl's father for permission to marry, see Jaclyn Geller, *Here Comes the Bride: Women, Weddings, and the Marriage Mystique* (New York: Four Walls Eight Windows, 2001), pp. 113–22.

23. Evelyn Millis Duvall, *Facts of Life and Love for Teen-Agers* (New York: Popular Library, 1956). The book went through seven printings between 1956 and 1957.

24. Ibid., pp. 5–8.

25. Winifred Richmond, *The Adolescent Girl: A Book for Parents and Teachers* (New York: Macmillan, 1925), p. 55.

26. Ruth Fedder, *A Girl Grows Up* (New York: McGraw-Hill, 1939), p. 114. In *Growing up with Our Children: For Parents of Teen Age Young People* (New York: Association Press, 1932), W. H. Burger spends a chapter discussing the importance of "emotional weaning" at adolescence.

27. On the question of "emotional maturing," see C. M. Fleming, *Adolescence: Its Social Psychology* (New York: International Universities Press, 1949); on "adjustment," see Lester D. Crow and Alice Crow, *Our Teen-Age Boys and Girls: Suggestions for Parents, Teachers, and Other Youth Leaders* (New York: McGraw-Hill, 1945).

28. Duvall, *Facts of Life*, p. 179.

29. Marynia F. Farnham, *The Adolescent* (New York: Harper, 1951), p. 23.

30. Elizabeth Douvan and Joseph Adelson, *The Adolescent Experience* (New York: John Wiley, 1966), p. 150.

31. Institute for Social Research, *Adolescent Girls: A Nation-wide Study of Girls between Eleven and Eighteen Years of Age* (Ann Arbor: University of Michigan, 1958), p. 80. For a discussion of the report, see Marguerite M. Dixon, "Adolescent Girls Tell about Themselves," *Journal of Marriage and Family Living* 20 (November 1958): 400–401.

32. Institute for Social Research, *Adolescent Girls*, p. 81.

33. Duvall, *Facts of Life*, p. 183. For a discussion of perspectives on internationalism in the wake of the explosion of the first atomic bomb, see Paul Boyer, *By the Bomb's Early Light: American Thought and Culture at the Dawn of the Atomic Age* (New York: Pantheon, 1985).

34. Barbara Ehrenreich, *The Hearts of Men: American Dreams and the Flight from Commitment* (New York: Anchor, 1983), p. 17.

35. For boys, maturity did involve an explicit break from an "infantile" dependence upon their mothers. See ibid., p. 20.

36. Grace Loucks Elliott, *Understanding the Adolescent Girl* (New York: Henry Holt, 1930), p. 34. For a contrasting, postwar view that emphasized the extent to which girls needed "direction" from their parents, see Alice Barr Grayson [Jean Schick Grossman], *Do You Know Your Daughter?* (New York: Appleton-Century, 1944), p. 1. For a perspective on the special need for parental "aid" during adolescence, see Frances Bruce Strain, *"But You Don't Understand": A Dramatic Series of Teen-Age Predicaments* (New York: Appleton-Century-Crofts, 1950).

37. Survey of *Seventeen*, 1945–65. In the 1950s, the regular column, "You and Your Parents," which discussed bedtimes, allowance, bringing dates home, choosing a college, and negotiations over buying clothes, was discontinued and replaced with the column "From a Boy's Point of View—A Guide to Appro-

priate Behavior on Dates." References to power struggles with parents quite simply disappeared.

38. Dick Ashbaugh, "The Dangerous Date," *Seventeen*, February 1959, p. 122.

39. Ibid.

40. Ibid., p. 126.

41. Ibid., p. 122.

42. Grace Hechinger and Fred M. Hechinger, *Teen-Age Tyranny* (New York: William Morrow, 1962), p. 101.

43. Kaspar Monahan, "Laugh Riot Comes to Nixon Theater," *New York Herald Tribune*, BRTC.

44. Ibid.

45. Richard Watts Jr., "The Theater: A Chronicle of Youth," *New York Herald Tribune*, 1943, BRTC.

46. Ashbaugh, "Dangerous Date," pp. 96–97, 120–27.

47. Filene, *Him/Her/Self*, p. 198.

48. Hechinger and Hechinger, *Teen-Age Tyranny*, p. 101.

49. On the connections between domestic consumption, family togetherness, and emasculation, see Robert Griswold, *Fatherhood in America: A History* (New York: Basic Books, 1993), pp. 199–202. On the crisis of masculinity, see Ehrenreich, *Hearts of Men*, and Bailey, *From Front Porch to Back Seat*, pp. 97–118.

50. Margaret Mead, *And Keep Your Powder Dry: An Anthropologist Looks at America* (New York: William Morrow, 1943), p. 44.

51. Edward Streeter, "Mr. Banks' Other Daughter: The Sequel to Father of the Bride," *Good Housekeeping* 130 (April 1950): 50.

52. "Photogravure Picture Section," *New York Times*, November 18, 1923, p. 1. See also, for instance, "Miss Elise Hughs" and "Miss Polly Thayer," *Town and Country* 77 (September 1920): 37; and "Miss Sheila Byrne," *Town and Country* 77 (December 10, 1920): 28. Stories about the heavy social schedules of mothers of debutantes were also common before the war. "It's no snap to be the mother of a popular debutante!" began one article on Mrs. George F. Barker Jr. in the November 25, 1930, edition of the *Daily News*, p. 16. Stories also listed events sponsored and/or hosted by mothers, aunts, and women friends in the prewar period. After the war, attention to these adult female figures, aunts, mothers, and grandmothers waned.

53. "Eva Seed Married in St. James: Escorted by Father at Her Wedding to James Auchincloss," *New York Times*, December 11, 1955, p. 90; "Mrs. Post Married in Ceremony Here: Escorted by Father, J. Harold Wheeler," *New York Times*, January 23, 1955, p. 80; survey of society pages from the *New York Times* and the *New York Daily News*, 1923 and 1930, and the *New York Times* and the *New York Herald Tribune*, 1949 and 1955.

54. "Evelyn Hanes Moore . . . arrives at the clubhouse with her father,

Thomas O. Moore," in "Debutantes in Winston-Salem," *Town and Country* 110 (September 1956): 170; "Wedding Days," *Town and Country* 112 (May 1958): 50; "Lake Forest," *Town and Country* 112 (November 1958): 90.

55. Captions read, for example, "Gail Whitney, the beautiful guest of honor, on the arm of her father, Cornelius Vanderbilt Whitney, ready to welcome their guests," in "Debutante Parties," *Town and Country* 110 (September 1956): 135; or "bride alights at the church on the arm of her father, Thomas Fortune Ryan III," in *Town and Country* 106 (January 1952): 38.

56. These conventions situated girls with their fathers (and to a lesser extent their mothers). The photographs announced the father's gaze, his subjective, but ultimately objectifying, view of his daughter, a perspective informed by both prewar and postwar filmic conventions for displaying images of women. This kind of gaze—upon a woman emerging at the top of a staircase, a man's first glimpse of her person—was typical of a perspective meant to announce, in Laura Mulvey's classic formulation, male "visual pleasure," an all-encompassing male sexual gaze that was, in the 1920s and 1930s, presented within the context of adult, or young adult, romance (as viewed through the eye of the camera). It could be argued that what we see in these postwar wedding and debutante photographs—particularly the device of the bride being glimpsed at the top of the stairs by her father—are visual conventions transcribed from romance films onto a moment between father and daughter. See Laura Mulvey, "Visual Pleasure and Narrative Cinema," in John Caughie and Annette Kuhn, eds., *The Sexual Subject: A "Screen" Reader in Sexuality* (New York: Routledge, 1992), pp. 22–34.

57. Bossard and Boll, "Rite of Passage," p. 225.

58. One woman recollecting her own debut in 1908 observed that whereas at the turn of the century an upper-class young woman could not "date" before her debut, by 1948 virtually all junior debutantes—or teenage girls—dated before their debut (Bossard and Boll, "Rite of Passage," p. 248).

59. Ibid., p. 249.

60. For a history of the debutante in the United States, see Karal Ann Marling, *Debutante: Rites and Regalia of American Debdom* (Lawrence: University Press of Kansas, 2004).

61. Bossard and Boll, "Rite of Passage," p. 253. A rare report on a debutante function is in *Time*: "Part of a Dream," January 3, 1955, p. 18.

62. William Davidson, "Our Negro Aristocracy," *Saturday Evening Post*, January 13, 1962.

63. Walter C. Daniel, *Black Journals of the United States* (Westport, Conn.: Greenwood Press, 1982), p. 159.

64. Ibid., p. 213.

65. Roland E. Wolseley, *The Black Press, U.S.A.* (Ames: Iowa State University Press, 1971), p. 145; Daniel, *Black Journals*, p. 159.

66. "Mission Statement," *Ebony*, February 1946, p. 1.

67. Gilmore, *Gender and Jim Crow*, p. 3.

68. For an analysis of the importance of marriage to black citizenship, see Nancy F. Cott, *Public Vows: A History of Marriage and the Nation* (Cambridge: Harvard University Press, 2000), pp. 31–44.

69. "Ebony Photo Editorial," *Ebony*, December 1945, pp. 15–16.

70. See, for example, "Track Whiz," *Ebony*, January 1947, p. 47.

71. Wolseley, *Black Press*, p. 142.

72. One headline reads, "Negro Pulchritude Ranks High Despite U.S. Lily White Standards, Picture Proves," *Ebony*, July 1946. On the question of beauty pageants and the publicizing of black beauty before World War II, see Kathy Peiss, *Hope in a Jar: The Making of America's Beauty Culture* (New York: Metropolitan Books, 1998). For an analysis of beauty queens within black political efforts to "reclaim the honor due to the race," see Maxine Leeds Craig, *Ain't I a Beauty Queen? Black Women, Beauty, and the Politics of Race* (New York: Oxford University Press, 2002), p. 14.

73. "Sit-In Student Freedom Fighters," *Jet*, April 21, 1960, cover.

74. *Jet*, April 2, 1959, cover.

75. "Shopping for That College Look," *Ebony*, November 1946, p. 24.

76. "Almost Seventeen," *Ebony*, February 1958, p. 39.

77. "Belafonte's Daughter Campaigns to Aid NAACP," *Jet*, September 14, 1961, cover; "Jesse Owens' Daughter Is a Campus Queen," *Ebony*, December 1960, p. 113; "Cookie Cole Meets Society," *Ebony*, February 1962, pp. 73–74.

78. *Ebony*, January 1951, p. 71.

79. *Jet*, December 27, 1962, cover.

80. "N.Y. Jazz Musician's Daughter Weds White Swiss Sweetheart," *Jet*, April 18, 1954, p. 26; "Artist's Daughter Models," *Jet*, September 21, 1961, cover.

81. "Beauty Has Prominent Dad," *Ebony*, July 1960, p. 113.

82. *Ebony*, April 1946, p. 6.

83. Ibid.

84. Ibid., p. 7.

85. Eric Foner, *Reconstruction: America's Unfinished Revolution, 1863–1867* (New York: Harper Collins, 1989).

86. Lerone Bennett Jr., "The Negro Woman: Crumbling Matriarchate Poses New Problems," *Ebony*, July 1960, pp. 38–46. For an interpretation of the role of masculinity as it has been connected to ideas about racial progress among black intellectuals, see Hazel Carby, *Race Men* (Cambridge: Harvard University Press, 1998).

87. Bennett, "Negro Woman," p. 46.

88. E. Franklin Frazier, *The Negro Family in the United States* (New York: Citadel, 1948), p. 87. On the "matriarchate," see ibid., ch. 7. See also St. Clair Drake and Horace R. Cayton, *Black Metropolis: A Study of Negro Life in a Northern City* (New York: Harcourt, Brace, 1945); Allison Davis and John Dollard, *Children of Bondage: The Personality Development of Negro Youth in the Urban South* (Washington, D.C.: American Council on Education, 1940); Abram Kardiner and Lionel Ovesey, *The Mark of Oppression* (New York: Norton, 1951); and Harold Lief, Daniel Thompson, and William Thompson, *The Eighth Generation: Cultures and Personalities of New Orleans Negroes* (New York: Harper, 1960). For a sociological and psychological comparison between white and black patterns of child rearing, see Allison Davis and Robert J. Havinghurst, *Father of the Man: How Your Child Gets His Personality* (Boston: Houghton Mifflin, 1947).

89. "Teens Make Debut for Grown-Up Cause," *Ebony*, February 1965, p. 70. The emphasis on the father occurred despite the fact that women's clubs were responsible for far more debutante balls than men's clubs. The Smart Set and The Girl Friends were two of the most important women's clubs. For information on women's clubs, see "Girl Friends at Greenbrier," *Ebony*, April 1958, pp. 73–78; and "Texas Deb Ball," *Ebony*, April 1958, pp. 118–21. See also Lawrence Otis Graham, *Our Kind of People: Inside America's Black Upper Class* (New York: Harper Collins, 1999).

90. "Kansas City Cotillion," *Ebony*, March 1962, p. 73.

91. "Who Are the Newly Rich?" *Ebony*, March 1954, p. 27; *Ebony*, September 1954, p. 58.

92. "Cookie Cole Meets Society," p. 74.

93. The physical and sexual distance implied by this absence is reinforced in other pictorial conventions of family life in *Ebony*. While in the white media the family was increasingly heterosexualized—that is, in family photographs mothers were pictured with sons at their side and fathers with daughters—in *Ebony*, daughters were almost always pictured next to their mothers, and sons, when pictured at all, with their fathers. For instance, in 1955, *Ebony* celebrated its tenth anniversary with an article trumpeting its own success, as well as the kind of family life it promoted. In the large picture accompanying the article, which was meant to be representative and was, in fact, exemplary, a "typical Negro family" is shown "marching forward into the future of unlimited possibilities" with the mother paired with daughter, and father with son (November 1955 issue, p. 134).

94. "Sarah Lawrence College Student President: Sue McClain Is First Negro Elected at Exclusive School," *Ebony*, October 1957, pp. 98–104; "How Serious Are Our Teen-Agers?" *Ebony*, October 1958, pp. 95–100; "A Coed for a Day," *Ebony*, November 1958, pp. 53–58; "The School That Was Too Good to Die,"

Ebony, March 1958, cover; "Teens Fight Bias in Oklahoma City," *Jet*, September 11, 1958, pp. 14–19; "Sit-in Student Freedom Fighters," *Jet*, April 21, 1960, cover; "The Revolt of Negro Youth," *Ebony*, May 1960, pp. 36–42; "Coed Who Gave Up College to Fight for Rights," *Jet*, June 29, 1961, cover.

95. Gilmore, *Gender and Jim Crow*, p. 151.

96. Stephen J. Whitfield, *A Death in the Delta: The Story of Emmett Till* (Baltimore: Johns Hopkins University Press, 1988).

97. Sander Gilman, "Black Bodies, White Bodies: Toward an Iconography of Female Sexuality in Late Nineteenth-Century Art, Medicine, and Literature," in Henry Louis Gates Jr., ed., *"Race," Writing, and Difference* (Chicago: University of Chicago Press, 1986); Jacqueline Dowd Hall, "The Mind That Burns in Each Body: Women, Rape, and Racial Violence," in *Powers of Desire: The Politics of Sexuality*, ed. Ann Snitow, Christine Stansell, and Sharon Thompson (New York: Monthly Review Press, 1983); Robyn Wiegman, *American Anatomies: Theorizing Race and Gender* (Durham: Duke University Press, 1995), ch. 3; Saidiya V. Hartman, *Scenes of Subjection: Terror, Slavery, and Self-Making in Nineteenth-Century America* (New York: Oxford University Press, 1997), pp. 86–94.

98. Lorraine Hansberry's play, *A Raisin in the Sun*, which is about the internal struggles of a black family, appeared in 1959. Until the late 1950s, serious black characters in films were mostly portrayed in terms of their relationship to the problem of integration. See, for instance, *Pinky*, directed by Elia Kazan (Twentieth Century Fox, 1949), and *Blackboard Jungle* (Metro-Goldwyn-Mayer, 1955).

99. For an exhaustive list of plays that were influenced by or explicitly addressed psychoanalytic ideas, see David Sievers, *Freud on Broadway* (New York: Hermitage House, 1955).

100. "A Hit in Harlem," *Ebony*, December 1945, p. 18.

101. Ibid.

102. "A Date with Anna," *Ebony*, December 1945, p. 17.

103. Errol G. Hill and James V. Hatch, *A History of African American Theatre* (New York: Cambridge University Press, 2003), p. 352.

104. Philip Yordan, *Anna Lucasta* (New York: Random House, 1945), p. 22.

105. Ibid., pp. 5–6.

106. Ibid., p. 24.

107. When Anna asks him to dance, "he freezes, and something akin to terror seizes him" (ibid., p. 75).

108. Burton Rascoe, "Anna Lucasta Impresses as Significant Drama," *New York World-Telegram*, August 31, 1944, BRTC.

109. Louis Kronenberger, "'Anna Lucasta' Scores Again," *New York Newspaper PM*, August 31, 1944, BRTC.

110. Rascoe, "Anna Lucasta."

111. Gatewood, *Aristocrats of Color*, p. 182.

112. E. Anthony Rotundo, *American Manhood: Transformations in Masculinity from the Revolution to the Modern Era* (New York: Basic Books, 1993), introduction.

CHAPTER FIVE

Epigraph. Grace Metalious, *Peyton Place* (New York: Julian Messner, 1956), p. 27.

1. F. Hugh Herbert, *Meet Corliss Archer* (New York: Random House, 1944), p. 1.

2. *The National Cyclopaedia of American Biography*, vol. 48 (New York: James White and Co., 1965).

3. F. Hugh Herbert, "Private Affair," *Good Housekeeping*, March 1943, pp. 32–33, 205–7.

4. *Kiss and Tell* (Columbia Pictures, 1945); *A Kiss for Corliss* (United Artists, 1948).

5. John Dunning, *On the Air: The Encyclopedia of Old-Time Radio* (New York: Oxford University Press, 1998), p. 444. "*Meet Corliss Archer*," according to Dunning, was "the CBS answer to NBC's *A Date with Judy*. . . . Corliss Archer and Judy Foster were cut from the same log: both were charming and breathless, prone to endless exasperation. But the men in her life set Corliss apart. First there was Dexter Franklin, the boy next door. . . . The other man in Corliss's life was her father." What "truly inspired" Corliss's father, Dunning writes, "was the eternal war with the female gender." His war was waged with his daughter.

6. "People Are Talking About . . . ," *Vogue*, April 1943; Wolcott Gibbs, "Tarkington Revisited," *New Yorker*, March 25, 1943, BRTC.

7. One of the few exceptions was Mary Chase's play about a group of boys, *Bernardine* (1953), which was a moderate success. Although more attention has been paid to the mother-daughter melodramas and their transformation from the 1930s to the 1940s, especially the connections between the films *Stella Dallas* (United Artists, 1937), *Mildred Pierce* (Metro-Goldwyn-Mayer, 1945), and *Imitation of Life* (Universal, 1959), it should be pointed out that film musicals and comedies of the 1930s were often centered around fathers and daughters, as well as mothers and daughters and fathers and sons. The father/father figure himself, especially in the Judy Garland and Deanna Durbin musicals, mostly played a critical role in the plot without making an appearance until the very end of the narrative. These men usually stepped in at the end of the film to fix problems in a behind-the-scenes way, often solving their daughters' adolescent dilemmas. For instance, in *First Love* (Universal, 1933), a modern version of the Cinderella fairy tale, Durbin's adoptive father secretly produces gowns, furs, and slippers for Durbin, thwarting his frivolous wife's designs for their biologi-

cal daughter as the social set's best catch and paving the way for Durbin to show off her beautiful voice at the Christmas ball. In *Stella Dallas*, Laurel's father, who is divorced from her mother, arranges for Laurel to enter the educated, upper-class society to which she is innately drawn, again, simply by providing the means at the appropriate moment. The father-daughter relationship is not intimate in any of these films; rather, the father plays an instrumental role in ways that do not involve much interaction. On the mother-daughter relationship in film, see Jackie Byars, *All that Hollywood Allows: Re-Reading Gender in the 1950s Melodrama* (Chapel Hill: University of North Carolina Press, 1991).

8. Eugene O'Neill, *Ah, Wilderness!* in *Eugene O'Neill: Complete Plays, 1932–1943* (New York: Library of America, 1988); Booth Tarkington, *Seventeen: A Tale of Youth and Summer Time and the Baxter Family, Especially William* (1915; New York: Harper and Brothers, 1932). Clarence Day's *Life with Father* (New York: Random House, 1920), a popular book and long-running hit on Broadway, is another good example of this kind of depiction of fatherhood. See also the film *Four Daughters* (Warner Brothers, 1938).

9. O'Neill, *Ah, Wilderness!* pp. 15, 67, 101.

10. Ibid., p. 194. Paternal denial in the instance of adolescent male consumer demands was also portrayed in most of the Andy Hardy movies. Much of the plot in those movies, as in *Seventeen*, revolved around Andy's attempts to procure items that will help him appear attractive to the opposite sex—a car, cuff links, and cash to go on dates. He usually fails in these endeavors, and his father ultimately helps him out. However, in the process, valuable lessons about telling the truth, treating others with respect, and the value of a dollar are learned. Because these plots center around the attempt to make money rather than the transformative power of the desired object, the act of consumption in these male coming-of-age stories had a different meaning from that in the female coming-of-age story. In the latter, the meaning of consumerism was lodged within the act of acquisition and adornment itself, whereas in the male coming-of-age story, the meaning of consumerism was found in the act of finding a way to pay for what was desired.

11. Jerome Chodorov and Joseph Fields, *Junior Miss* (New York: Random House, 1942), p. 133.

12. Josephine Bentham and Herschel William, *Janie* (1942), act 1, scene 1, p. 13 (script from BRTC).

13. F. Hugh Herbert, *Kiss and Tell* (New York: Dramatists Play Service, 1945), p. 36.

14. For a different kind of adult commentary on youthful behavior, see F. Scott Fitzgerald, "Bernice Bobs Her Hair," in *The Crack Up* (New York: James Laughlin, 1945).

15. *Kiss for Corliss*, p. 40.

16. Ibid., p. 33.

17. Ibid., p. 156.

18. Ibid., p. 70.

19. Ibid., pp. 31 and 36.

20. Herbert, *Meet Corliss Archer*, p. 6.

21. Ibid.

22. One possible explanation for such narrow concerns on both sides of this relationship is that Herbert did not mean for his stories to be comedies about adolescent problems so much as satire. In satirical situations, characters usually undergo severe stylization; personal attributes are isolated and exaggerated so that they can be held up for mockery. Self-esteem is very often impregnable (which holds true for both Corliss and Mr. Archer), and the capacity to feel pain is truncated (Penelope Gilliatt, *To Wit: Skin and Bones of Comedy* [New York: Scribner's, 1990], pp. 36–50).

23. *Meet Corliss Archer* (radio program), n.d., The Museum of Television and Radio. The segment is starring Janet Waldo, so it must have aired after 1943.

24. Herbert, *Meet Corliss Archer*, p. 11.

25. F. Hugh Herbert, *For Keeps* (1944), produced by Gilbert Miller, The Henry Miller Theatre, BRTC.

26. Elliot Norton, "Writer at Work: Alters 'For Keeps,' Newest Comedy," *Boston Post*, June 4, 1944, BRTC.

27. "Domestic Relations," *New Yorker*, June 24, 1944, BRTC.

28. *For Keeps*, act 1, scene 1, p. 33.

29. Ibid., act 2, scene 1, p. 7.

30. Ibid., act 2, scene 2, pp. 39–40.

31. Ibid., p. 51.

32. Title appears on original script (1944), BRTC.

33. *For Keeps*, act 2, scene 1, p. 12.

34. Ibid., act 1, scene 2, p. 5.

35. For a good description of the dynamics between men and women in the comedies of the 1930s, see Maria DiBattista, *Fast-Talking Dames* (New Haven: Yale University Press, 2001).

36. *For Keeps*, act 1, scene 1, p. 5.

37. Ibid., act 2, scene 1, p. 8.

38. When the novel was published in the United States it was praised most for its humor. Dorothy Parker called the novel "wildly funny" in "Sex—without the Asterisks," *Esquire*, October 1958, p. 103, cited in Harold Bloom, ed., *Lolita* (New York: Chelsea House, 1993), p. 10. Alfred Appel Jr. concentrates on its darker side in his introduction to his annotated edition of the book, *The Annotated Lolita* (New York: Vintage, 1991).

39. According to a list compiled by the Modern Library published in the *New*

York Times (July 20, 1998, p. 1), *Lolita* is the fourth greatest novel of the twentieth century.

40. Appel, ed., *Annotated Lolita*, p. xi.

41. Ibid., p. l.

42. Ibid., p. xlvii.

43. The reflection on Charlotte Haze is from ibid.; the impersonation of the international novel from F. W. Dupee in *Anchor Review* (1957) in Norman Page, ed., *Nabokov: The Critical Heritage* (Boston: Routledge and Kegan Paul, 1982), p. 86; the "external ambiance" of Lolita from Kingsley Amis in *Spectator* (1959) in Page, ed., *Nabokov*, p. 106.

44. Page, ed., *Nabokov*, p. 90.

45. Alfred Appel has been Lolita's harshest critic (though others have also been taken in by Humbert Humbert's sulking criticisms of her and his assessment that American culture is responsible for having produced a corrupted person). Appel says: "Humbert's terrible demands notwithstanding, [Lolita] is as insensitive as children are to their parents; sexuality aside, she demands anxious parental placation in an all too American way. . . . She affords Nabokov an ideal opportunity to comment on the Teen and Sub-Teen Tyranny" (*Annotated Lolita*, p. xlviii). Brian Boyd claims that Nabokov, rather than Humbert Humbert, made distinctions between the "passing fads of youth" that made up Lolita's exterior and the person who managed to show "remarkable patience under [Humbert's] tyranny and confinement." He also claims that Nabokov said that "of all the thousands of characters in his work . . . Lolita came second in his list of those he admired most as people." However, what makes Lolita much like other adolescent female characters discussed in this book is the faddish consumerism *combined* with her ability to be a "courageous victim." See Brian Boyd, *Vladimir Nabokov: The American Years* (Princeton: Princeton University Press, 1991), p. 237. Citations from the text of *Lolita* are from the Vintage International edition.

46. Boyd, *Nabokov*, p. 211.

47. Appel, ed., *Annotated Lolita*, p. xlviii.

48. Nabokov, *Lolita*, p. 187.

49. Ibid., p. 45.

50. Ibid., pp. 113 and 115.

51. Ibid., p. 148.

52. Lolita is rude to her mother but does not banter with her in a cynical manner the way she does with Humbert Humbert. Charlotte and Dolores are described as "rivals" (ibid., p. 48). Humbert Humbert receives a verbal report from the headmistress at the Beardsley school that "schoolmates find Dolly antagonistic," but we never actually see her act this way among peers (ibid., 196). The same holds true for representations of juvenile delinquency. Though there

were reports of girls misbehaving in groups and at school, the emphasis was on problems at home and relationships with fathers. See Chapter 1.

53. Nabokov, *Lolita*, p. 60.

54. Ibid., pp. 39 and 24.

55. On Humbert's moodiness see Boyd, *Nabokov*, p. 229.

56. Nabokov, *Lolita*, p. 49.

57. On the ways in which critics have been attracted to Humbert, see Boyd, *Nabokov*, p. 233 and ff.

58. Nabokov, "On a Book Entitled *Lolita*," *Lolita*, p. 312.

59. Appel, ed., *Annotated Lolita*, p. xxxviii.

60. Nabokov, *Lolita*, p. 174.

61. Appel, ed., *Annotated Lolita*, p. xlvii.

62. Alice Barr Grayson [Jean Schick Grossman], *Do You Know Your Own Daughter?* (New York: Appleton-Century, 1944).

63. Ibid., p. 99.

64. Page, ed., *Nabokov*, p. 87.

65. Appel, ed., *Annotated Lolita*; Boyd, *Nabokov*; Richard H. Bullock, "Humbert the Character, Humbert the Writer," in Bloom, ed., *Lolita*, pp. 90–104.

66. By the time Stanley Kubrick directed the film version in 1962, the identity of Quilty had been changed into something much more fashionable and appropriate to the period, a writer for television. This development points to what has been lost in our understanding of the status of the playwright in the 1940s, before the advent of TV.

67. This free-standing magazine was later folded into *New York* magazine, BRTC.

68. Humbert Humbert discovers Herbert's identity in the volume "*Who's Who in the Limelight*—actors, producers, playwrights, and shots of static scenes" (*Lolita*, p. 31).

69. On Nabokov's scientific work on "natural mimicry" and the possibilities it presented for "metaphysical speculation," see Boyd, *Nabokov*, pp. 35–57. In a *Playboy* interview, Nabokov claimed that the redundancy in Humbert Humbert's name was "nasty" and "suggestive" and lent itself to a number of puns. To my knowledge, this is the only information he has ever given on his choice of names (*Playboy*, January 1964, cited in Bloom, ed., *Lolita*, p. 23).

70. On Nabokov and deliberation, see Trevor McNeely, "'Lo' and Behold: Solving the Lolita Riddle," in Bloom, ed., *Lolita*, pp. 134–48.

71. Maxwell Geismar, "Domestic Tragedy in Virginia," *Saturday Review*, September 15, 1951, p. 12; Louis D. Rubin, Jr., "Notes on a Southern Writer in Our Time," in Robert K. Morris and Irving Malin, eds., *The Achievement of William Styron* (Athens: University of Georgia Press, 1975), p. 53.

72. Malcolm Cowley, "The Faulknerian Pattern," *New Republic* 125 (October 8, 1951), p. 19.

73. William Styron, *Lie Down in Darkness* (Indianapolis: Bobbs-Merrill, 1951; New York: Vintage, 1952), p. 153.

74. Ibid., p. 49.

75. Ibid., p. 329.

76. It is noteworthy that Loftis's revulsion at his wife's middle-aged body and contempt for her churchgoing ways will be reproduced exactly in Nabakov's description of Charlotte Haze. Critics have pointed out Humbert Humbert's particular dissatisfaction with the middle-aged female body, but his moral criticisms of Charlotte's religious rectitude have not been particularly well considered, nor linked to Styron's portrayal of Helen Loftis.

77. Styron, *Lie Down in Darkness*, pp. 47–48.

78. Nabokov, *Lolita*, pp. 58–59.

79. Styron, *Lie Down in Darkness*, p. 215.

80. Ibid., p. 290.

81. Ibid., p. 286.

82. Ibid., p. 267.

83. Nabokov, *Lolita*, pp. 112, 114, 133.

84. Styron, *Lie Down in Darkness*, p. 262; Nabokov, *Lolita*, p. 114.

85. See especially Alfred Appel, ed., *Annotated Lolita*, preface.

86. Emily Toth, *Inside Peyton Place: The Life of Grace Metalious* (New York: Doubleday, 1981), p. 83.

87. Ibid., p. 76.

88. On Styron's biography, see Geismar, "Domestic Tragedy in Virginia," p. 12.

89. Harold Strauss, "The Tale of a Western Town," *New York Times Book Review*, April 14, 1940, p. 4.

90. William Graebner, *The Age of Doubt: American Thought and Culture in the 1940s* (Boston: Twayne, 1991), p. 18.

91. Ibid., p. 25.

92. Robert K. Morris and Irving Malin, eds., *The Achievement of William Styron* (Athens: University of Georgia Press, 1975), p. 5.

93. Ibid., p. 1.

94. *Atlantic*, October 1951, pp. 78–80.

95. Linda Nochlin, *Women, Art, and Power, and Other Essays* (Boulder, Colo.: Icon Editions, 1989), p. 2.

96. Page, ed., *Nabokov*, p. 93; Lionel Trilling, from an essay published in *Encounter* in 1958.

97. "Who's Mature?" *Time*, November 17, 1957, p. 17.

98. Selma Fraiberg, "Two Modern Incest Heroes," *Partisan Review* 28 (1961): pp. 646–47.

99. Ibid., p. 647.

100. Ibid., p. 651.

101. Ralph Ellison, *Invisible Man* (1947; New York: Vintage, 1995), p. 66.

102. Ibid., p. 52. It is possible that Ellison's depiction of the unrepentant and sane sharecropper was inspired by, or meant to comment upon, the portrayal of the insane Mr. Lucasta in *Anna Lucasta*.

103. Fraiberg, "Two Modern Incest Heroes," p. 659.

104. Ibid., pp. 660–61.

105. Ibid., p. 650.

106. Page, ed., *Nabokov*, pp. 90–91.

EPILOGUE

Epigraph. Philip Roth, *American Pastoral* (New York: Vintage, 1997), p. 272.

1. Marjorie Leonard, "Fathers and Daughters: The Significance of 'Fathering' in the Psychosexual Development of the Girl," *International Journal of Psychoanalysis* 47 (1966): 325 (emphasis added).

2. Ibid., p. 332.

3. Ibid., p. 333.

4. "Golden Girl: A Success Story—Or at Least Ought to Be," *Life*, October 11, 1963, p. 65.

5. Ibid., p. 71.

6. Ibid., pp. 73–74.

7. In the recent past, examinations of the psychological impact of father-daughter incest, especially abuse occurring in early childhood, have played an important role in the feminist critique of patriarchy, while some of that writing has come under attack in debates surrounding the nature of "repressed memory syndrome." The overall impact of these debates on the contemporary construction of the father-daughter relationship remains to be seen. Nevertheless, the question of the role of the sexual within the father-daughter relationship continues to inform current discourses on fathers and daughters. See, among many others, Judith Lewis Herman, *Father-Daughter Incest* (Cambridge: Harvard University Press, 1981); Lenore Terr, *Unchained Memories: True Stories of Traumatic Memories, Lost and Found* (New York: Basic Books, 1994); and Frederick Crews, "The Revenge of the Repressed," pts. 1 and 2, *The New York Review of Books*, November and December 1994.

8. See, for example, Joan Jacobs Brumberg, *The Body Project: An Intimate History of American Girls* (New York: Random House, 1997); Leora Tanenbaum, *Slut! Growing up Female with a Bad Reputation* (New York: Perennial, 2000); Sharon Lamb, *The Secret Lives of Girls: What Good Girls Really Do—Sex Play, Ag-*

gression, and Their Guilt (New York: Free Press, 2000); Terr, *Unchained Memories*; and Crews, "Revenge of the Repressed."

9. Joan Jacobs Brumberg, introduction to *Girl Culture*, by Laura Greenfield (New York: Chronicle Books, 2002), p. 3.

10. Mary Pipher, jacket review for Joe Kelly, *Dads and Daughters: How to Inspire, Understand, and Support Your Daughter When She's Growing up So Fast* (New York: Broadway Books, 2002).

Bibliography

Primary Sources

MANUSCRIPT AND ARCHIVAL COLLECTIONS
Lincoln Center Library for the Performing Arts, New York, New York
    The Billy Rose Theater Collection
New Haven, Connecticut
    Mudd Library, Yale University Library
New York State Archives, Albany, New York
    Records of the Bedford Hills Correctional Facility
Smithsonian Institution, Washington, D.C.
    Estelle Ellis Collection

GOVERNMENT DOCUMENTS
Federal Bureau of Investigation. *The Uniform Crime Reports of the United States*. Washington, D.C.: Government Printing Office, 1945–65.
New York Public Library and the Library of Congress
    New York City Magistrates Courts. Patrick J. Shelly. "The Wayward Minors' Court: An Evaluative Review of Procedures and Purposes, 1936–1941." 1942.
    ———. Anna M. Cross. "Procedures for Dealing with Wayward Minors in New York City." 1936.
    New York City Probation Bureau. "Justice for the Wayward Minor Girl in the City Magistrates' Courts: Facts and Figures for 1939." 1941.
    New York City Youth Board. "Pattern for Prevention." ca. 1955.
    ———. "Police and Children: A Study of the Juvenile Aid Bureau." 1951.
    ———. "Reaching Adolescents Through a Court Clinic." Monograph Number 3, 1955.
    ———. "Reaching the Unreached Family: A Study of Service to Families and Children." Monograph Number 5, 1957.
United States Congress. Senate. *Hearings before the Senate Subcommittee to Investigate Juvenile Delinquency*. "National, Federal and Youth Serving Agencies: Boston." 83rd Cong. Washington, D.C.: Government Printing Office, 1954.
———. *Hearings before the Senate Subcommittee to Investigate Juvenile Delinquency*. "National, Federal and Youth Serving Agencies: Denver, Colorado." 83rd Cong. Washington, D.C.: Government Printing Office, 1953.

————. *Hearings before the Senate Subcommittee to Investigate Juvenile Delinquency.* "National, Federal and Youth Serving Agencies: Philadelphia." 83rd Cong. Washington, D.C.: Government Printing Office, 1954.

————. *Hearings before the Senate Subcommittee to Investigate Juvenile Delinquency.* "Juvenile Violence in California," Citizens Advisory Committee to the Attorney General on Crime Prevention. Washington, D.C., Government Printing Office, 1958.

United States Department of Health, Education and Welfare. Children's Bureau. *Juvenile Court Statistics.* Washington, D.C.: Government Printing Office, 1927–65.

United States Department of Labor. Bureau of Labor Statistics. *Annual Report of the Secretary of Labor.* Washington, D.C.: Government Printing Office, 1941–45.

————. Merritt, Ella Arvilla, and Edith S. Gray. "Child Labor Trends in an Expanding Market." *Monthly Labor Review* 67 (December 1948).

————. "Trend in Child Labor, 1940–1944." *Monthly Labor Review* 60 (1944).

————. Children's Bureau. *The National Go-to-School Drive, 1944–1945.* Washington, D.C.: Government Printing Office, 1944.

————. Children's Bureau with the Office of Education. *Back to School! Suggestions for a Fall Campaign.* Washington, D.C.: Government Printing Office, 1943.

United States Census of Population. *Special Reports: Employment and Personal Characteristics.* 1950.

JOURNALS

American Journal of Orthopsychiatry, 1945–65
American Journal of Psychiatry, 1945–65
Journal of the American Psychoanalytic Association, 1945–65
Journal of Marriage and Family Living, 1955–65
Psychoanalytic Study of the Child, 1945–65

MAGAZINES

Ebony, 1945–65
Jet, 1950–65
Life, 1945–55
Parents' Magazine, 1920–65
Seventeen Magazine, 1944–65
Town and Country, 1920, 1930, 1945–65

ARTICLES

Abraham, Karl. "The Experiencing of Sexual Traumas as a Form of Sexual Activity." In *The Selected Papers of Karl Abraham*, edited by Ernest Jones, 47–63. London: Hogarth, 1965.

————. "Neurotic Exogamy." *Psychoanalytic Review* 8 (1921): 101–20.

Ackley, Ethel G., and Beverly R. Fliegel. "A Social Work Approach to Street-Corner Girls." *Social Work* 5 (1960): 27–36.

Ahlbum, Sumner. "Are You Afraid of Your Teenager?" *Cosmopolitan*, November 1957, 41.

Alexander, Anne. "How Our Daughter Spends Her Allowance." *Parents' Magazine*, April 1954, 40–41, 133.

"All Our Children." *Newsweek*, November 9, 1953, 28.

Ashbaugh, Dick. "The Dangerous Date." *Seventeen*, February 1959, 96–127.

Atkinson, Brooks. "Junior Miss." *New York Times*, November 19, 1941, 28.

Barker, Gordon H. "Comparison of the Delinquencies of Boys and Girls." *Journal of Criminal Law, Criminology and Police Science* 53 (1962): 472.

Bibring, Grete L. "On the Passing of the Oedipus Complex in a Matriarchal Setting." In *Drives, Affects, Behavior: Essays in Honor of Marie Bonaparte*, edited by Rudolph M. Lowenstein, 278–84. New York: International Universities Press, 1953.

Blos, Peter. "Preoedipal Factors in the Etiology of Female Delinquency." *Psychoanalytic Study of the Child* 12 (1957): 229–49.

Bohlke, Robert H. "Social Mobility, Stratification Inconsistency and Middle Class Delinquency." *Social Problems* 8 (Spring 1961): 351–63.

Bossard, James H. S., and Eleanor S. Boll. "Rite of Passage: A Contemporary Study." *Social Forces* 26 (March 1948): 247–55.

Brown, Charles H. "Self-Portrait: The Teen-Type Magazine." *Annals of the American Academy of Political and Social Science* 338 (November 1961): 13–21.

Buxbaum, Edith. "Panel Reports: The Psychology of Adolescence." *Journal of the American Psychoanalytic Association* 6 (1958): 111–20.

Cateora, Philip R. "An Analysis of the Teen-Age Market." *Studies in Marketing*. Austin: Bureau of Business Research, 1963.

Cavallin, Hector. "Incestuous Fathers: A Clinical Report." *American Journal of Psychiatry* 122 (April 1966): 1132–38.

Chidester, Ann. "Journey to the Heart of This Earth." *Seventeen*, May 1961, 139–201.

Chivers, Walter. "The Negro Delinquent." In *Yearbook of the National Probation Association*, 46–59. New York: National Probation Association, 1942.

Clarke, Dorris. "Treatment of the Delinquent Adolescent Girl: By Court or Administrative Tribunal?" *New York University Law Quarterly Review* (January and April 1946): 96–103.

Clenenden, Richard. "The Shame of America." *Saturday Evening Post*, January 8, 1955, 17–21, 101–10.

Cohen, Albert K., and James Short Jr. "Research in Delinquent Subcultures." *Journal of Social Issues* 14 (1958): 20–36.

Coleman, Rose W., Ernst Kris, and Sally Provence. "The Study of Variations of Early Parental Attitudes." *Psychoanalytic Study of the Child* 8 (1953): 20–47.

Coolidge, John C. "Brother Identification in an Adolescent Girl." *American Journal of Orthopsychiatry* 24 (July 1954): 611–45.

Cormier, Bruno, Miriam Kennedy, and Jadwiga Sangowicz. "Psychodynamics of Father-Daughter Incest." *Canadian Psychiatric Association Journal* 7 (October 1962): 203–17.

Cowley, Malcolm. "The Faulknerian Pattern." *New Republic* 125 (October 8, 1951): 19.

"Delinquency Trends." *Youth Service News*, July 1960, 9.

Denney, Reuel. "American Youth Today: A Bigger Cast, a Wilder Screen." *Daedalus* 91 (1962): 124–44.

De Rascovsky, Matilde Wencelblat, and Arnaldo de Rascovsky. "On Consummated Incest." *International Journal of Psycho-Analysis* 31 (1950): 45–54.

Dixon, Marguerite M. "Adolescent Girls Tell about Themselves." *Journal of Marriage and Family Living* 20 (November 1958): 400–401.

Dooley, Lucille. "Analysis of a Case of Manic-Depressive Psychosis Showing Well-Marked Regressive Stages." *Psychoanalytic Review* 5 (1918): 1–46.

Duvall, Evelyn Millis. "Keeping Up with Teenagers." Public Affairs Pamphlet No. 127, The National Council on Family Relations (1947), 26.

Eissler, Ruth S. "Riots: Observation in a Home for Delinquent Girls." *Psychoanalytic Study of the Child* 4 (1949): 451–67.

Erikson, Erik Homburger. "The Problem of Ego Identity." *Journal of the American Psychoanalytic Association* 4 (1956): 56–121.

———. "Reality and Actuality: An Address." *Journal of the American Psychoanalytic Association* 10 (1962): 451–73.

Farrell, James. "What Makes Them That Way?" *Coronet*, January 1958, 71–80.

Fraiberg, Selma. "Two Modern Incest Heroes." *Partisan Review* 28 (1961): 646–61.

Frank, Lawrence. "How Much Do We Know about Men?" *Look*, May 17, 1955, 30–34.

Freud, Anna. "Adolescence." *Psychoanalytic Study of the Child* 13 (1958): 255–78.

Freud, Sigmund. "The Aetiology of Hysteria." In *The Standard Edition of the Complete Works of Sigmund Freud*. Vol. 3, translated and edited by James Strachey, 191–21. London: Hogarth, 1962.

———. "The Dissolution of the Oedipus Complex." In *Standard Edition of the Complete Psychological Works of Sigmund Freud*. Vol. 9, translated and edited by James Strachey, 173–79. London: Hogarth, 1924.

———. "Femininity (1933)." In *Introductory Lectures on Psycho-Analysis*, translated and edited by James Strachey, 139–67. New York: Norton, 1989.

———. "Some Psychological Consequences of the Anatomical Distinction between the Sexes." In *Standard Edition of the Complete Psychological Works of Sigmund Freud*. Vol. 17, translated and edited by James Strachey, 186–97. London: Hogarth, 1925.

———. *Three Essays on the Theory of Sexuality*. New York: Basic Books, 1962.

Friedan, Betty. "Teenage Girl in Trouble." *Coronet*, March 1958, 163–68.

Gagnon, John H. "Female Child Victims of Sex Offenses." *Social Problems* 13 (1965): 176–92.

Geismar, Maxwell. "Domestic Tragedy in Virginia." *Saturday Review*, September 15, 1951, 12.

Geleerd, Elisabeth R. "Some Aspects of Ego Vicissitudes in Adolescence." *Journal of the American Psychoanalytic Association* 9 (1961): 394–405.

———. "Some Aspects of Psychoanalytic Technique in Adolescence." *Psychoanalytic Study of the Child* 12 (1957): 394–405.

Gilbert, Eugene. "Why Today's Teen-Agers Seem So Different." *Harper's Magazine*, November 1959, 77–86.

"Golden Girl: A Success Story—Or at Least Ought to Be." *Life*, October 11, 1963, 65–85.

Gordon, Lillian. "Incest as Revenge against the Pre-Oedipal Mother." *Psychoanalytic Review* 42 (1955): 284–92.

Greenacre, Phyllis. "The Prepuberty Trauma in Girls." *Psychoanalytic Quarterly* 19 (July 1950): 278–300.

"Group Case Work: An Experiment." *New York Youth Board News* (December 1957): 1, 5.

Hall, G. Stanley. "Flapper Americana Novissima." *Atlantic*, June 1922, 771–80.

"Handling the Make-Up Situation." *Seventeen*, January 1945, 112–13.

Hannegan, Robert E. "Prognosis for Parents." *Seventeen*, November 1945, 32–33, 100.

Henting, Hans von. "The Criminality of Colored Women." *University of Colorado Studies, Series C: Studies in the Social Sciences* 1 (November 1935–46): 231–64.

Herbert, F. Hugh. "Private Affair." *Good Housekeeping*, March 1943, 32–33, 205–7.

"High-School Fads." *Life*, May 15, 1944, 65–69.

Hill, Reuben. "The Returning Father and His Family." *Journal of Marriage and Family Living* (Spring 1945): 28–45.

Himes, Joseph S. "Negro Teen-Age Culture." *Annals of the American Academy of Political and Social Science* 338 (November 1961): 91–101.

Hoover, J. Edgar. "Major Crime Wave Due." *New York Times*, December 11, 1945.

———. "Wild Children." *American Magazine* 136 (July 1943): 39–41, 103–5.

"How America Lives: Meet a Sub-Deb." *Ladies Home Journal*, December 1944, 138–42.

Howard, Harry S. "Incest: The Revenge Motive." *Delaware State Medical Journal* 31 (1959): 223–25.

Jones, Ernest. "The Early Development of Female Sexuality." *International Journal of Psycho-Analysis* 8 (1927): 459–72.

Josselyn, Irene. "The Ego in Adolescence." *American Journal of Orthopsychiatry* 24 (April 1954): 223–37.

Kaufman, Irving, Alice L. Peck, and Consuelo K. Tagiuri. "The Family Constellation and Overt Incestuous Relations between Father and Daughter." *American Journal of Orthopsychiatry* 24 (April 1954): 273–89.

Kaufman, S. Harvard. "Aggression in the Girl Delinquent." *American Journal of Orthopsychiatry* 15 (January 1945): 167–71.

Keiser, Sylvan. "A Manifest Oedipus Complex in an Adolescent Girl." *Psychoanalytic Study of the Child* 8 (1953): 92–106.

Khan, Masud R. "Ego Distortion, Cumulative Trauma and the Role of Reconstruction in the Analytic Situation." *International Journal of Psycho-Analysis* 45 (1964): 272–85.

"The Kids Grow Worse." *Newsweek*, December 6, 1954, 31, 133.

Klein, Malcolm W., and Barbara C. Myerhoff. "The Nature and Roles of Female Delinquent Gangs." *A Proposal Submitted to the National Institutes of Health*. Youth Studies Center. University of Southern California, 1963.

Klein, Melanie. "Early Stages of the Oedipus Conflict." *International Journal of Psycho-Analysis* 9 (1928): 167–80.

———. "Early Stages of the Oedipus Frustration." *International Journal of Psycho-Analysis* 8 (1927): 459–72.

Kris, Ernst. "Helene Deutsch—Birthday Greetings." *Journal of the American Psychoanalytic Association* 12 (October 1964): 875.

———. "Notes on the Development and on Some Current Problems of Psychoanalytic Child Psychology." *Psychoanalytic Study of the Child* 5 (1950): 31.

———. "To Helene Deutsch on Her Seventieth Birthday." *International Journal of Psycho-Analysis* 36 (1955): 209.

Lampl-De Groot, J. "The Evolution of the Oedipus Complex in Women." In *The Psychoanalytic Reader: An Anthology of Essential Papers, with Critical Introductions*, edited by Robert Fleiss, 207–22. New York: International Universities Press, 1962.

Leary, Lewis Gaston. "A Girl Needs Her Father." *Parents' Magazine*, April 1936, 60–62.

Leonard, Marjorie. "Fathers and Daughters: The Significance of 'Fathering' in the Psychosexual Development of the Girl." *International Journal of Psycho-Analysis* 47 (1966): 325–34.

"Letters to the Editor." *Senior Scholastic* 47 (October 22 and 29, 1945): 42, 80.

Levy, Kata. "Simultaneous Analysis of a Mother and Her Adolescent Daughter: The Mother's Contribution to the Loosening of the Infantile Object Tie." *Psychoanalytic Study of the Child* 15 (1960): 378–91.

Lidner, Robert. "Rebels or Psychopaths?" *Time*, December 6, 1954, 64.

"*Life* Goes to a Slumber Party." *Life*, January 4, 1943, 72–75.

"Little Women." *Time*, October 29, 1951, 24.

Lumpkin, Katharine Du Pre. "Parental Conditions of Wisconsin Girl Delinquents." *American Journal of Sociology* 38 (September 1932): 232–39.

Lyndon, Louis. "Uncertain Hero: The Paradox of the American Male." *Woman's Home Companion*, November 1956, 107–11.

Macdonald, Dwight. "Profiles: A Caste, a Culture, a Market." *New Yorker*, November 22, 1958, 71–87.

Maller, J. B. "The Trend of Juvenile Delinquency in New York City." *Journal of Juvenile Research* 17 (January 1933): 10–18.

Markey, Oscar B. "A Study of Aggressive Sex Misbehavior in Adolescents Brought to Juvenile Court." *American Journal of Orthopsychiatry* 20 (October 1950): 719–31.

Martin, Linton. "The Age of Adolescence Yields Charming Comedy." *Philadelphia Inquirer*, January 3, 1943, A11.

McKenzie, Catherine. "Teen-Age Daughters." *New York Times Magazine*, January 14, 1945, 29.

Meiss, Margaret L. "The Oedipal Problem of a Fatherless Child." *Psychoanalytic Study of the Child* 7 (1952): 216–29.

Morgan, Murray. "Nice Girls Can Be Delinquent." *Woman's Home Companion*, April 1955, 48–64.

Murphy, Fred. "Delinquency Off the Record." in *Yearbook of the National Probation Association*, 184–85. New York: National Probation Association, 1946.

"A New, $10-Billion Power: The U.S. Teen-Age Consumer," *Life*, August 31, 1959, 77–85.

"The New Three R's." *Time*, March 15, 1954, 68–69.

Reference Papers on Children and Youth, 243–49. Washington, D.C.:
  Government Printing Office, 1960.

Podhoretz, Norman. "Our Changing Ideas, As Seen on TV." In *The Scene
  before You: A New Approach to American Culture*, edited by Chandler
  Brossard, 92–103. New York: Rinehart and Co., 1955.

Porges, Irwin. "Your Teenager Is Big Business." *American Mercury* 87
  (July 1958): 94–96.

"Prognosis for Parents." *Seventeen*, November 1945, 98–100.

"Put Father Back." *America*, March 15, 1958, 682.

Rhinehart, John W. "Genesis of Overt Incest." *Comprehensive Psychiatry*
  2 (December 1961): 338–49.

Robbins, Jhan, and June Robbins. "Why Girls Are So Good." *Popular Science
  Monthly* 172 (January 1958): 158–61.

Robey, Ames. "The Runaway Girl." In *Family Dynamics and Female Sexual
  Delinquency*, edited by Otto Pollak and Alfred S. Friedman, 124–37. Palo
  Alto: Science and Behavior Books, 1969.

———. "The Runaway Girl: A Reaction to Family Stress." *American Journal of
  Orthopsychiatry* 34 (July 1964): 762–67.

Rubin, Sol. "The Legal Character of Juvenile Delinquency." *Annals of the
  American Academy of Political and Social Science* 261 (January 1949): 1–18.

Samuels, Gertrude. "Tangled Problem of the Gang Girl." *New York Times
  Magazine*, July 10, 1960, 13.

Schlesinger, Arthur. "The Crisis of American Masculinity." *Esquire*, November
  1958, 133.

Schwartz, Edward E. "A Community Experiment in the Measurement of
  Juvenile Delinquency." *Yearbook of the National Probation Association*,
  157–81. New York: National Probation Association, 1946.

Sentman, Everette Edgar. "Pity Poor Dad." *Parents' Magazine* 1960, 52–53, 78.

"*Seventeen*: A Unique Case Study." *Tide: The News Magazine of Advertising and
  Marketing*, April 15, 1945, 119.

Sloan, Paul, and Eva Karpinski. "Effects of Incest on the Participants."
  American Journal of Orthopsychiatry 12 (October 1942): 666–73.

Sloman, Sophie Schroeder. "Reactions of Children to a Highly Publicized
  Crime against a Child." *American Journal of Psychiatry* 105 (April 1949):
  779–81.

Spence, William Henry. "Fathers and Daughters." *Parents' Magazine*,
  September 1937, 80.

Spiegel, Leo A. "Comments on the Psychoanalytical Psychology of
  Adolescence." *Psychoanalytic Study of the Child* 13 (1958): 296–300.

———. "A Review of the Contributions to a Psychoanalytic Theory of
  Adolescence." *Psychoanalytic Study of the Child* 6 (1951): 375–93.

Stern, Edith M. "Danger! Children at Work." *Woman's Home Companion*,
January 1944, 66–69.

"Sub-Deb Clubs: The Midwest Is Full of Them." *Life*, April 2, 1945, 87–93.

"Subdebs: They Live in a Jolly World of Gangs, Games, Gadding, Movies,
Malteds and Music." *Life*, January 27, 1941, 74–79.

Tappan, Paul W. "Children and Youth in the Criminal Court." *Annals of the
American Academy of Political and Social Science* 261 (January 1949):
128–36.

Tasch, Ruth. "The Role of the Father in the Family." *Journal of Experimental
Education* 20 (June 1952): 318–61.

"Teenage Boys." *Life*, June 11, 1945, 33–37.

"Teen-Age Girls: They Live in a Wonderful World of Their Own." *Life*,
December 11, 1944, 91–99.

"Three Smart Girls." *Newsweek*, October 29, 1951, 25.

Tompkins, J. Butler. "Penis Envy and Incest: A Case Report." *Psychoanalytic
Review* 27 (1940): 319–25.

Trilling, Lionel. "The Other Margaret." *Partisan Review* 12 (Fall 1945):
481–501.

Weiner, Irving B. "Father-Daughter Incest: A Clinical Report." *Psychiatric
Quarterly* 36 (1962): 607–32.

Winnicott, D. W. "Paediatrics and Psychiatry." *British Journal of Medicine and
Psychology* 21 (1948): 23–33.

———. "Primary Maternal Preoccupation." *Through Paediatrics to
Psychoanalysis: Collected Papers*. 1956. New York: Brunner Mazel, 1992.

Wise, Nancy Barton. "Juvenile Delinquency among Middle-Class Girls." In
Middle-Class Juvenile Delinquency, edited by Edmund W. Vaz, 179–88.
New York: Harper and Row, 1967.

"Youth." *Time*, October 29, 1951, 54.

BOOKS AND PLAYS

Ackerman, Nathan, M.D. *The Psychodynamics of Family Life: Diagnosis and
Treatment of Family Relationships*. New York: Basic Books, 1958.

Atkinson, Brooks. *Broadway*. New York: Macmillan, 1970.

Barron, Milton L. *The Juvenile in Delinquent Society*. New York: Knopf, 1954.

Benson, Sally. *Junior Miss*. New York: Random House, 1939.

Benson and Benson. *Life with Teena*. Vols. 1 and 2. Princeton: Benson and
Benson Opinion Research Corp., 1945–46.

Blanchard, Phyllis. *The Adolescent Girl: A Study from the Psychoanalytic
Viewpoint*. New York: Dodd, Mead, 1924.

Blanchard, Phyllis, and Carlyn Manasses. *New Girls for Old*. New York:
Macaulay, 1930.

Blanshard, Paul, and Edwin J. Lukas. *Probation and Psychiatric Care for Adolescent Offenders in New York City.* New York: Society for the Prevention of Crime, 1942.

Blos, Peter. *On Adolescence: A Psychoanalytic Interpretation.* New York: Free Press of Glencoe, 1962.

Breckinridge, Sophinisba, and Edith Abbott. *The Delinquent Child and the Home.* New York: Charities Publication, 1912.

Brooks, William Allan. *Girl Gangs.* New York: Padell, 1952.

Burger, W. H. *Growing up with Our Children: For Parents of Teen Age Young People.* New York: Association Press, 1932.

Burgess, Ernest W., and Harvey J. Locke. *The Family: From Institution to Companionship.* New York: American Book Company, 1945.

Chodorov, Jerome, and Joseph Fields. *Junior Miss.* New York: Random House, 1942.

Cohen, Albert K. *Delinquent Boys: The Culture of the Gang.* New York: Free Press of Glencoe, 1955.

Coleman, James S. *The Adolescent Society: The Social Life of the Teenager and Its Impact on Education.* New York: Free Press, 1961.

Coward, Richard A., and Lloyd E. Ohlin. *Delinquency and Opportunity.* Glencoe: Free Press, 1960.

Crow, Lester D., and Alice Crow. *Our Teen-Age Boys and Girls: Suggestions for Parents, Teachers, and Other Youth Leaders.* New York: McGraw-Hill, 1945.

Daly, Maureen, ed. *Profile of Youth.* New York: J. B. Lippincott, 1951.

Davis, Allison, and John Dollard. *Children of Bondage: The Personality Development of Negro Youth in the Urban South.* Washington, D.C.: American Council on Education, 1940.

Davis, Allison, and Robert J. Havinghurst. *Father of the Man: How Your Child Gets His Personality.* Boston: Houghton Mifflin, 1947.

Day, Clarence. *Life with Father.* New York: Random House, 1920.

Deutsch, Helene. *The Psychology of Women.* Vol. 1. New York: Grune and Stratton, 1944.

Douvan, Elizabeth, and Joseph Adelson. *The Adolescent Experience.* New York: John Wiley, 1966.

Drake, St. Clair, and Horace R. Cayton. *Black Metropolis: A Study of Negro Life in a Northern City.* New York: Harcourt, Brace, 1945.

Duvall, Evelyn Millis. *Facts of Life and Love for Teen-Agers.* New York: Popular Library, 1956.

Elliott, Grace Loucks. *Understanding the Adolescent Girl.* New York: Henry Holt, 1930.

English, O. Spurgeon, and Constance J. Foster. *Fathers Are Parents, Too: A*

Constructive Guide to Successful Fatherhood. New York: G. P. Putnam's Sons, 1951.

Erikson, Erik H. *Childhood and Society*. New York: Norton, 1950.

Farnham, Marynia F. *The Adolescent*. New York: Harper, 1951.

Fedder, Ruth. *A Girl Grows Up*. New York: McGraw-Hill, 1939.

Fisher, Bernard C. *Justice for Youth: The Courts for Wayward Youth in New York City*. New York: Community Service Society, Bureau of Public Affairs, 1955.

Fleming, C. M. *Adolescence: Its Social Psychology*. New York: International Universities Press, 1949.

Frazier, E. Franklin. *Black Bourgeoisie: The Rise of a New Middle Class*. New York: Free Press, 1957.

———. *The Negro Family in the United States*. New York: Citadel, 1948.

Freud, Anna. *The Ego and the Mechanisms of Defense*. New York: International Universities Press, 1946.

Freud, Sigmund. *Dora: An Analysis of a Case of Hysteria*, ed. Philip Rieff. New York: Collier, 1963.

———. *A General Introduction to Psychoanalysis*. New York: Washington Square Press, 1952.

Friedan, Betty. *The Feminine Mystique*. New York: Norton, 1963.

Friedenberg, Edgar Z. *The Vanishing Adolescent*. Boston: Beacon Press, 1959.

Friedlander, Kate. *The Psycho-Analytical Approach to Juvenile Delinquency*. London: Keegan Paul, 1947.

Gilbert, Eugene. *Advertising and Marketing to Young People*. New York: Printer's Ink, 1957.

Goodman, Paul, *Growing up Absurd: The Problems of Youth in an Organized Society*. New York: Vintage Books, 1960.

Gorer, Geoffrey. *The American People: A Study in National Character*. New York: Norton, 1948.

Grayson, Alice Barr [Jean Schick Grossman]. *Do You Know Your Daughter?* New York: Appleton-Century, 1944.

Greenacre, Phyllis. *Trauma, Growth, and Personality*. London: Hogarth, 1953.

Hansberry, Lorraine. *A Raisin in the Sun*. New York: Random House, 1959.

Hart, Moss. *Act One: An Autobiography*. New York: Random House, 1959.

Hechinger, Grace, and Fred M. Hechinger. *Teen-Age Tyranny*. New York: William Morrow, 1962.

Henry, Jules. *Culture against Man*. New York: Random House, 1963.

Herbert, F. Hugh. *For Keeps*. Produced by Gilbert Miller, The Henry Miller Theatre, New York, 1944.

———. *Kiss and Tell*. New York: Dramatists Play Service, 1945.

———. *Meet Corliss Archer*. New York: Random House, 1944.

Hewitt, Lester E., and Richard L. Jenkins. *Fundamental Patterns of Maladjustment*. Illinois: n.p., 1946.

Hood, Mary G. *For Girls and the Mothers of Girls; A Book for the Home and the School Concerning the Beginnings of Life*. Indianapolis: Bobbs-Merrill, 1914.

Hunt, Morton M. *The Talking Cure: Psychoanalysis Today, What It Is and What It Can Mean to You*. New York: Pyramid, 1964.

Institute for Social Research. *Adolescent Girls: A Nation-wide Study of Girls between Eleven and Eighteen Years of Age*. Ann Arbor: University of Michigan, 1958.

Jones, Ernest. *Papers on Psychoanalysis*. 4th ed. Baltimore: William Wood, 1938.

Kardiner, Abram, and Lionel Ovesey. *The Mark of Oppression*. New York: Norton, 1951.

Keats, John. *The Crack in the Picture Window*. Boston: Houghton Mifflin, 1956.

Kinsey, Alfred C. *Sexual Behavior in the Human Female*. Philadelphia: Saunders, 1953.

Knight, John. *The Story of My Psychoanalysis*. New York: Pocket Books, 1952.

Levy, David. *Maternal Overprotection*. New York: Columbia University Press, 1943.

Lief, Harold, Daniel Thompson, and William Thompson. *The Eighth Generation: Cultures and Personalities of New Orleans Negroes*. New York: Harper, 1960.

Lundberg, Ferdinand, and Marynia F. Farnham. *Modern Woman: The Lost Sex*. New York: Harper, 1947.

Mead, Margaret. *And Keep Your Powder Dry: An Anthropologist Looks at America*. New York: William Morrow, 1943.

Merrill, Maud. *Problems of Child Delinquency*. New York: Houghton Mifflin, 1947.

Metalious, Grace. *Peyton Place*. New York: Julian Messner, 1956.

Nabokov, Vladimir. *The Enchanter*. 1939. New York: Putnam's, 1986.

———. *Lolita*. New York: Putnam, 1958.

Nathan, Robert. *Winter in April*. New York: Knopf, 1938.

The National Cyclopaedia of American Biography. Vol. 48. New York: James White and Co., 1965.

O'Neill, Eugene. *Ah, Wilderness!* In *Eugene O'Neill: Complete Plays, 1932–1943*. New York: Library of America, 1988.

Parsons, Talcott. *Social Structure and Personality*. New York: Free Press, 1964.

Porterfield, Austin L. *Youth in Trouble: Studies in Delinquency and Despair*. Fort Worth: Leo Potishman Foundation, 1946.

Remmers, H. H., and D. H. Radler. *The American Teenager*. New York: Bobbs-Merrill, 1957.

Rhinehart, Mary. *Bab: A Sub-Deb*. New York: George H. Doran, 1917.

Richmond, Winifred. *The Adolescent Girl: A Book for Parents and Teachers*. New York: Macmillan, 1925.

Riesman, David. *The Lonely Crowd*. New Haven: Yale University Press, 1961.

Salinger, J. D. *Catcher in the Rye*. Boston: Little, Brown, 1951.

Schlesinger, Arthur. *The Vital Center: The Politics of Freedom*. 1949. New Brunswick, N.J.: Transaction, 1998.

Shulman, Harry. *Juvenile Delinquency in American Society*. New York: Harper, 1961.

Sievers, David. *Freud on Broadway*. New York: Hermitage House, 1955.

Simpson, Sally. *Popularity Plus: Good Manners for Young Moderns*. New York: Pocket Books, 1950.

Smith, Robert Paul, *"Where Did You Go?" "Out" "What Did You Do?" "Nothing."* New York: Norton, 1957.

Spock, Dr. Benjamin. *Baby and Child Care*. New York: Merideth, 1968.

Strain, Frances Bruce. *"But You Don't Understand": A Dramatic Series of Teen-Age Predicaments*. New York: Appleton-Century-Crofts, 1950.

Stratton-Porter, Gene. *Her Father's Daughter*. New York: Doubleday, 1921.

Streeter, Edward. *Chairman of the Bored*. New York: Harper, 1961.

———. *Daily Except Sundays*. New York: Simon and Shuster, 1938.

———. *Father of the Bride*. New York: Simon and Schuster, 1948.

———. *Merry Christmas, Mr. Baxter*. New York: Harper, 1956.

———. "Mr. Banks' Other Daughter: The Sequel to Father of the Bride." *Good Housekeeping* 130 (April 1950): 50.

Styron, William. *Lie Down in Darkness*. Indianapolis: Bobbs-Merrill, 1951.

Sullivan, Katharine. *Girls on Parole*. Boston: Houghton Mifflin, 1956.

Tappan, Paul. *Delinquent Girls in Court*. New York: Columbia University Press, 1947.

Tarkington, Booth. *Alice Adams*. New York: Doubleday, 1921.

———. *Seventeen: A Tale of Youth and Summer Time and the Baxter Family, Especially William*. 1915. New York: Harper and Brothers, 1932.

Terman, Lewis. *Psychological Factors in Marital Happiness*. New York: McGraw-Hill, 1938.

Trilling, Lionel. *The Liberal Imagination*. New York: Viking, 1950.

Truitt, Ralph P. *The Child Guidance Clinic and the Community: A Group of Papers Written from the Viewpoints of the Clinic, the Juvenile Court, the School, the Child Welfare Agency, and the Parent*. New York: Commonwealth Fund, 1928.

Waller, Willard. *The Family: A Dynamic Interpretation*. New York: The Cordon Company, 1938.

Wattenberg, William W. *The Adolescent Years*. New York: Harcourt, Brace, 1955.

Whyte, William, Jr. *The Organization Man*. New York: Simon and Schuster, 1956.

Wood, A. E., and J. B. Waite. *Crime and Its Treatment: Social and Legal Aspects of Criminology*. New York: American Book Company, 1941.

Wylie, Philip. *Generation of Vipers*. New York: Farrar and Rinehart, 1942.

Yordan, Philip. *Anna Lucasta*. New York: Random House, 1945.

FILMS

Ah, Wilderness! Metro-Goldwyn-Mayer, 1935.

A Raisin in the Sun. Columbia, 1961.

The Bachelor and the Bobby Soxer. RKO, 1948.

Blackboard Jungle. Metro-Goldwyn-Mayer, 1955.

The Catered Affair. Warner Brothers, 1956.

Daddy Long Legs. Universal, 1955.

A Date with Judy. Metro-Goldwyn-Mayer, 1948.

Father of the Bride. Metro-Goldwyn-Mayer, 1950.

Father Was a Fullback. Twentieth Century Fox, 1949.

First Love. Universal, 1933.

Four Daughters. Warner Brothers, 1938.

Girl's Town. Metro-Goldwyn-Mayer, 1959.

Imitation of Life. Universal, 1959.

Kiss and Tell. Columbia Pictures, 1945.

A Kiss for Corliss. United Artists, 1948.

Lady on a Train. Universal, 1945.

Listen, Darling. Metro-Goldwyn-Mayer, 1938.

Lolita. Metro-Goldwyn-Mayer, 1962.

Love Finds Andy Hardy. Metro-Goldwyn-Mayer, 1938.

Mad about Music. Universal, 1938.

Margie. Twentieth Century Fox, 1946.

Mildred Pierce. Metro-Goldwyn-Mayer, 1945.

Naked Youth. RKO, 1956.

Peyton Place. Universal, 1957.

Pinky. Twentieth Century Fox, 1949.

Rebel Without a Cause. Warner Brothers, 1955.

The Reluctant Debutante. Metro-Goldwyn-Mayer, 1958.

Stella Dallas. United Artists, 1937.

Teenage Crime Wave. RKO, 1959.

Teenage Devil Dolls. RKO, 1957.

"Teenage Girls." March of Time newsreels, 1945.

Three Smart Girls. Universal, 1936.
Wife vs. Secretary. Metro-Goldwyn-Mayer, 1936.
The Wild One. Columbia, 1955.

Secondary Sources

Alexander, Ruth M. *The Girl Problem: Female Sexual Delinquency in New York: 1900–1930.* Ithaca: Cornell University Press, 1995.

American Psychiatric Association. *Biographical Dictionary of Fellows and Members of the American Psychoanalytic Association.* New York: American Psychoanalytic Association, 1977.

Anderson, Karen. *Wartime Women: Sex Roles, Family Relations and the Status of Women during World War II.* Westport, Conn.: Greenwood Press, 1981.

Appel, Alfred, Jr., ed. *The Annotated Lolita.* New York: Vintage, 1991.

———. *Nabokov's Dark Cinema.* New York: Oxford University Press, 1974.

Bailey, Beth. *From Front Porch to Back Seat: Courtship in Twentieth-Century America.* Baltimore: Johns Hopkins University Press, 1988.

Barton, Nancy Jo. "Disregarded Delinquency: A Study of Self-Reported Middle-Class Female Delinquency in a Suburb." Ph.D. dissertation, Indiana University, 1965.

Basinger, Jeanine. "The Girls Next Door." *New York Times Magazine,* November 24, 1996, 64.

Bederman, Gail. *Manliness and Civilization: A Cultural History of Gender and Race in the United States, 1880–1917.* Chicago: University of Chicago Press, 1995.

Benson, Susan Porter. "Living on the Margin: Working-Class Marriages and Family Survival Strategies in the United States, 1919–1941." In *The Sex of Things: Gender and Consumption in Historical Perspective,* edited by Victoria de Grazia, 212–43. Berkeley: University of California Press, 1996.

Biskind, Peter. *Seeing Is Believing: How Hollywood Taught Us to Stop Worrying and Love in the Fifties.* New York: Pantheon, 1983.

Bloom, Harold, ed. *Lolita.* New York: Chelsea House, 1993.

Boose, Lynda E., and Betty S. Flowers, eds. *Daughters and Fathers.* Baltimore: Johns Hopkins University Press, 1989.

Boruchoff, David A., ed. *Isabel La Catolica, Queen of Castile: Critical Essays.* New York: Palgrave, 2003.

Boyd, Brian. *Vladimir Nabokov: The American Years.* Princeton: Princeton University Press, 1991.

Boyer, Paul. *By the Bomb's Early Light: American Thought and Culture at the Dawn of the Atomic Age.* New York: Pantheon, 1985.

Breines, Wini. *Young, White, and Miserable: Growing up Female in the Fifties*. Boston: Beacon Press, 1992.

Brown, Kathleen M. *Good Wives, Nasty Wenches, and Anxious Patriarchs: Gender, Race, and Power in Colonial Virginia*. Chapel Hill: University of North Carolina Press, 1996.

Brumberg, Joan Jacobs. *The Body Project: An Intimate History of American Girls*. New York: Random House, 1997.

———. Introduction to *Girl Culture*, by Laura Greenfield. New York: Chronicle Books, 2002.

Buhle, Mari Jo. *Feminism and Its Discontents: A Century of Struggle with Psychoanalysis*. Cambridge: Harvard University Press, 1998.

Burnham, John. *Paths into American Culture: Psychology, Medicine, and Morals*. Philadelphia: Temple University Press, 1988.

Carby, Hazel. *Race Men*. Cambridge: Harvard University Press, 1998.

———. *Reconstructing Womanhood: The Emergence of the Afro-American Woman Novelist*. New York: Oxford University Press, 1987.

Caughie, John, and Annette Kuhn, eds. *The Sexual Subject: A "Screen" Reader in Sexuality*. New York: Routledge, 1992.

Chafe, William H. *The Paradox of Change: American Women in the Twentieth Century*. New York: Oxford University Press, 1991.

Chodorow, Nancy. *The Reproduction of Mothering: Psychoanalysis and the Sociology of Gender*. Berkeley: University of California Press, 1978.

Cohan, Steve. "Cary Grant in the Fifties: Indiscretions of the Bachelor's Masquerade." *Screen* 33 (1992): 394–412.

———. *Masked Men: Masculinity and the Movies in the Fifties*. Bloomington: Indiana University Press, 1997.

Cott, Nancy F. *Public Vows: A History of Marriage and the Nation*. Cambridge: Harvard University Press, 2000.

Craig, Maxine Leeds. *Ain't I a Beauty Queen? Black Women, Beauty, and the Politics of Race*. New York: Oxford University Press, 2002.

Crews, Frederick. "The Revenge of the Repressed." Parts 1 and 2, *The New York Review of Books*, November and December 1994.

Daniel, Walter C. *Black Journals of the United States*. Westport, Conn.: Greenwood Press, 1982.

De Grazia, Victoria, ed. *The Sex of Things: Gender and Consumption in Historical Perspective*. Berkeley: University of California Press, 1996.

D'Emilio, John, and Estelle B. Freedman. *Intimate Matters: A History of Sexuality in America*. New York: Harper and Row, 1988.

Demos, John. "Oedipus in America: Historical Perspectives on the Reception of Psychoanalysis in the United States." *Annual of Psychoanalysis* 6 (1978): 23–39.

———. *Past, Present and Personal: The Family and the Life Course in American History*. New York: Oxford University Press, 1986.

Diamond, Irene, and Lee Quinby. *Feminism and Foucault: Reflections on Resistance*. Boston: Northeastern University Press, 1988.

DiBattista, Maria. *Fast-Talking Dames*. New Haven: Yale University Press, 2001.

Doss, Erika, ed., *Looking at Life Magazine*. Washington, D.C.: Smithsonian Institution Press, 2001.

Douglas, Susan. *Where the Girls Are: Growing up Female with the Mass Media*. New York: Random House, 1994.

Driscoll, Catherine. *Girls: Feminine Adolescence in Popular Culture and Cultural Theory*. New York: Columbia University Press, 2002.

Dunning, John. *On the Air: The Encyclopedia of Old-Time Radio*. New York: Oxford University Press, 1998.

Ehrenreich, Barbara. *The Hearts of Men: American Dreams and the Flight from Commitment*. New York: Anchor, 1983.

Ehrenreich, Barbara, and Deirdre English. *For Her Own Good: 150 Years of the Experts' Advice to Women*. New York: Doubleday, 1978.

Enstad, Nan. *Ladies of Labor, Girls of Adventure: Working Women, Popular Culture, and Labor Politics at the Turn of the Twentieth Century*. New York: Columbia University Press, 1999.

Erickson, Erik Homburger. *Identity, Youth and Crisis*. New York: Norton, 1968.

Fass, Paula. *The Damned and the Beautiful: American Youth in the 1920's*. New York: Oxford University Press, 1977.

Filene, Peter Gabriel. *Him/Her/Self: Sex Roles in Modern America*. Baltimore: Johns Hopkins University Press, 1974.

Fischer, Lucy, ed. *Imitation of Life*. New Brunswick, N.J.: Rutgers University Press, 1991.

Forman-Brunell, Miriam, ed. *Girlhood in America: An Encyclopedia*. Santa Barbara, Calif.: ABC-CLIO, 2001.

———. "Truculent and Tractable: The Gendering of Babysitting in Postwar America." In *Delinquents and Debutantes: Twentieth Century Girls' Cultures*, edited by Sherrie Inness, 61–82. New York: New York University Press, 1998.

Foucault, Michel. *The History of Sexuality*. Vol. 1. New York: Vintage, 1985.

Freedman, Estelle B. "'Uncontrolled Desires': The Response to the Sexual Psychopath, 1920–1960." In *Passion and Power*, edited by Kathy Peiss and Christina Simmons, 199–225. Philadelphia: Temple University Press, 1987.

Gale Literary Data Bases. *Contemporary Authors*. New York: Gale Group, 1999.

Gates, Henry Louis, Jr. *"Race," Writing, and Difference*. Chicago: University of Chicago Press, 1986.

Gatewood, Willard. *Aristocrats of Color: The Black Elite, 1880–1920*. Bloomington: Indiana University Press, 1990.

Geller, Jaclyn. *Here Comes the Bride: Women, Weddings, and the Marriage Mystique*. New York: Four Walls Eight Windows, 2001.

Giddings, Paula. *When and Where I Enter: The Impact of Black Women on Race and Sex in America*. New York: William Morrow, 1984.

Gilbert, James. *A Cycle of Outrage: America's Reaction to the Juvenile Delinquent in the 1950s*. New York: Oxford University Press, 1986.

Gilliatt, Penelope. *To Wit: Skin and Bones of Comedy*. New York: Scribner's, 1990.

Gillis, John R. *For Better, For Worse: British Marriages 1600 to the Present*. New York: Oxford University Press, 1985.

Gilmore, Glenda. *Gender and Jim Crow: Women and the Politics of White Supremacy in North Carolina, 1896–1920*. Chapel Hill: University of North Carolina Press, 1996.

Gordon, Linda. *Heroes of Their Own Lives: The Politics and History of Family Violence, Boston, 1880–1960*. New York: Viking Press, 1988.

———. *Woman's Body, Woman's Right: Birth Control in America*. New York: Penguin, 1974.

Gordon, Linda, and Allen Hunter. "Not All Male Dominance Is Patriarchal." *Radical History Review* 71 (Spring 1998): 71–76.

Graebner, William. *The Age of Doubt: American Thought and Culture in the 1940s*. Boston: Twayne, 1991.

Graham, Lawrence Otis. *Our Kind of People: Inside America's Black Upper Class*. New York: Harper Collins, 1999.

Graver, Lawrence. *An Obsession with Ann Frank: Meyer Levin and the "Diary."* Berkeley: University of California Press, 1995.

Griswold, Robert. *Fatherhood in America: A History*. New York: Basic Books, 1993.

Haag, Pamela. *Consent: Sexual Rights and the Transformation of American Liberalism*. Ithaca: Cornell University Press, 1999.

———. "In Search of 'The Real Thing': Ideologies of Love, Modern Romance, and Women's Sexual Subjectivity in the United States, 1920–1940." *Journal of the History of Sexuality* 2 (1992): 558.

Hale, Nathan G., Jr. *The Rise and Crisis of Psychoanalysis in the United States: Freud and the Americans, 1917–1985*. New York: Oxford University Press, 1995.

Hall, Jacquelyn Dowd. "'The Mind that Burns in Each Body': Women, Rape, and Racial Violence." In *Powers of Desire: The Politics of Sexuality*, edited by Ann Snitow, Christine Stansell, and Sharon Thomson. New York: Monthly Review Press, 1983.

———. *Revolt against Chivalry: Jessie Daniel Ames and the Women's Campaign against Lynching.* New York: Columbia University Press, 1993.

Halttunen, Karen. *Confidence Men and Painted Women: A Study of Middle-Class Culture in America, 1830–1870.* New Haven: Yale University Press, 1982.

Hartman, Saidiya V. *Scenes of Subjection: Terror, Slavery, and Self-Making in Nineteenth-Century America.* New York: Oxford University Press, 1997.

Herman, Judith Lewis. *Father-Daughter Incest.* Cambridge: Harvard University Press, 1981.

Hill, Errol G., and James V. Hatch. *A History of African American Theatre.* New York: Cambridge University Press, 2003.

Hine, Thomas. *The Rise and Fall of the American Teenager.* New York: Avon, 1999.

Hobsbawm, Eric, and Terence Ranger, eds. *The Invention of Tradition.* New York: Cambridge University Press, 1983.

Hoganson, Kristin L. *Fighting for American Manhood: How Gender Politics Provoked the Spanish-American and Philippine-American Wars.* New Haven: Yale University Press, 1998.

Huyssen, Andrea. *After the Great Divide: Modernism, Mass Culture, Postmodernism.* Bloomington: Indiana University Press, 1986.

Jacobson, Matthew Frye. *Whiteness of a Different Color: European Immigrants and the Alchemy of Race.* Cambridge: Harvard University Press, 1998.

Jameson, Frederic. *Postmodernism or the Cultural Logic of Late Capitalism.* Durham: Duke University Press, 1992.

———. "Reification and Utopia in Mass Culture." *Social Text* 1 (1979): 141.

Jones, Kathleen W. *Taming the Troublesome Child: American Families, Child Guidance, and the Limits of Psychiatric Authority.* Cambridge: Harvard University Press, 1999.

Jones, Langdon Y. *Great Expectations: America and the Baby Boom Generation.* New York: Coward, McCann and Geoghegan, 1980.

Justice-Malloy, Rhona. "Little Girl Bound: Costume and Coming of Age in the Sears Catalog 1906–1927." In *Delinquents and Debutantes: Twentieth Century Girls' Cultures,* edited by Sherrie Inness, 109–33. New York: New York University Press, 1998.

Kaplan, E. Ann. *Motherhood and Representation: The Mother in Popular Culture and Melodrama.* New York: Routledge, 1992.

Kelley, Robin D. G. *Race Rebels: Culture, Politics, and the Black Working Class.* New York: Free Press, 1994.

Kesselman, Amy. *Fleeting Opportunities: Women Shipyard Workers in Portland*

and Vancouver during World War II and Reconversion. New York: State University of New York Press, 1990.

Kessler-Harris, Alice. *Out to Work: A History of Wage-Earning Women in the United States*. New York: Oxford University Press, 1982.

Kett, Joseph. *Rites of Passage: Adolescence in America, 1790 to the Present*. New York: Basic Books, 1977.

Kunzel, Regina. *Fallen Women, Problem Girls: Unmarried Mothers and the Professionalization of Social Work, 1890–1945*. New Haven: Yale University Press, 1993.

————. "Pulp Fictions and Problem Girls: Reading and Rewriting Single Pregnancy in the Postwar United States." *American Historical Review* 100 (December 1995): 1487.

Ladd-Taylor, Molly, and Lauri Umansky, eds. *"Bad" Mothers: The Politics of Blame in Twentieth-Century America*. New York: New York University Press, 1998.

Lamb, Sharon. *The Secret Lives of Girls: What Good Girls Really Do—Sex Play, Aggression, and Their Guilt*. New York: Free Press, 2000.

LaRossa, Ralph. "The Culture of Fatherhood in the Fifties: A Closer Look." *Journal of Family History* 29 (January 2004): 47–70.

————. *The Modernization of Fatherhood: A Social and Political History*. Chicago: University of Chicago Press, 1997.

Lasch, Christopher. *Haven in a Heartless World: The Family Besieged*. New York: Basic Books, 1977.

Leach, William. "Transformations in a Culture of Consumption: Women and Department Stores, 1890–1925." *Journal of American History* 71 (September 1984): 319–42.

Lunbeck, Elizabeth. "'A New Generation of Women': Progressive Psychiatrists and the Hypersexual Female." *Feminist Studies* 13 (Fall 1987): 513–39.

————. *The Psychiatric Persuasion: Knowledge, Gender, and Power in Modern America*. Princeton: Princeton University Press, 1994.

Lynch, Nancy. "A Walk in a Dark Room." *Mademoiselle*, October 1957, 98, 146–53.

Marling, Karal Ann. *Debutante: Rites and Regalia of American Debdom*. Lawrence: University Press of Kansas, 2004.

Marsh, Margaret. *Suburban Lives*. New Brunswick, N.J.: Rutgers University Press, 1990.

Masson, Jeffrey Moussaieff. *The Assault on Truth: Freud's Suppression of the Seduction Theory*. New York: Pocket, 1984.

May, Elaine Tyler. *Homeward Bound: American Families in the Cold War Era*. New York: Basic Books, 1988.

Mazon, Mauricio. *The Zoot Suit Riots.* Austin: University of Texas Press, 1984.

McFadden, Margaret T. "America's Boy Friend Who Can't Get a Date: Gender, Race and the Cultural Work of the Jack Benny Program, 1932–1946." *Journal of American History* 80 (June 1993): 113–34.

McGee, Mark Thomas, and R. J. Robertson. *The J.D. Films: Juvenile Delinquency in the Movies.* Jefferson, N.C.: McFarland and Co., 1982.

Merril, Hugh. *Esky: The Early Years at Esquire.* New Brunswick, N.J.: Rutgers University Press, 1995.

Meyerowitz, Joanne. "Beyond the Feminine Mystique: A Reassessment of Postwar Mass Culture, 1946–1958." *Journal of American History* 79 (March 1993): 1455–81.

————, ed. *Not June Cleaver: Women and Gender in Postwar America, 1945–1965.* Philadelphia: Temple University Press, 1994.

Millett, Kate. *Sexual Politics.* Garden City, N.Y.: Doubleday, 1970.

Mintz, Steven, and Susan Kellogg. *Domestic Revolutions: A Social History of American Family Life.* New York: Free Press, 1988.

Modell, John. *Into One's Own: From Youth to Adulthood in the United States, 1920–1975.* Berkeley: University of California Press, 1989.

Moore, Burness E., ed. *Psychoanalytic Terms and Concepts.* New Haven: Yale University Press, 1990.

Morris, Robert K., and Irving Malin, eds. *The Achievement of William Styron.* Athens: University of Georgia Press, 1975.

Morrison, Toni. *Playing in the Dark: Whiteness in the Literary Imagination.* New York: Vintage, 1992.

Nash, Illana. "'Nowhere Else to Go': *Gidget* and the Construction of Adolescent Femininity." *Feminist Media Studies* 2 (2002): 341–56.

Nochlin, Linda. *Women, Art, and Power, and Other Essays.* Boulder, Colo.: Icon Editions, 1989.

O'Connell, Agnes N., ed. *Women in Psychology: A Bio-Bibliographic Sourcebook.* New York: Greenwood, 1990.

Odem, Mary. *Delinquent Daughters: Protecting and Policing Adolescent Female Sexuality in the United States, 1885–1920.* Chapel Hill: University of North Carolina Press, 1995.

Page, Norman, ed. *Nabokov: The Critical Heritage.* Boston: Routledge and Kegan Paul, 1982.

Palladino, Grace. *Teenagers: An American History.* New York: Basic Books, 1996.

————. *Social Structure and Personality.* New York: Free Press of Glencoe, 1964.

Patterson, James T. *Grand Expectations: The United States, 1945–1974.* New York: Oxford University Press, 1996.

Peiss, Kathy. *Hope in a Jar: The Making of America's Beauty Culture*. New York: Metropolitan Books, 1998.

———. "Making Up, Making Over: Cosmetics, Consumer Culture, and Women's Identity." In *The Sex of Things: Gender and Consumption in Historical Perspective*, edited by Victoria de Grazia, 311–36. Berkeley: University of California Press, 1996.

Peterson, Theodore. *Magazines in the Twentieth Century*. Urbana: University of Illinois Press, 1964.

Pfister, Joel, and Nancy Schnog, ed. *Inventing the Psychological: Toward a Cultural History of Emotional Life in America*. New Haven: Yale University Press, 1997.

Plant, Rebecca. "The Repeal of Mother-Love: Momism and the Reconstruction of Motherhood in Philip Wylie's America." Ph.D. dissertation, Johns Hopkins University, 2001.

Pleck, Elizabeth. *Domestic Tyranny: The Making of American Social Policy against Family Violence from Colonial Times to the Present*. New York: Oxford University Press, 1987.

Pleck, Joseph. "American Fathering in Historical Perspective." In *Changing Men: New Directions in Research on Men and Masculinity*, edited by Michael Kimmel. Newbury Park, Calif.: Sage, 1987.

Poovey, Mary. *Uneven Developments: The Ideological Work of Gender in Mid-Victorian England*. Chicago: University of Chicago Press, 1988.

Rich, Frank. "Oh, What a Miserable Mornin'." *New York Times Magazine*, October 28, 2001, 58.

Roazen, Paul. *Helene Deutsch: A Psychoanalyst's Life*. New York: Anchor/Doubleday, 1985.

Roediger, David. *The Wages of Whiteness: Race and the Making of the American Working Class*. New York: Verso, 1991.

Rogin, Michael Paul. *"Ronald Reagan," the Movie: And Other Episodes of Political Demonology*. Berkeley: University of California Press, 1987.

Rotundo, E. Anthony. *American Manhood: Transformations in Masculinity from the Revolution to the Modern Era*. New York: Basic Books, 1993.

Rupp, Leila J., and Verta Taylor. *Survival in the Doldrums: The American Women's Rights Movement, 1945 to the 1960s*. New York: Oxford University Press, 1987.

Ryan, Mary. *The Cradle of the Middle Class: The Family in Oneida County, New York, 1790–1865*. New York: Cambridge University Press, 1981.

Scanlon, Jennifer, ed. *The Gender and Consumer Culture Reader*. New York: New York University Press, 2000.

Scheiner, Georganne. *Signifying Female Adolescence: Film Representations and Fans, 1920–1950*. Westport, Conn.: Praeger, 2000.

Schlossman, Steven L., and Stephanie Wallach. "The Crime of Precocious Sexuality: Female Juvenile Deliquency in the Progressive Era." *Harvard Educational Review* 48 (February 1978): 65–94.

Schrum, Kelly. "Teena Means Business: Teenage Girls' Culture and *Seventeen* Magazine, 1944–1950." In *Delinquents and Debutantes: Twentieth Century Girls' Cultures*, edited by Sherrie Inness, 134–63. New York: New York University Press, 1998.

Simmons, Christina. "Modern Sexuality and the Myth of Victorian Repression." In *Passion and Power: Sexuality in History*, edited by Christina Simmons and Kathy Peiss, 157–77. Philadelphia: Temple University Press, 1989.

Snitow, Ann, Christine Stansell, and Sharon Thompson, eds. *Powers of Desire: The Politics of Sexuality*. New York: Monthly Review Press, 1993.

Solinger, Rickie. *Wake up Little Susie: Single Pregnancy and Race before Roe v. Wade*. New York: Routledge, 1992.

Spigel, Lynn. *Make Room for TV: Television and the Family Ideal in Postwar America*. Chicago: University of Chicago Press, 1992.

Sprengnether, Madelon. "Enforcing Oedipus: Freud and Dora." In *In Dora's Case: Freud—Hysteria—Feminism*, edited by Charles Bernheimer, 254–76. New York: Columbia University Press, 1985.

Steele, Valerie. *The Corset: Cultural History*. New Haven: Yale University Press, 2001.

Stone, Lawrence. *The Family, Sex and Marriage in England, 1500–1800*. New York: Harper and Row, 1977.

Tanenbaum, Leora. *Slut! Growing up Female with a Bad Reputation*. New York: Perennial, 2000.

Terr, Lenore. *Unchained Memories: True Stories of Traumatic Memories, Lost and Found*. New York: Basic Books, 1994.

Thomas, Keith. *History and Literature*. Swansea, England: University College of Swansea, 1988.

Toth, Emily. *Inside Peyton Place: The Life of Grace Metalious*. New York: Doubleday, 1981.

Townsend, Kim. *Manhood at Harvard: William James and Others*. Cambridge: Harvard University Press, 1996.

Tuttle, William. *"Daddy's Gone to War": The Second World War in the Lives of America's Children*. New York: Oxford University Press, 1993.

Ugland, Richard. "The Adolescent Experience during World War II: Indianapolis as a Case Study." Ph.D. dissertation, Indiana University, 1977.

Walkerdine, Valerie. *Daddy's Girl: Young Girls and Popular Culture*. Cambridge: Harvard University Press, 1997.

Weiner, Lynn. *From Working Girl to Working Mother: The Female Labor Force in the United States, 1820–1980*. Chapel Hill: University of North Carolina Press, 1985.

Weiss, Jessica. *To Have and to Hold: Marriage, the Baby Boom, and Social Change*. Chicago: University of Chicago Press, 2000.

Whitfield, Stephen J. *The Culture of the Cold War*. Baltimore: Johns Hopkins University Press, 1991.

———. *A Death in the Delta: The Story of Emmet Till*. Baltimore: Johns Hopkins University Press, 1988.

Wiegman, Robyn. *American Anatomies: Theorizing Race and Gender*. Durham: Duke University Press, 1995.

Wolseley, Roland E. *The Black Press, U.S.A*. Ames: Iowa State University Press, 1971.

Zusne, Leonard, ed. *The Biographical Dictionary of Psychology*. Westport, Conn.: Greenwood Press, 1984.

Index

Abraham, Karl, 186 (n. 82)

Abuse. *See* Childhood sexual abuse; Incest

Ackerman, Nathan, 193–94 (n. 85)

Acting out: and mother-daughter relationship, 29; sexual, 41–42, 46, 50, 193–94 (n. 85); female rebellion as, 52, 68, 69–70, 72. *See also* Delinquent girls

Adelson, Joseph, 118

Adolescence. *See* Girls' culture; Puberty; Teenagers

Advertising. *See* Consumerism

Advice books, 116–19

Affection, 2, 148–56, 165

Aggression, 32, 68

Ah, Wilderness! (O'Neill), 146

Aichorn, August, 26

Alice Adams (Tarkington), 146, 204 (n. 9)

Alienation, 5

"Amateur Girls," 23, 55

American Negro Theatre, 136

Anger, 29, 67, 147

Anna Lucasta (Yordan), 112, 135–40, 218 (n. 102)

Annotated Lolita (Appel), 156, 214 (n. 38)

Antisocial behavior. *See* Delinquent boys; Delinquent girls; Rebellion

Appel, Alfred, Jr., 156, 157, 160, 214 (n. 38), 215 (n. 45)

Archer, Corliss (fictional character), 14, 141–45, 148–51, 152, 158, 163

As I Lay Dying (Faulkner), 161

Atkinson, Brooks, 88

Autonomy. *See* Independence

Bachelor and the Bobby Soxer, The (film), 86, 102

Back-to-School Campaign, 93

Bailey, Beth L., 5

Barnes, Cynthia, 108

Basinger, Jeanine, 82

Bellamann, Henry, 146, 165, 166, 167

Bennett, Lerone, 131

Benson, Sally, 84–85, 148, 198 (n. 31)

Bernardine (Chase), 212–13 (n. 7)

Bibring, Edward, 26

Blackboard Jungle (film), 74

Black middle-class culture, 127–40; and debutantes, 11, 127, 131–34, 210 (n. 89); and father-daughter relationship, 11–12, 112–13, 129–31, 134–40; and delinquent girls, 74, 194 (n. 90); and family life, 130–39, 205 (n. 14), 210 (n. 93), 211 (n. 98); film and play portrayals of, 211 (n. 98)

Blanchard, Phyllis, 27

Blos, Peter, 12, 69, 194 (n. 85)

Bobby-soxers, 102, 127, 198 (n. 38)

Body image, 172

Bossard, James, 127

Bossiness, 82, 111, 151

Boyd, Brian, 215 (n. 45)

Boys, 90, 91, 198 (n. 42); and father-son relationships, 3; father's relationship with, 3, 146–47, 213 (n. 10); mother's relationship with,

8, 46–47, 169; and Oedipus complex, 12, 23–24; independence as goal of, 23, 112, 117, 118; and delinquency, 49, 52, 53, 59–60, 64, 65, 74; and teenage consumerism, 94, 146–47, 213 (n. 10); black press treatment of, 128–29

Brando, Marlon, 50, 75

Brattiness, 158

Brumberg, Joan Jacobs, 172

Brunswick, Ruth Mack, 26

Buhle, Mary Jo, 22

Burnham, John, 21

Calling All Girls (magazine), 96, 200 (n. 54)

Carby, Hazel, 205 (n. 15)

Catcher in the Rye (Salinger), 3, 5

Catered Affair, The (film), 112

Ceremonial roles, 10, 124, 131, 134, 208 (n. 56)

Chase, Mary, 212–13 (n. 7)

Child guidance clinics, 23, 191–92 (n. 62)

Childhood and Society (Erikson), 3, 25

Childhood sexual abuse, 172, 186 (n. 82), 218 (n. 7); and Oedipal traumata, 35–37, 39–40

Child labor, 92

Children's agencies, 23, 54, 55

Children's Bureau (U.S.), 53, 93

Children's Court (N.Y.C.), 53

Chodorov, Jerome, 84

Chodorow, Nancy, 183 (n. 41)

Civil rights, 131, 134–35, 211 (n. 98)

Clarke, Dorris, 62, 63

Class. *See* Social class

Clothing. *See* Fashion

Cole, Cookie, 130, 134

Cole, Nat King, 130, 134

Coleman, James, 108, 203 (n. 104)

Comedies, father-daughter, 84–88, 102–7, 141–56, 214 (n. 22)

Coming-of-age, 109–40; postwar view of, 5, 11, 86–88, 197 (n. 27); and sexual maturity, 110–11, 119–22; and adolescence, 111–12, 116–19; and fathers' ceremonial roles, 124, 131, 134, 208 (n. 56); clothing and hairstyle symbols of, 203 (n. 96)

Common Sense Book of Baby and Child Care (Spock), 20

Connecticut, 74, 192 (n. 65)

Conservatism, 5–6

Consumer citizens, 82, 94

Consumerism, 9, 11, 78–108; father-daughter, 11, 13, 78–94, 102–8, 122, 150–51; and girls' culture, 88–102; and teenage boys, 94, 146–47, 213 (n. 10)

Corliss Archer (radio program), 141

Cosmetics. *See* Makeup

Court clinics, 13, 65–66, 67, 191–92 (nn. 62, 65, 66)

Crime, 12, 53–54, 62. *See also* Juvenile justice system

Daddy Long Legs (film), 202 (n. 94)

Daly, Maureen, 107, 200 (n. 54)

"Dangerous Date, The" (short story), 119–21

Date with Judy, A (film), 82, 86, 102–7, 116, 120

Dating, 4, 23

Daughters. *See* Father-daughter relationship; Girls' culture; Mother-daughter relationship

Day, Clarence, 213 (n. 8)

Dean, James, 50, 76

Death of a Salesman (Miller), 3

Debutantes, 110, 124, 127, 207 (n. 52), 208 (nn. 56, 58); in black middle-class culture, 11, 127, 131–34, 210 (n. 89)

Delinquent boys, 49, 52, 53, 59–60, 64, 65, 74

Delinquent girls, 20, 23, 48–77, 158, 188 (n. 10); and psychoanalytic theory, 3, 12–13, 50–52, 64–77; and Oedipus complex, 3, 13, 19, 49, 50–52, 68–73, 75, 76–77, 88; media reports on, 48, 50, 55–61, 74; and father-daughter relationship, 49, 69–73, 75–77; and popular culture, 50, 73–77, 87; and acting out, 52; rates of, 53–55, 188 (n. 13), 189 (n. 14); and class, 56, 75; and race and, 74, 194 (n. 90). See also Juvenile justice system

Deutsch, Helene, 4, 22–35, 44, 85, 96, 160, 197 (n. 29); Oedipal theory of, 12, 25, 29–34, 38; "feminine-erotic woman" concept of, 27–33, 38; on mother-daughter relationship, 28, 183 (n. 41); and delinquent girls, 49

Dinwiddie, Jill, 171–72

Domestic dominance, 83, 97

"Dora" (Freud case history), 22

Douglas, Susan, 82

Douvan, Elizabeth, 118

Do You Know Your Daughter? (Grayson), 96, 160

Dramatists Play Service, 86

Dress. See Fashion

Dunning, John, 212 (n. 5)

Dupee, F. W., 160

Durbin, Deanna, 102, 195–96 (n. 4), 204 (n. 9), 212–13 (n. 7)

Duvall, Evelyn Millis, 117

Ebony (magazine), 11, 127–28, 130–32, 134–36, 139, 210 (n. 93)

Ehrenreich, Barbara, 118

Eliot, Martha, 57

Elliott, Grace, 118

Ellis, Estelle, 101

Ellison, Ralph, 146, 168–69

Employment: of women, 26–27, 199 (n. 47); of teenage girl, statistics, 92

Erikson, Erik, 3, 5, 25, 198 (n. 42)

Eroticism: father-daughter, 2, 3, 4, 5–11, 13, 14, 15, 20, 31, 33, 38, 52, 70, 76, 83–84, 110–11, 120, 137, 139–40, 145, 150, 173–74, 208 (n. 56); mother-son, 8; and feminine woman, 28, 30. See also Incest

Facts of Life and Love for Teen-Agers (Duvall), 116–17

Family life, 5, 6, 9, 21, 94, 152; post-war ideal of, 6; dominant member in, 83, 97; teenage girl's role in, 98–102, 106–8; and black family portrayals, 130–39, 210 (n. 93), 211 (n. 98). See also Father-daughter relationship; Father-son relationship; Mother-daughter relationship; Mothers; Mother-son relationship; Paternal authority

Fantasy, 30, 33, 39–41, 42

Farnham, Marynia F., 26

Farrell, James, 55, 57–58, 59, 69

Fashion: teenage girls as leaders in, 13, 101–2; fathers' interest in, 81, 83–84, 100–101, 108, 173, 195–96 (n. 4), 203 (n. 97); mother-daughter relationship and, 81, 195–96 (n. 4); and coming-of-age symbolism, 203 (n. 96). See also Makeup

Fass, Paula, 91

Father-daughter relationship, 1–15; and paternal affection, 2, 148–56, 165; and ceremonial roles, 10, 124, 131, 134, 208 (n. 56); and consumerism, 11, 13, 78–94, 102–8, 122, 150–51; in black families, 11–12, 112–13, 129–31, 134–40; and female rebellion, 75–77; and domestic dominance, 83, 97; comedies about, 84–88, 102–7, 141–51, 152–56, 214 (n. 22); and coming-of-age events, 109–40; and male identity, 111, 113, 151–52, 159; and stepfather figure, 156–61; and commercial sexualization of girls, 172; critics of Oedipalization of, 172 (*see also* Oedipus complex). *See also* Eroticism; Incest; Paternal authority

Father-fixation, 34

Father of the Bride, The (Streeter), 4, 109–10, 113–16, 118–19

"Fathers and Daughters" (Leonard), 171

Father-son relationship, 3, 146–47, 213 (n. 10)

Father Was a Fullback (film), 102, 107

Faulkner, William, 161, 166

Female sexuality. *See* Sexuality, female

"Feminine-erotic woman," 27–33, 38

Feminism, 26

Feminist theory, 178 (n. 37), 218 (n. 7)

Fields, Joseph, 84

Film: portrayal of father-daughter relationship in, 4, 14, 95–96, 102–4, 105–7, 195–96 (n. 4), 204 (n. 9), 212–13 (n. 7); portrayal of mother-son relationship in, 8; portrayal of delinquent girl in, 50, 73, 74–76, 195 (n. 93); portrayal of teenage girl in, 82, 85, 86, 94–96, 102–7; portrayal of mother-daughter relationship in, 195 (n. 5), 212–13 (n. 7); and male gaze, 208 (n. 56). *See also titles of specific films*

First Love (film), 204 (n. 9), 212–13 (n. 7)

For Keeps (Herbert), 145, 152–55

Fraiberg, Selma, 168, 169

Frazier, E. Franklin, 131

Freedman, Estelle, 185 (n. 73)

Freud, Anna, 23, 24, 26

Freud, Sigmund, 18, 21, 22, 24, 25, 31, 39–40, 168; and seduction theory, 40, 185 (nn. 75, 76); on female sexual development stages, 184 (n. 55)

Friedan, Betty, 72–73

Frigidity, 194 (n. 85)

Frustration. *See* Oedipal frustration

Gable, Clark, 86

Gangs, 56, 58–59

Garland, Judy, 102, 204 (n. 9), 212–13 (n. 7)

Gatewood, Willard, 139

Gaze, theory of, 208 (n. 56)

Genital transference, 22

Gidget (television program and film), 82, 197 (n. 24), 202 (n. 94)

Gigi (film), 202 (n. 94)

Gilbert, James, 49, 82, 97, 202 (n. 77)

Gilmore, Glenda, 112, 128, 135

Girl delinquents. *See* Delinquent girls

Girl Friends, The (women's club), 210 (n. 89)

Girl Scouts of America, 118

Girls' culture, 11, 82–92, 94–97, 108, 121, 160; and "Sub-Deb" category,

90, 91, 198 (n. 33); and fashion leadership, 101–2; 1990s reemergence of, 172. *See also* Consumerism; Magazines

Girl's Term (N.Y.C. court), 50, 61–66, 68

Gluek, Eleanor and Sheldon, 59

Going steady, 4, 23

Good Housekeeping (magazine), 151

Goodman, Paul, 3

Gordon, Lillian, 43–45, 46

Gordon, Linda, 178 (n. 37)

Gorer, Geoffrey, 9

Graebner, William, 166

Graves, Judy (fictional character), 101–5

Grayson, Alice Barr, 96, 160

Greenacre, Phyllis, 12, 35–38, 42

Gribble, Harry Wagstaff, 136

Griswold, Robert, 10, 50–51

Growing Up Absurd (Goodman), 3

Guilt, 186 (n. 82)

Hale, Nathan, 21

Hall, G. Stanley, 1–2

Hansberry, Lorraine, 211 (n. 98)

Hardy, Andy (film character), 146, 213 (n. 10)

Harper's Bazaar (magazine), 93, 111

Hartmann, Heinz, 26

Haven in a Heartless World (Lasch), 5

Healy, William, 23

Hellcats (female gang), 58–59

Henry, Jules, 78

Hep Cats (magazine), 203 (n. 104)

Hep culture, 5

Herbert, F. Hugh, 14, 116, 141–45, 146, 148–56, 161, 163, 170, 214 (n. 22)

Hill, Abram, 136

Hobsbawm, Eric, 110

Hollander, John, 169

Hoover, J. Edgar, 55–56

Horney, Karen, 22, 25

Hostility, 146–48

Humor. *See* Comedies, father-daughter

Hypersexual females, 66

Imitation of Life (Sirk), 4, 194 (n. 91), 212–13 (n. 7)

Incest: literary portrayals of, 3, 7, 20, 138, 145–46, 156–70; and father-daughter eroticism, 15, 31, 140; and Oedipus complex, 19, 22, 38–47, 168, 169, 185 (nn. 73, 75, 76), 186 (n. 82); mother-son, 46–47, 169; and feminist theory, 218 (n. 7)

Independence, 4–5, 83, 117–19; as male vs. female goal, 23, 112, 117, 118; and paternal authority, 51, 73, 108, 173; makeup as sign of, 105–7; interdependence vs., 117–19

Institute for Social Research, University of Michigan, 117–18

Integration, 134–35

Interdependence, 117–19

Invented traditions, 110

Invisible Man (Ellison), 146, 168

Jameson, Frederic, 6

Janie (play and film), 4, 86, 146, 147

Jet (magazine), 127–35

Johnson, John H., 127

Jones, Ernst, 22, 31, 41

Judge Baker Children's Center (Boston), 49, 71, 191–92 (n. 62)

Junior Miss (play), 84–88, 93, 94, 114, 121, 124–25, 145–48, 157, 198 (n. 31); immense popularity of, 1, 85–86

Juvenile delinquency *See* Delinquent boys; Delinquent girls
Juvenile justice system, 13, 50, 53–55, 61–68, 191–92 (nn. 62, 65, 66)

Kardiner, Abram, 131
"Kathy" (comic strip), 201 (n. 71)
Kazan, Elia, 211 (n. 98)
Keiser, Sylvan, 42–43, 46
Kennedy, John F., 134
Kett, Joseph, 5
King's Row (Bellamann), 146, 165–68, 170
Kiss and Tell (play and film), 4, 86, 102, 116, 141, 142–43, 146–48, 152, 155
Kiss for Corliss, A (play), 86, 102, 141
Klein, Melanie, 22, 31, 37
Kubrick, Stanley, 216 (n. 66)
Kunzel, Regina, 66

Ladies Home Journal (magazine), 93, 107, 200 (n. 54)
Lampl–De Groot, Jeanne, 22, 31
Lasch, Christopher, 5
Leibowitz, Samuel S., 60
Leonard, Marjorie, 171, 172
Levy, David, 19
Levy, Kata, 17–18
Lie Down in Darkness (Styron), 4, 14, 20, 145, 146, 161–68, 170
Life (magazine), 1, 78–79, 88, 90, 91, 92, 93, 129, 171–72
Life with Father (Day), 213 (n. 8)
Literary criticism, 165–70
Literature: portrayal of father-daughter relationship in, 3, 4, 14–15, 20, 113–16, 148–51, 204 (n. 9); portrayal of father-son relationship in, 3, 146–47; portrayal of incest in, 3, 7, 20, 138, 145–46, 156–

70; on teenager alienation, 5. *See also specific titles*
Lolita (Nabokov), 14, 145, 146, 156–61, 163–70, 217 (n. 76)
Love prize, 32
Lowell, Robert, 17
Loy, Myrna, 86
Lundberg, Ferdinand, 26

Macdonald, Dwight, 81
Magazines: for girls, 5, 13, 83, 93–94, 96, 97–102, 105, 119–21, 200 (n. 54), 203 (nn. 97, 104), 206–7 (n. 37); coverage of teenage girls by, 78–81, 88–93, 97–102, 127–35, 171–72, 198–99 (n. 45); for black middle class, 112, 127–35; coverage of society events by, 124, 127, 131–34, 208 (n. 56). *See also specific titles*
Makeup, 71–72, 82, 83, 84, 103–7, 203 (n. 97)
Male gaze, 208 (n. 56)
Male identity, 111, 113, 151–52, 159
Manchurian Candidate, The (film), 8
March of Time (newsreel series), 94–96
Marriage, 7, 23, 34, 202 (n. 74); decline in age at, 4, 20. *See also* Weddings
Marsh, Margaret, 9
"Masculine domesticity" ideal, 9, 15
Masculinity. *See* Male identity
Masochism, 28
Massachusetts, 192 (n. 66)
Mass media. *See* Popular culture
Matriarchate, 131
Maturity, 117, 118. *See also* Sexual maturity
May, Elaine Tyler, 5
McCullers, Carson, 4, 20
Mead, Margaret, 122

Meet Corliss Archer (Herbert), 141, 149–50, 151, 152, 214 (n. 22)
Member of the Wedding, The (McCullers), 4, 20, 86
Metalious, Grace, 4, 145, 165, 166, 167
Meyerowitz, Joanne, 5
Mildred Pierce (film), 212–13 (n. 7)
Miller, Arthur, 3
Millett, Kate, 178 (n. 37)
Miranda, Carmen, 103
Miscegenation, 135
Modell, John, 4
Modern Woman: The Lost Sex (Farnham and Lundberg), 26
"Momism," 8
Mother-daughter relationship, 33–34, 43–46, 69–70, 98–99, 183 (n. 41), 212–13 (n. 7); and overprotection, 17–18, 19; and the reemergence of the Oedipal complex, 24–25; disengagement from, 28–29; and acting out, 29, 195 (n. 93); and fashion, 81, 195–96 (n. 4); and debutantes, 207 (n. 52)
Mothers, 8, 17–19; primacy of, 9; and overprotection, 19; in workforce, 199 (n. 47)
Mother-son relationship, 8, 46–47, 169
Movies. *See* Film
"Mr. Banks' Other Daughter" (Streeter), 122–24
Mulvey, Laura, 208 (n. 56)
Murphy, Mary, 75
My Son John (film), 8

Nabokov, Vladimir, 14, 96, 145, 156–61, 163–70, 217 (n. 76)
Nash, Illana, 197 (n. 24)
Nathan, Robert, 204 (n. 9)

Negro Family in the United States, The (Frazier), 131
New York City, 50, 53, 61–66, 68, 85–86, 189 (n. 14)
Niebuhr, Reinhold, 166
Nochlin, Linda, 167

Odem, Mary, 66
Oedipal conflict, 12, 19, 34, 37, 52, 76, 84, 171
Oedipal frustration, 37–38, 50
Oedipal impasse, 50, 52, 69, 70, 72–73, 194 (n. 85)
Oedipal traumata, 35–38
Oedipus complex, 17–47; and father-daughter attachment, 1–2, 6, 8, 10, 12, 25, 29–35, 44; and delinquent girls, 3, 12–13, 19, 49, 50, 51–52, 68–73, 75, 76–77, 88; and boys, 12, 23–24; phases of, 12, 24–25; as founding psychoanalytic principle, 12–13; and incest, 19, 22, 38–47, 168, 169, 185 (nn. 73, 75, 76), 186 (n. 82); and prepuberty trauma, 35–38, 42; and girls' emotional development, 38, 171–73, 183 (n. 41); postwar popular ideas about, 137–38; critics of overuse of, 172
O'Neill, Eugene, 146
Our Dancing Daughters (film), 195 (n. 5)
Ovesey, Lionel, 131

Palladino, Grace, 81
Parents' Magazine, 78, 80, 93, 200 (n. 54)
Parker, Dorothy, 214 (n. 38)
Parody, *Lolita* as, 157, 160, 161
Parsons, Talcott, 46–47
Passivity: female, 28, 31–32, 33, 55,

184 (n. 55); paternal, 111, 114, 122, 140

Paternal authority, 48–52, 111, 177–78 (nn. 34, 37); erosion of, 9–10, 20, 50–51, 121–22, 177–78 (nn. 34, 37); and delinquent girls, 48–49, 60–61; cultural transformation of, 78–108; and teenage consumerism, 82–84, 122, 213 (n. 10); and black families, 131

Patriarchy: feminist theory on, 178 (n. 37), 218 (n. 7). *See also* Paternal authority

Patty Duke Show, The (television program), 82

Peardon, Patricia, 1, 89

Peiss, Kathy, 82, 104

Peyton Place (Metalious), 4, 145, 146, 165–68, 170

Pfister, Joel, 20

Pinky (film), 211 (n. 98)

Pipher, Mary, 172

Plant, Rebecca, 8

Plays, 1, 3, 4, 14, 84–88, 121, 135–39, 141–46, 152–56, 160–61

Pleasure of His Company, The (play), 86, 153

Poitier, Sidney, 74

Popular culture: and portrayals of father-daughter relationship, 3, 4, 8, 10, 14–15, 20, 78–82, 84–88, 95–96, 102–4, 105–8, 121, 141–45, 151, 158, 197 (n. 24); and psychoanalytic theory, 3, 8, 11, 20, 73–77; and focus on teenage girls, 13–14, 78–89, 90–108, 151, 171–72, 198–99 (n. 45); and portrayals of delinquent girls, 48, 50, 55–61, 73–77, 74, 88. *See also* Comedies, father-daughter; Film; Literature; Magazines; Plays; Radio

Powell, Jane, 82, 102

Power, Tyrone, 87

Pregnancy, out-of-wedlock, 51, 172

Prepuberty, 28, 29, 35–38

"Prepuberty Trauma in Girls, The" (Greenacre), 35–38, 42

Prescott, William H., 15

Presley, Elvis, 5

"Private Affair" (Herbert), 141

Progressive reformers, 66

Promiscuity, 49, 55, 63, 66, 69

Pseudoheterosexuality, 69, 70, 194 (n. 85)

Psychoanalytic Study of the Child (Blos), 69

Psychoanalytic theory, 17–47; and father-daughter relationship, 1–3, 7–8; and delinquent girls, 3, 12–13, 49–52, 64–77; and popular culture, 8, 11, 20–21, 73–77; Oedipus complex as founding theory of, 12; and teenage girls, 22–25, 49, 154; and female sexuality, 31–33. *See also* Oedipus complex

Psychology of Women, The (Deutsch), 4, 12, 25–34, 35, 38, 85, 197 (n. 29)

Puberty, 12, 18; and Oedipus complex reemergence, 24–25, 35–38, 42. *See also* Prepuberty; Teenagers

Race. *See* Black middle-class culture

Radio, 141, 145, 150–51

Raisin in the Sun, A (Hansberry), 211 (n. 98)

Rascoe, Burton, 138

Rascovsky, Arnoldo, 46

Rebellion, 55, 67, 68, 75, 76–77. *See also* Delinquent girls

Rebel Without a Cause (film), 50, 74, 75–76

Reich, Wilhelm, 26

Rejection, girls and feelings of, 64, 68, 69–70, 71
Repressed memory syndrome, 172, 218 (n. 7)
Reproduction of Mothering, The (Chodorow), 183 (n. 41)
Reynolds, Debbie, 82
Rhinehart, Mary, 204 (n. 9)
Rites of passage, 109–10, 113–16
Rogin, Michael, 8
Rooney, Mickey, 102
Roth, Philip, 171
Rubin, Louis D., 161
Ryan, Mary, 9

Salinger, J. D., 3
Sarcasm, 147, 151, 155
Scheiner, Georganne, 102, 195 (n. 93)
Schlesinger, Arthur, 166
School phobia, 192
Seduction theory, 40, 185 (nn. 75, 76)
Self-image, 64
Seventeen (magazine), 5, 13, 93, 97–102, 105, 119–21, 203 (n. 97), 206–7 (n. 37)
Seventeen (Tarkington), 146–47
Sex offenses, 53–54
Sexual assault. *See* Childhood sexual abuse; Incest
Sexual dysfunction, 37, 38
Sexuality, female: and precocious behavior, 4–5, 20, 23, 69; and postwar conservatism, 5; and puberty, 12, 18, 24–25; and psychoanalytic theories, 18–19, 22–25, 27–38, 84, 173; and Deutsch's theories, 25–34, 197 (n. 29); and prepuberty trauma, 35–38, 42; and acting out, 41–42, 46, 50, 193–94 (n. 85); and promiscuity, 49, 55, 63, 66, 69; and delinquency, 55–56, 66; and autonomy, 73; postwar advice books on, 116–17; contemporary provocative images of, 172. *See also* Eroticism; Incest
Sexual liberalism, 10, 27, 54, 63, 116, 191 (n. 56); gradual acceptance of, 4, 5
Sexual maturity, 2, 3, 6, 10, 11, 30–31, 34, 68, 70–73, 83–84, 88, 110–11, 119–22, 173; signifiers of, 106, 120
Shulman, Harry, 64
Simms, Hilda, 136
Sirk, Douglas, 4, 194 (n. 91)
Situation comedies, 82
Skepticism, 151, 152, 155–56
Slang, 91
Smart Set, The (women's club), 210 (n. 89)
Social class: and father-daughter relationship, 11–12, 112–13, 127–31, 139–40; and delinquent girls, 49, 50, 55, 56–58, 66–67, 73–75; and "Sub-Deb" designation, 91, 124; and debutante balls, 124, 127, 131, 134
Society events, 124, 127, 131–34, 208 (n. 56)
Solinger, Ricky, 51
Spock, Benjamin, 20
"Squire Clubs," 89
Status crimes, 53, 62
Stella Dallas (film), 212–13 (n. 7)
Stepfathers, 156–61
Stern, Edith, 92
Stratton-Porter, Gene, 204 (n. 9)
Streeter, Edward, 4, 109, 110, 113, 116, 122–24
Sturges, Ethel, 23
Styron, William, 4, 14, 20, 145, 161–65, 166, 167

"Sub-Deb" designation and clubs, 89, 91, 124, 198 (n. 33)

Tammy and the Bachelor (film), 82
Tappan, Paul, 63, 64, 192 (n. 62)
Tarkington, Booth, 146–47, 204 (n. 9)
Taylor, Elizabeth, 109
Teena (promotional character), 97–101, 102, 201 (n. 71)
Teenagers: postwar media focus on, 4–5, 7, 13, 20, 57, 82, 88–102, 108, 111–12, 116–19; increased autonomy of, 4–5, 83, 106, 112; postwar psychoanalytic interest in, 23–24, 49; and origin of term, 91; as new subculture, 97; commercialization of, 173. *See also* Boys; Consumerism; Delinquent girls; Girls' culture; Popular culture
Teen World (magazine), 203 (n. 104)
Television, 9, 82, 85, 179 (n. 44)
Thomas, Keith, 14
Three Daughters (film), 195 (n. 3)
Toth, Emily, 165
Town and Country (magazine), 124
Tracy, Spencer, 109
Tree Grows in Brooklyn, A (film), 112, 205 (n. 12)
Trilling, Lionel, 1, 166, 167, 168
Tuttle, William M., 7

Ugland, Richard, 91
United Service Organization (USO), 86

Waldo, Janet, 150
Wayward girls. *See* Delinquent girls
Wayward Minor Act of 1925 (N.Y.), 61, 62
Weddings, 109–10, 113–16, 124, 208 (n. 56)
Weiner, Lynn, 199 (n. 47)
Weiss, Jessica, 10–11
Wencelblat De Rascovsky, Matilde, 46
White, Jane, 130
White, Walter, 130
Whitfield, Stephen J., 6
Wife vs. Secretary (film), 86
Wildberg, John, 136
Wild One, The (film), 50, 74, 75–76
Wood, Natalie, 75
World War II, 22, 55–56, 86, 108; and interest in father-daughter relationships, 1–2; social climate following, 5–6; and interest in teenage girls, 88–94

Yordan, Philip, 136
Youth culture. *See* Girls' culture; Teenagers

Gender and American Culture

Relative Intimacy: Fathers, Adolescent Daughters, and Postwar American Culture, by Rachel Devlin (2005).

The Freedom of the Streets: Work, Citizenship, and Sexuality in a Gilded Age City, by Sharon E. Wood (2005).

Home on the Rails: Women, the Railroad, and the Rise of Public Domesticity, by Amy G. Richter (2005).

Worrying the Line: Black Women Writers, Lineage, and Literary Tradition, by Cheryl A. Wall (2005).

From Welfare to Workfare: The Unintended Consequences of Liberal Reform, 1945–1965, by Jennifer Mittelstadt (2005).

Choice and Coercion: Birth Control, Sterilization, and Abortion in Public Health and Welfare, by Johanna Schoen (2005).

Closer to Freedom: Enslaved Women and Everyday Resistance in the Plantation South, by Stephanie M. H. Camp (2004).

Masterful Women: Slaveholding Widows from the American Revolution through the Civil War, by Kirsten E. Wood (2004).

Manliness and Its Discontents: The Black Middle Class and the Transformation of Masculinity, 1900–1930, by Martin Summers (2004).

Citizen, Mother, Worker: Debating Public Responsibility for Child Care after the Second World War, by Emilie Stoltzfus (2003).

Women and the Historical Enterprise in America: Gender, Race, and the Politics of Memory, 1880–1945, by Julie Des Jardins (2003).

Free Hearts and Free Homes: Gender and American Antislavery Politics, by Michael D. Pierson (2003).

Ella Baker and the Black Freedom Movement: A Radical Democratic Vision, by Barbara Ransby (2003).

Signatures of Citizenship: Petitioning, Antislavery, and Women's Political Identity, by Susan Zaeske (2003).

Love on the Rocks: Men, Women, and Alcohol in Post–World War II America, by Lori Rotskoff (2002).

The Veiled Garvey: The Life and Times of Amy Jacques Garvey, by Ula Yvette Taylor (2002).

Working Cures: Health, Healing, and Power on Southern Slave Plantations, by Sharla Fett (2002).

Southern History across the Color Line, by Nell Irvin Painter (2002).

The Artistry of Anger: Black and White Women's Literature in America, 1820–1860, by Linda M. Grasso (2002).

Too Much to Ask: Black Women in the Era of Integration, by Elizabeth Higginbotham (2001).

Imagining Medea: Rhodessa Jones and Theater for Incarcerated Women, by Rena Fraden (2001).

Painting Professionals: Women Artists and the Development of Modern American Art, 1870–1920, by Kirsten Swinth (2001).

Remaking Respectability: African American Women in Interwar Detroit, by Victoria W. Wolcott (2001).

Ida B. Wells-Barnett and American Reform, 1880–1930, by Patricia A. Schechter (2001).

Taking Haiti: Military Occupation and the Culture of U.S. Imperialism, 1915–1940, by Mary A. Renda (2001).

Before Jim Crow: The Politics of Race in Postemancipation Virginia, by Jane Dailey (2000).

Captain Ahab Had a Wife: New England Women and the Whalefishery, 1720–1870, by Lisa Norling (2000).

Civilizing Capitalism: The National Consumers' League, Women's Activism, and Labor Standards in the New Deal Era, by Landon R. Y. Storrs (2000).

Rank Ladies: Gender and Cultural Hierarchy in American Vaudeville, by M. Alison Kibler (1999).

Strangers and Pilgrims: Female Preaching in America, 1740–1845, by Catherine A. Brekus (1998).

Sex and Citizenship in Antebellum America, by Nancy Isenberg (1998).

Yours in Sisterhood: Ms. Magazine and the Promise of Popular Feminism, by Amy Erdman Farrell (1998).

We Mean to Be Counted: White Women and Politics in Antebellum Virginia, by Elizabeth R. Varon (1998).

Women Against the Good War: Conscientious Objection and Gender on the American Home Front, 1941–1947, by Rachel Waltner Goossen (1997).

Toward an Intellectual History of Women: Essays by Linda K. Kerber (1997).

Gender and Jim Crow: Women and the Politics of White Supremacy in North Carolina, 1896–1920, by Glenda Elizabeth Gilmore (1996).

Delinquent Daughters: Protecting and Policing Adolescent Female Sexuality in the United States, 1885–1920, by Mary E. Odem (1995).

U.S. History as Women's History: New Feminist Essays, edited by Linda K. Kerber, Alice Kessler-Harris, and Kathryn Kish Sklar (1995).

Common Sense and a Little Fire: Women and Working-Class Politics in the United States, 1900–1965, by Annelise Orleck (1995).

How Am I to Be Heard?: Letters of Lillian Smith, edited by Margaret Rose Gladney (1993).

Entitled to Power: Farm Women and Technology, 1913–1963, by Katherine Jellison (1993).

Revising Life: Sylvia Plath's Ariel Poems, by Susan R. Van Dyne (1993).

Made From This Earth: American Women and Nature, by Vera Norwood (1993).

Unruly Women: The Politics of Social and Sexual Control in the Old South, by Victoria E. Bynum (1992).

The Work of Self-Representation: Lyric Poetry in Colonial New England, by Ivy Schweitzer (1991).

Labor and Desire: Women's Revolutionary Fiction in Depression America, by Paula Rabinowitz (1991).

Community of Suffering and Struggle: Women, Men, and the Labor Movement in Minneapolis, 1915–1945, by Elizabeth Faue (1991).

All That Hollywood Allows: Re-reading Gender in 1950s Melodrama, by Jackie Byars (1991).

Doing Literary Business: American Women Writers in the Nineteenth Century, by Susan Coultrap-McQuin (1990).

Ladies, Women, and Wenches: Choice and Constraint in Antebellum Charleston and Boston, by Jane H. Pease and William H. Pease (1990).

The Secret Eye: The Journal of Ella Gertrude Clanton Thomas, 1848–1889, edited by Virginia Ingraham Burr, with an introduction by Nell Irvin Painter (1990).

Second Stories: The Politics of Language, Form, and Gender in Early American Fictions, by Cynthia S. Jordan (1989).

Within the Plantation Household: Black and White Women of the Old South, by Elizabeth Fox-Genovese (1988).

The Limits of Sisterhood: The Beecher Sisters on Women's Rights and Woman's Sphere, by Jeanne Boydston, Mary Kelley, and Anne Margolis (1988).